BOOKWORMS

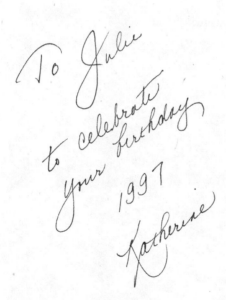

To Julie
to celebrate
your birthday
1997
Katherine

BOOKWORMS

Great Writers and Readers
Celebrate Reading

Edited by

Laura Furman and Elinore Standard

CARROLL & GRAF PUBLISHERS, INC.
NEW YORK

Copyright © 1997 by Laura Furman and Elinore Standard

All rights reserved

First Carroll & Graf edition 1996

Carroll & Graf Publishers, Inc.

260 Fifth Avenue

New York, NY 10001

Library of Congress Cataloging-in-Publication Data

Bookworms : great writers and readers celebrate reading / edited by
Laura Furman and Elinore Standard. — 1st Carroll & Graf ed.
p.   cm.
ISBN 0-7867-0395-4 (trade paper)
1. Books and reading—Literary collections.   2. American literature.
3. English literature.   I. Furman, Laura.   II. Standard, Elinore.
PS509.B66B66   1996
820.8—dc20   96-32523
CIP

Manufactured in the United States of America

ACKNOWLEDGMENTS

The editors and publisher are grateful for permission to include the following copyrighted material in this volume.

From *Katherine Mansfield: A Biography* by Antony Alpers. Copyright © Antony Alpers, 1980. Reprinted by permission of John Johnson, Ltd.

From *The Pleasures of Reading in an Ideological Age* by Robert Alter. Copyright © 1989 by Robert Alter. Reprinted by permission of Georges Borchardt, Inc. for the author.

From *The Dyer's Hand and Other Essays* by W.H. Auden. Copyright © 1948, 1950, 1952, 1953, 1954, 1956, 1957, 1958, 1960, 1962 by W.H. Auden. Reprinted by permission of Random House, Inc.

"The Treachery of Books" from *Writing Home* by Alan Bennett. First published in 1994 by Faber and Faber Ltd. Copyright © Forelake Ltd.1994. Reprinted by permission of the publisher and Random House, Inc.

From *Literary Taste: How to Form It* by Arnold Bennett. First published by A.P. Watt, 1909. Reprinted by permission of A.P. Watt on behalf of Mme. V.M. Eldin.

"Paging the Self: Privacies of Reading" from *The Gutenberg Elegies: The Fate of Reading in an Electronic Age* by Sven Birkerts. Copyright © 1994 by Sven Birkerts. Reprinted by permission of Faber and Faber Ltd.

From "A Nation of Readers" remarks by Daniel Boorstin at a dinner on April 21, 1982, in the Great Hall of the Library of Congress. Copyright © 1982 by Daniel Boorstin. Used by permission of the Library of Congress.

From *Bury Me Standing: The Gypsies and their Journey* by Isabel Fonseca. Copyright © 1995 by Isabel Fonseca. Reprinted by permission of Alfred A. Knopf, Inc.

From *The Commonplace Book* by E. M. Forster, edited by Philip Gardner. First published in the USA by the Stanford University Press, 1985. Reprinted by permission of the publisher.

From "Beyond the Book?", a review by Don Fowler, in *The Future of the Book* by Geoffrey Nunberg. First published by the *Times Literary Supplement* May 10, 1996. Copyright © 1996 by Don Fowler. Reprinted by permission of the author and the *Times Literary Supplement*.

From "The Reader in Exile" by Jonathan Franzen. First published by *The New Yorker,* March 6, 1995. Copyright © 1995 by Jonathan Franzen. Reprinted by permission of the author and *The New Yorker*.

From "A Child's Reading in South Africa" by Lynn Freed. First published in *The Washington Post Book World,* December 10, 1995. Copyright © 1995 by Lynn Freed. Reprinted by permission of the author.

"Mrs. Darling's Kiss" by Laura Furman. Copyright © 1996 by Laura Furman. n.p. n.p. 1996. Used by permission of the author.

From "Through West Indian Eyes" by Leslie Garis. First published in *The New York Times Magazine,* October 7, 1990. Copyright © by Leslie Garis. Reprinted by permission of the author.

From *Anne Frank Remembered* by Miep Gies with Alison Leslie Gold. Copyright © 1987 by Miep Gies and Alison Leslie Gold. Reprinted with the permission of Simon & Schuster.

From *Autobiography* by Eric Gill. Copyright © 1941 by the Devin-Adair Publishers, Inc. All rights reserved. Reprinted by permission of the publisher.

From *The Woman Within* by Ellen Glasgow. Copyright © 1954, 1982 by Harcourt Brace & Company. Reprinted by permission of the publisher.

From *The Reader Over Your Shoulder: A Handbook for Writers of English Prose* Second Edition by Robert Graves and Alan Hodge. Copyright ©

1971 by Robert Graves and Alan Hodge. Reprinted by permission of A.P.Watt Ltd. on behalf of the Trustees of the Robert Graves Copyright Trust and Jane Aiken Hodge.

The poem "The Ideal Reader" by Jonathan Greene is taken from his book *Idylls,* published by the North Carolina Wesleyan College Press and is used by permission of the author. Copyright © 1983, 1990 by Jonathan Greene.

From "A Place Elsewhere: Reading in the Age of the Computer," an address by Vartan Gregorian to the April 3, 1995 meeting of the American Academy of Arts and Sciences. Copyright © by Vartan Gregorian. Used by permission of Vartan Gregorian, President, Brown University, Providence, RI.

From "The Cradle and the Bookcase" by Rachel Hadas. Copyright © 1989 by Rachel Hadas. First published in *Southwest Review,* subsequently included in *Living in Time* by Rachel Hadas, Rutgers University Press, 1990. Reprinted by permission of Rutgers University.

From "The New World" from *Lost in Translation* by Eva Hoffman. Copyright © 1989 by Eva Hoffman. Reprinted by permission of Dutton Signet, a division of Penguin Books USA, Inc.

From "Diary" by Michael Holroyd. First published in *London Review of Books,* XVIII, 5, March 7, 1996. Reprinted by permission.

From *Holmes-Laski Letters* edited by Mark DeWolfe Howe. Copyright © 1953 by the President and Fellows of Harvard College. Reprinted by permission of Harvard University Press.

From "The Inside Search" from *Dust Tracks on a Road* by Zora Neale Hurston. Copyright © 1942 by Zora Neale Hurston, renewed 1970 by John C. Hurston. Reprinted by permission of HarperCollins Publishers, Inc.

From *Henry James: Selected Letters* Vol. IV by Henry James, edited by Leon Edel. Copyright © 1984 by Alexander R. James. Reprinted by permission of The Belknap Press of Harvard University Press.

The poem "Destinations" by Laura Jensen is taken from *Shelter*. Copyright © 1985 by Laura Jensen. Reprinted by permission from Dragon Gate Publishers, Inc., Port Townsend, WA.

From *A Portrait of the Artist as a Young Man* by James Joyce. Copyright © 1916 by B.W. Heubsch, © 1944 by Nora Joyce, © 1964 by the Estate of James Joyce. Reprinted by permission of Viking Penguin, a division of Penguin Books USA, Inc.

From *The Diaries of Franz Kafka, 1910–1913* and *1914–1923* by Franz Kafka, edited by Max Brod. Copyright © 1948, renewed 1976 by Schocken Books, Inc. Reprinted by permission of Schocken Books, a division of Random House, Inc.

From "Return of the Luddites" by Jon Katz. First appeared in *Wired*. Copyright © 1995 by John Katz. Reprinted by permission of Sterling Lord Literistic, Inc.

From "Interview with the Luddite" by Kevin Kelly. Copyright © 1995 Wired Ventures, Inc. Reprinted by permission of *Wired*.

The poem "Insomnia at the Solstice" is taken from *Otherwise: New and Selected Poems* by Jane Kenyon. Copyright © 1996 by the Estate of Jane Kenyon. Reprinted by permission of Graywolf Press, St. Paul, MN.

From the Introduction to *Bird by Bird* by Anne Lamott. Copyright © 1994 by Anne Lamott. Reprinted by permission of Pantheon Books, a division of Random House, Inc.

From *Nine Gates to the Chassidic Mysteries* by Jiri Langer. First published in Czech in the City of Prague by Elk under the title *Devet Bran;* first English translation 1961 by Stephen Jolly. Copyright © 1961 by James Clarke & Co., Ltd. Reprinted by permission of James Clarke & Co., Ltd.

From "Texts" by Ursula K. Le Guin. First published in *American Short Fiction* 1, 1, Spring 1991. Copyright © 1990 by Ursula K. Le Guin.

From *The Letters and Journals of Katherine Mansfield: A Selection* edited by C.K. Stead. First published by Allen Lane, London, 1977. This collection copyright © C.K. Stead, 1977. Reprinted by permission.

The poem "Reading Braille" by Mary McGinnis was first published in *The Disability Rag,* August 1993, and subsequently reprinted in *The Ragged Edge*, published by The Advocado Press. Copyright © 1996 by Mary McGinnis. Reprinted by permission of The Advocado Press and the author.

From *Down Cobbled Streets* by Philomena O'Keeffe. First published in 1995 by Brandon Book Publishers, Dingle, IRE. Copyright © 1995 by Phil O'Keefe. Reprinted by permission of Brandon Book Publishers Ltd.

The poem "McGuffey's First Eclectic Reader" by Linda Pastan was taken from *PM/AM: New and Selected Poems* by Linda Pastan. Copyright © 1981 by Linda Pastan. Reprinted by permission of W.W. Norton & Company, Inc.

From *Difficult Women: A Memoir of Three* by David Plante. Copyright © 1979, 1983 by David Plante. Reprinted by permission of the author.

From "The Country House" from *Etiquette* by Emily Post. Copyright © 1922, 1927, 1931, and 1934 by Funk & Wagnalls Company. Reprinted by permission of HarperCollins Publishers, Inc.

From *A Cab at the Door* by V.S. Pritchett. First published by Chatto & Windus, 1968. Copyright © V.S. Pritchett, 1968, 1971. Reprinted by permission of the publisher and the Peters Fraser and Dunlop Group Ltd.

The poem *Der Lesende* (The Reader) by Rainer Maria Rilke is taken from *Das Buch Der Bilder* (The Book of Images), first published in 1902. Original English translation for this edition by Markus Frank and John Zuern copyright © 1996. Reprinted by permission of the translators.

From "The Achievement of Desire" from *Hunger of Memory* by Richard Rodriguez. Copyright © 1981 Richard Rodriguez. Reprinted by permission of Georges Borchardt, Inc. for the author.

From *Lives on the Boundary: The Struggles and Achievements of America's Underprepared* by Mike Rose. Copyright © 1989 by Mike Rose. Abridged with the permission of The Free Press, a division of Simon & Schuster.

For

Joel and Michael, Sam and Solomon

Great Readers

THANKS

The editors would like to thank the following for their kind help and good advice:

Linda Anderson; Sam Antupit; Kathryn Blount; Emily Furman; Clare Gregorian; Kurt Heinzelman; Cathy Henderson and Jake Baxter of the Humanities Research Center, University of Texas at Austin; Daniel Kaderka, CPA; Terry Kelley; the librarians at the The Bedford Village Free Library; the librarians at the The Hiram Halle Memorial Library; Zora Molitor, University of Texas Press; Mrs. Ann Malamud; Polly Robertus; Diane Lane Root; Elvira Schadlow; Rabbi Chaim Stern; Willard Spiegelman; Marcia Thomas; Catherine Vanhentenryck; Natasha Waxman; and Susan Williamson.

CONTENTS

VI. THE PRIVILEGED PLEASURE 281

INTRODUCTION

We take the title of our book from Katherine Mansfield, one of the world's great readers. In June 1922, suffering from tuberculosis in Switzerland, she examined her loneliness in terms of reading:

> Should I be as happy with anyone at my side? No. I'd begin to talk, and it's far nicer not to talk. Or, if it were J. he'd open a little blue book by Diderot, *Jacques le Fataliste,* and begin to read it, and that would make me wretched. . . . Why the devil want to read stuffy, snuffy Diderot when there is this other book before one's eyes? I do not want to be a book *worm.* If its book is taken away from it, the little blind head is raised; it wags, hovers, terribly uneasy, in a void—until it begins to burrow again.

Bookworms sometimes regret that they do not live in what Ralph Waldo Emerson called an "original relation" to the world, unmediated by reading. For the true bookworm it is sometimes hard to distinguish between what one has experienced and what one has read. We know that this is odd and even a little demented. But there it is. We are uneasy in a void with no book.

Is reading like any other experience? We can say that it is not unlike hearing voices, or seeing apparitions. Reading is a socially accepted form of hallucination. Through words we react to the ideas, memories, and fantasies of people we'll never meet, whom we believe we know. We witness what we don't see, and we swear to the veracity of voices we'll never hear. Yet reading is such a quotidian activity that we forget even to notice its hallucinatory aspects or notice it at all as an act interesting for itself.

Our book about reading addresses another paradox that all readers face: The solitary activity of reading, the private and silent taking-in of words, seems to be an immediate communication, sometimes a communion, between reader and writer. We believe, at least as readers, that we have caught the ball the writer has thrown especially to us. Readers ask writers about their writing habits, as if by knowing what time of day and where their work takes place, readers might better understand the text that results. We want to know how the thing we love was created and when, the way we want to know everything about a new friend or lover. It is not the writer we want more of, but our own reading experience, the experience the writer's words gave to us. In bad writing, the writer's personality stands between the reader and the book. Details about the writer's flat feet and unhappy sex life don't add to the intimacy of reading his or her best work—unless the biography is another wonderful book to read.

Even in a public reading by an author or an actor the words are still received silently and privately. In several accounts that we've included of being a young reader, the writers mention their surprise at discovering, as Eudora Welty says, that books are not "natural wonders" but are the creations of human beings. Such is the power of the story for a child, even more so when the story is read aloud. In our best experiences of reading the sense returns of literature as a natural wonder.

Reading may be the last private act of our lives. We talk openly—and our fellow citizens are polled constantly—about sex, marriage, family troubles, political and religious beliefs. But few people are asked about their reading habits: Where do you like to read and at what time of day or night? Does it drive you crazy if there's music playing? Do you do it lying down or sitting up? Do you eat or drink while you read?

Reading is the great escape, annoying sometimes to those who live with bookworms. For many readers, the time when they read before sleep is an encapsulation of what happens on an ideal vacation. The daily round of obligations, duties, and appointments is over; however well or badly you've done, the day is in the past. Reading before sleep is a safe blue harbor of oblivion where you forget where you are and who you are, for so long as you manage to stay awake. It doesn't seem to matter if what you read is disturbing, moving, or tragic; the troubles are not yours, though for a moment you believe in them. It is a sign of intimacy to be able to read in the same room with another person, as trusting as dreaming with someone right beside you.

Through reading, we intensify our capacity for pleasure, for sympathy, and for comprehension. What we read utterly changes our relation to the world. There is a thirst in all readers for stories that teach us about the world and ourselves.

We have divided our book of reading experiences into six sections, each with a short introduction.

In "The Young Reader," we present the literacy narrative—recollections of first decoding the words on a page and the memories of exactly where and when this magical act occurred.

In "Sorts of Readers," we look at styles of reading—skipping, slogging through the boring parts, forgetting everything, forgetting nothing, and addicted serial reading.

The thought of being read to by another person inspires in most of us nostalgia for the sound of a lost voice. Others recoil when someone threatens to read to them. Both reactions can be found in "Reading Aloud."

"Reading Ahead" includes some of the voices lifted now in argument, grief, and/or exaltation at the presence of electronic media in our reading lives.

Reading sometimes provides the velocity for an escape from humble beginnings, from oppression, from physical disability, from madness, and such experiences we've included in "Queen Lear."

Our final section, "The Privileged Pleasure," is a celebration of the activity that makes our lives better and sometimes possible.

No one could omit "On First Looking Into Chapman's *Homer*" by John Keats from a book about reading. But as we dug, we discovered ever rarer and more unusual things. We traveled the world with our writers. We discovered kindred spirits, brother and sister readers, kids like we were who wouldn't be stopped from reading, and adults like we've become who read as addicts, who read to save their lives.

There is so much we have not included. We could continue searching forever because—thank God—there is no end of things to read. This collaboration of old friends has doubled our energy for reading. Thanks to the miracles and speed of modern electronics, we can almost read each other's minds.

Laura Furman   *Austin, Texas*
Elinore Standard   *Pound Ridge, New York*

I
THE YOUNG
READER

Jane Austen
(1775–1817)

> ". . . you . . . may perhaps be brought to acknowledge that it is very well worthwhile to be tormented for two or three years of one's life, for the sake of being able to read all the rest of it."
>
> NORTHANGER ABBEY

We recently asked someone who, at the age of six, is a lot closer to the primal reading experience than we are, to explain the difference between being able and not being able to read. "Well," he said, "when you can't read, you don't, and when you can, you can." Notice the self-assurance in this reply! The ability to make sense of those two-dimensional squiggles on a page is a giant step toward independence and power.

George Bernard Shaw remarked that he couldn't remember actually learning to read and therefore wondered if he was born able to read. Few of us remember the process of learning to read but we usually recall the sensation we had when the marks and scribbles suddenly took on meaning.

The young person's slow awareness of the chasm between the lives of people in books and what can be called "real life" is a theme within the literacy narratives in "The Young Reader." By reading about other lives, children locate themselves in a place, time, and context larger than their families; they continuously cross and recross the borders between worlds. The young reader can try on different—sometimes wild or bizarre—aspirations, and engage in what has been called "self-translation."

As we grow, we shuttle back and forth between the real and the unreal, between insider and outsider, between past and present. Through the ability to read, a child is introduced to time and place, to the clash of identity and culture, to what Penelope Lively says is the "transforming element of identification."

3

Alan Bennett

(b. 1934)

Alan Bennett was born and brought up in Leeds where his father was a butcher. Bennett first appeared on the stage in the early 1960s in the revue Beyond the Fringe. *He has written many plays and in 1994,* Writing Home, *a collection of memoirs, diaries, talks, reminiscences, and reviews that was on the best seller list in Britain and the U.S. for months.*

"What you want to be", Mam said to my brother and me, "is gentlemen farmers. They earn up to £10 a week." It was in Leeds some time in the early years of the war, when my father, a butcher at Armley Lodge Road Co-op, was getting £6 a week and they thought themselves not badly off. So it's not the modesty of my mother's aspirations that seems surprising now but the direction. Why gentlemen farmers? And the answer, of course, was books.

We had, it's true, had some experience of a farm. I was five when the war started, and Monday 4 September 1939 should have been my first day at school; but that was not to be. I wish I could record our family was gathered anxiously round the wireless, as most were at eleven o'clock that Sunday morning, but I already knew at the age of five that I belonged to a family that without being in the least bit remarkable or eccentric yet managed never to be quite like other families. If we had been, my brother and I would have been evacuated with all the other children the week before, but Mam and Dad hadn't been able to face it. So, not quite partaking in the national mood and, as ever, unbrushed by the wings of history, Mr. Chamberlain's broadcast found us on a tram going down Tong Road into Leeds. Fearing the worst, my parents had told my brother and me that we were all going out into the country that day and we

5

were to have a picnic—something I had hitherto only come across in books. So on that fateful Sunday morning what was occupying my mind was the imminent conjunction of life with literature; that I should remember nothing of the most momentous event in the twentieth century because of the prospect of an experience found in books was, I see now, a melancholy portent.

Nor was the lesson that life was not going to live up to literature slow in coming, since the much-longed-for picnic wasn't eaten as picnics were in books, on a snowy tablecloth set in a field by a stream, but was taken on a form in the bus station at Vicar Lane, where we waited half that day for any bus that would take us out of the supposedly doomed city.

Early that afternoon a bus came, bound for Pateley Bridge, the other side of Harrogate. Somewhere along the way and quite at random the four of us got off and our small odyssey was ended. It was a village called Wilsill, in Nidderdale. There were a few houses, a shop, a school and a church and, though we were miles from any town even here the stream had been dammed to make a static water tank in readiness for the firefighters and the expected bombs. Opposite the bus-stop was a farm. My father was a shy man and, though I'm sure there were many larger acts of bravery being done elsewhere that day, to knock at the door of the farm and ask some unknown people to take us in still seems to me to be heroic. Their name was Weatherhead and they did take us in and without question, as people were being taken in all over England that first week of the war.

That night Dad took the bus back to Leeds, my mother weeping as if he were returning to the front, and there at Wilsill we stayed—but for how long? My brother, then aged eight, says it was three weeks; to me, three years younger, it seemed months; but, weeks or months, very happy it was until, once it became plain nothing was going to happen for a while, we went back home, leaving Byril Farm (which is now, alas, not a farm and has carriage lamps) standing out in my mind as the one episode in my childhood that lived up to the story-books.

I had read quite a few story-books by this time, as I had

learned to read quite early by dint, it seemed to me, of staring over my brother's shoulder at the comic he was reading until suddenly it made sense. Though I liked reading (and showed off at it), it was soon borne in upon me that the world of books was only distantly related to the world in which I lived. The families I read about were not like our family (no family ever quite was). These families had dogs and gardens and lived in country towns equipped with thatched cottages and mill-streams, where the children had adventures, saved lives, caught villains, and found treasure before coming home, tired but happy, to eat sumptuous teas off chequered tablecloths in low-beamed parlours presided over by comfortable pipe-smoking fathers and gentle aproned mothers, who were invariably referred to as Mummy and Daddy.

Ellen Glasgow
(1874–1945)

When or where I learned to read, I could never remember. When I look back, it seems to me that one day the alphabet was merely a row of black or red marks on paper, and the next day I was earnestly picking out the letters in *Old Mortality*.

THE WOMAN WITHIN

In an effort to bring this fabulous world closer to my own, more threadbare, existence, I tried as a first step substituting "Mummy" and "Daddy" for my usual "Mam" and "Dad", but was pretty sharply discouraged. My father was hot on anything smacking of social pretension; there had even been an argument at the font because my aunties had wanted my brother given two Christian names instead of a plain one.

Had it been only stories that didn't measure up to the world it wouldn't have been so bad. But it wasn't only fiction that was fiction. Fact too was fiction, as textbooks seemed to bear no more relation to the real world than did the story-books. At school or in my *Boy's Book of the Universe* I read of the minor wonders of nature—the sticklebacks that haunted the most ordinary pond, the newts and toads said to lurk under every stone, and the dragonflies that flitted over the dappled surface. Not, so far as I could see, in Leeds. There were owls in hollow trees, so the nature books said, but I saw no owls—and hollow trees were in pretty short supply too. The only department where nature actually lined up with the text was frog-spawn. Even in Leeds there was that, jamjars of which I duly fetched home to stand beside great wilting bunches of bluebells on the backyard windowsill. But the tadpoles never seemed to graduate to the full-blown frogs the literature predicted, invariably giving up the ghost as soon as they reached the two-legged stage when, unbeknownst to Mam, they would have to be flushed secretly down the lav.

It was the same when we went on holiday. If the books were to be believed, every seashore was littered with starfish and delicately whorled shells, seahorses in every rockpool and crabs the like of which I had seen only in Macfisheries' window. Certainly I never came across them at Morecambe, nor any of the other advertised treasures of the seashore. There was only a vast, untenanted stretch of mud and somewhere beyond it the sea, invisible, unpaddleable and strewn with rolls of barbed wire to discourage any parachutist undiscerning enough to choose to land there.

These evidences of war and the general shortage of treats and toys made me somehow blame the shortcomings of the natural world on the current hostilities. I don't recall seeing a magnolia tree in blossom until I was fifteen or so, and when I did I found myself thinking "Well, they probably didn't have them during the war." And so it was with shells and starfish and all the rest of Nature's delights: she had put these small treasures into storage for the duration, along with signposts, neon lights and the slot machines for Five Boys chocolate that stood, invariably empty, on every railway platform.

This sense of deprivation, fully developed by the time I was seven or eight, sometimes came down to particular words. I had read many stories, beginning I suppose with *Babes in the Woods*, how the childish hero and heroine, lost in the forest, had nevertheless spent a cosy night bedded down on *pine needles*. I had never come across these delightfully accommodating features and wondered where they were to be found. Could one come across them in Leeds? It was not short of parks after all—Gott's Park, Roundhay Park—surely one of them would have pine needles.

And then there was *sward,* a word that was always cropping up in *Robin Hood*. It was what tournaments and duels were invariably fought on. But what was sward? "Grass," said my teacher, Miss Timpson, shortly, but I knew it couldn't be. Grass was the wiry, sooty stuff that covered the Rec in Moorfield Road where we played at night after school. That was not sward. So once, hearing of some woods in Bramley, a few miles from where we lived, I went off on the trail of sward, maybe hoping to come across pine needles in the process. I trailed out past the rhubarb fields at Hill Top, over Stanningley Road then down into the valley that runs up from Kirkstall Abbey. But all I found were the same mouldy old trees and stringy grass that we had at Armley. Pine needles, sward, starfish and stickle-backs—they were what you read about in books.

Books are where the gentlemen farmers must have come from too, from Winifred Holtby's *South Riding* perhaps, or something by Phyllis Bentley, both novelists my mother favoured—local celebrities (as much later was John Braine), writers who had escaped the mill or the mine and made good, the making good invariably taking the form of going Down South. These books, and those my brother and I read, would be borrowed from Armley Library at the bottom of Wesley Road, a grand turn-of-the-century building with a marble staircase and stained-glass swing doors.

The Junior Library was in a room of its own, and an institution more intended to discourage children from reading could not have been designed. It was presided over by a fierce British

Legion commissionaire, a relic of the Boer War, who, with his medals and walrus moustache was the image of Hindenburg as pictured on the German stamps in my brother's album. The books were uniformly bound in stout black or maroon covers, so whether they were Henry, Captain Marryat or (my favourite) Hugh Lofting, they looked a pretty unenticing read.

In contrast the Adults' Library was a bright and cheerful place, where Dad would be looking for something funny by Stephen Leacock or what he called "a good tale", and Mam would be in Non-Fiction seeking her particular brand of genteel escape—sagas of couples who had thrown up everything to start a smallholding (gentlemen farmers in the making) or women like Monica Dickens who had struck out on their own. A particular favourite was William Holt, whose *I Haven't Unpacked* was one of the few books Mam ever bought, and again it was escape—the story of someone brought up, as she had been, in a mill town but who had bought a horse and gone off on his travels.

This theme of escape, very strong in Wells and Priestley, tantalized my parents for much of their lives. Dreams of leaving I suppose they had, and I now share them, feeling myself as nailed to my table as ever my Dad was to his shop counter. They never did escape quite, though they made a shot at it just once when, towards the end of the war, my father gave up his job at the Co-op, answered an advert in the *Meat Trades Journal* and got a job working for a private butcher in Guildford. And in Guildford for a year we lived. Down South. And there were thatched cottages and mill-streams and children who called their parents "Mummy" and "Daddy"—the world I had read about in my books, and the world Mam and Dad had read about in theirs.

But, thatched cottages or no thatched cottages, they were not happy, and one miserable December night in 1945 the four of us got off the train at Holbeck and trailed disconsolately back to my grandma's house and reality. It was another lesson that you should not believe what you read in books.

From time to time after this my mother's hands would be covered in terrible eczema, the joints cracked open, the skin scaling away. "My hands have broken out again," she would say, and put it down to the wrong soap. But it was as if she was now caged in and this the only "breaking out" she was capable of.

The few books we owned were largely reference books, bought by subscription through magazines: *Enquire Within, What Everybody Wants to Know* and, with its illustrations of a specimen man and woman (minus private parts and pubic hair), *Everybody's Home Doctor*. No book, whether from the library or otherwise, was ever on view. Anthony Powell's *Books Do Furnish a Room* was not my mother's way of thinking. "Books untidy a room" more like, or, as she would have said, "Books upset." So if there were any books being read they would be kept out of sight, generally in the cabinet that had once held a wind-up gramophone, bought when they were first married and setting up house.

Eudora Welty
(b. 1909)

. . . You could not take back a book to the Library on the same day you'd taken it out; it made no difference to her (the librarian) that you'd read every word in it and needed another to start. You could take out two books at a time and two only; that applied as long as you were a child and also for the rest of your life, to my mother as severely as to me.

ONE WRITER'S BEGINNINGS

This undercover attitude to books persisted long after I had grown up and had accumulated books of my own. I worked in the spare room, though it was never dignified as such and just known as the junk room. That was where the books were kept now, and there among the broken lampshades and bits of old carpet and hemmed in by the sewing-machine and the family suitcases I would set up a table and work. To begin with it was for my degree, then it was research in medieval history, and finally writing proper. But to my mother it was all the same: to her my life had not changed since I was fourteen and doing School Certificate, so degree, research or writing plays was always called "your swotting".

As a young man my father had some literary ambitions, going in for competitions in magazines such as *Tit-Bits* and even sending in little paragraphs and being paid. By the forties his efforts were concentrated on one competition, Bullets, a feature of the magazine *John Bull*, the point of which was to come up with a telling phrase on a given topic, the phrase to be witty, ironic or ambiguous—in effect a verbal cartoon. Once he had regularly won small prizes, but though he went on plugging away during the war, and until the magazine folded in the late forties, he won only a few pounds.

I couldn't get the hang of Bullets or see the point or the humour of the entries that won; they seemed like Tommy Handley's jokes—everybody said they were funny, but they never made you laugh. If I missed *John Bull* when it closed down it was for its cover paintings, in particular the landscapes of Rowland Hilder—idyllic downland farms, beech trees against a winter sky—or the townscapes of deaf and dumb artist A. R. Thomson, as English as Norman Rockwell was American.

In later life my father was often ill and this started him reading again, only now his taste was much more eclectic and he would try any book he found on my shelves. Knowing nothing of reputation and just judging a book by whether he could "get into it" or not, he lapped up Evelyn Waugh and Graham Greene, revelled in Nancy Mitford, but couldn't take (at opposite extremes) Buchan or E. F. Benson; Orwell he just about managed ("though there's not much of a tale to it"), and he liked Gavin Maxwell and especially Wilfred Thesiger. When he came to the episode in *Ring of Bright Water* when a Scots road-mender casually kills one of Maxwell's pet otters with a spade he burst out, "Why, the bad sod!"

This phrase had a literary history and was something of a family joke. As a child Dad had been taken to the Grand Theatre to see *Uncle Tom's Cabin* and in the scene in which Uncle Tom was being flogged by the overseer, Simon Legree, a woman sitting next to Dad in the gallery shouted out, "You bad sod!" The actor playing Simon Legree stopped, looked up at the gallery, leered, and then laid it on twice as hard.

Towards the end of his life I had so taken it for granted that our taste in reading coincided that I forgot how shy and fastidi-ous my father was and how far his world still was from mine. Though there may have been a priggish element of "I think you are now ready for this" about it, I did think that when I gave him Philip Roth's *Portnoy's Complaint* he would find it as funny as I did. Always anxious to talk about what he had read, on my next visit home he never mentioned it, and I later found it back on the shelf, the jacket marking the twenty pages or so that he had got through before deciding it was pornography and not something for him, and by implication not something for me, though nothing was ever said. It was a miscalculation that mor-tifies me to this day.

My mother was more broadminded and might have found *Portnoy's Complaint* quite funny, but Dad's literary renaissance never infected her, and for years her reading was largely con-fined to *Woman's Own* and in particular to the column written by Beverley Nichols, of whom she was a great fan. But seeing the Brontës frequently referred to in the *Yorkshire Evening Post* she began to persuade herself she had read them or perhaps would like to—maybe because (another escape story) if they hadn't got away from their surroundings they had at any rate transcended them. So on a bleak February day in the late forties she and I took the Keighley bus to Haworth to see the famous parsonage. Not so famous then, Haworth was still happily un-

aware of its potential as a tourist trap, its situation on the frontiers of *Last of the Summer Wine* country far in the future. The
place must have had some charm but it looked to me like any
other grim mill town and all I could think as we toiled up that
long hill was that it must be even more dismal on a Sunday.

We were the only visitors to the parsonage that day, and it
was as dark and damp as it must have been when the famous
trio lived there. Ramshackle and unrenovated, it was, even for
1948, a decidedly eccentric museum, looked after by a lady who,
if not actually a contemporary of the Brontës, seemed their
sister in suffering. Objects around the house were only haphazardly labelled: the sofa on which Emily died, for instance, just
had pinned to it a yellowing piece of paper that said starkly,
"Sofa Emily died on". Mam was horrified. The fireplace
wanted blackleading and the curtains were a disgrace. "Too
busy writing their books to keep the place up to scratch," was
her comment.

Michael Holroyd
(b. 1935)

In my teens I spent a lot of time at the new public
library. My aunt patronized the private lending library
at Boots the Chemist. But growing curious about my
library, she followed me there and was dazzled by
what she saw and, like many middle-class people
round the country, became a convert to the public library system. Being cautious, she would lightly roast
the books in our oven for the sake of the germs.

"DIARY"

Though this was long before the tasteful pall of heritage was
laid across the past, the parsonage can have survived in this

Victorian state only a few years longer. Had it been kept as it was then, it would today be in a museum itself, a museum of museums perhaps. It would certainly be more interesting and characteristic than the branch of Laura Ashley the parsonage is now, though there's not much doubt which Mam would have preferred.

My parents always felt that had they been educated their lives and indeed their characters would have been different. They imagined books would make them less shy and (always an ambition) able to "mix". Quiet and never particularly gregarious, they cherished a lifelong longing to "branch out", with books somehow the key to it. This unsatisfied dream they have bequeathed to me, so that without any conscious intention I find I am often including in plays or films what is essentially the same scene: someone is standing at a bookcase; it may be a boy with no education, not daring to choose a book, or a wife anxious to share in the literary world of men; it can be Joe Orton looking at Kenneth Halliwell's bookcase and despairing of ever catching up, or even Coral Browne, idly turning over the pages of Guy Burgess's books while being quizzed about Cyril Connolly, whom she does not know. One way or another they are all standing in for my parents and sharing their uncertainty about books. As for me, while I'm not baffled by books, I can't see how anyone can love them ("He loved books."). I can't see how anyone can "love literature". What does that mean? Of course, one advantage of being a gentleman farmer is that you seldom have to grapple with such questions.

—from *Writing Home*

Rita Ciresi

(b. 1960)

Mother Rocket, *Rita Ciresi's collection of short stories, won the Flannery O'Connor Short Story award from University of Georgia Press. She lives and teaches in Virginia.*

Books were rare sightings in my parents' house. Yellowed copies of *The Catholic Transcript*—the pages neat and intact—sat stacked upon a TV tray in the dining room. The Sunday edition of the *New Haven Register* hung around the living room until the end of the week, flung from one chair to another until the Saturday morning chore list dictated we toss it out. On top of a side table lay evidence that some relative or friend had given my father a year's subscription to *Sports Illustrated*—five or six Christmases ago. In 1973, visitors to our house still could read about the heartbreaks and triumphs of the 1968 Olympics.

Relatives jokingly referred to our bathroom as The Reading Room. The *gabinetto* held the working-class solution to the necessity of "reading a little something" every day—*The Reader's Digest*. At least a year's worth of the *Digest* was stacked on our wicker bathroom hamper, the covers of the magazines bubbled and buckled from the humidity. The *Digest* offered action and inspiration. Articles on grizzly bear attacks, plane crashes in the Andes, and little girls who had fallen down wells were interspersed with counsel from Erma Bombeck and Billy Graham to work hard and keep up the faith.

The jokes found in the *Digest*—a strange combination of mediocre middle-American comedy and crass Borscht Belt humor—broke up the drabness of our lives. My father, a Sicilian immigrant, worked in a warehouse from three in the morning until dinner time. My mother—one of nine children—completed nursing school, but gave up her career the moment she married, after which she gave birth to four girls in a span of five years. Who had time to read? Books were for *i bimbi*— strictly for kids.

Elinore Standard
(b. 1933)

We had a six-shelf bookcase on the stair landing, and I can picture the titles which faced me every time I went up or down. My parents had joined the Book-of-the-Month Club and new books came along regularly. When nobody packed them up for return, we wound up keeping many that were sent. So in addition to an encyclopedia my father used when he was a boy and other old works such as collections of poetry by Eugene Field and John Masefield, and the *Complete Shakespeare,* there were now new works of fiction which I had all to myself. I read Steinbeck's *The Red Pony,* Marjory Sharp's *Cluny Brown,* and I memorized all of the captions to the Willy and Joe cartoons in Bill Mauldin's *Up Front.* Somehow, a hilarious Max Schulman book got into the house: "Bang, bang, bang, bang, four shots rang out and I was off on another exciting adventure!"

"MY READING LIFE"

Like other children on our block, we had a small collection of classics—a distilled, incomprehensible account of *Alice's Adventures in Wonderland,* a badly-drawn version of *Cinderella* that made the fair maiden look just as hideous as her evil stepsisters, and a copy of *Peter Pan* whose cover showed the forever-young boy staring dolefully out a window. Peter Pan's treatment of Wendy and Tinker Bell inspired the wrath of one of my sisters, who took out her collection of Bic pens and gave Peter the long, dark eyelashes seen in Maybelline ads, and the full red lips found on photos of Marilyn Monroe in *Life*. Underneath Peter's picture, my sister wrote the ultimate Fourth-Street insult: *faggot*.

Although I sometimes resented my parents for not encouraging us to read, the truth must be told: It's probably *because* there was so little to read in the house that I became a writer. Literature—almost as inaccessible as Cadillacs and diamond rings—fascinated me. Each story was a magic-carpet ride to another world, a mythical place where the major concerns weren't who was getting married next June and which deli offered the most prosciutto for your dollar.

My mother distrusted the written word. But a library card was free and a visit to the Circular Avenue Branch kept us four girls busy on Saturdays, after all the chores were completed. So the library became a weekend habit, then an addiction. Alarmed by our greed—who wanted prodigy children?—my mother put strict boundaries on our acquisition of knowledge. Although the library limit was five, my mother restricted us to two books each. I checked out the same group over and over again. Now I can barely remember the plot lines, but the titles and the covers of these favorites remain vivid in my memory: *Wait for William, Strawberry Girl, The Boxcar Children.*

Organized visits to the library came to a halt when my sisters turned 10, 11, and 13, and preferred mooning over the men on baseball cards to reading *The Red Pony*. With great joy, I continued the weekly visits by myself. At the age of nine—with no one to reprimand me for overstepping my bounds—I graduated from the Early Reader and juvenile sections to the "teen stacks." Here I found books called *Sister of the Bride* and *Beanie Gets a Boyfriend*. Written in the 1950s, these novels told of girls—real American girls—who longed to own yellow slickers and cashmere sweaters and who dreamed of the happy day when their mothers would allow them to get pierced ears. The young heroine lusted after a letterman—usually the football captain, who typically was called something like Ken or Kevin—but by the end of the book she discovered that this boy drove fast and drank beer, so she settled on dating the nice nerd with glasses who sat next to her in math class—usually called George or Chip—who had lanky legs and a cowlick, but who played clarinet or trumpet like a dream.

My mother was not pleased with such books, or rather, the amount of time I spent reading them. If I had that many hours to devote to stories, I would do just as well to pick up a dust-cloth or dustpan. And how about playing outside? Jump rope or hopscotch were healthier than fantasizing about Ken and Kevin. I rolled my eyes, confirming my mother's fear that past *Curious George* and *My Friend Flicka* books somehow were sub-versive. Books made young people lazy, disrespectful, and dis-content with the world.

My mother grumbled. My father grumbled. These low, bes-tial, half-Italian, half-English noises translated into "Get your nose out of your book and get a job."

Someone once asked Graham Greene which classics formed him as a writer. He replied that he owed his inspiration to his love for boy's adventure stories. The books that formed my imagination had to be read, after my ridiculously early bedtime, by the pale beam of a metal flashlight, because they were con-demned by *The Catholic Transcript* and would have raised an-other ruckus with my mother. *The Godfather* and *Love Story* thrilled me.

The characters fought and loved, and best of all, swore! Each g—d— and f— illuminated by the flashlight seemed to send me further on the road to perdition. I was seduced by the foulness of the language, the thefts, the murders, the mad passionate forays into adultery. Had I not been raised in a house where rosary beads were strung on every bedpost and a plastic Pietà sat on top of the TV, these books probably would not have held such a grip on my imagination.

Reading always has been an act of rebellion for me, against Catholicism and other aspects of Italian American culture. All children rebel. I've heard tell that a young and even likable version of my father used to sneak down to my grandfather's cellar and suck the nasty, dandelion potion from the rubber hoses that came out of the wine casks. I've been informed that my tomboy mother once shaved her head.

But like most writers—Italian American or otherwise—I think I'm in a Peter Pan state of arrested development, adolescent forever. Each time I sit down at the computer I feel as stealthy as the girl who once discovered, beneath a mold-spotted shower curtain in my parents' basement, a stack of "pornographic" literature left behind by a more educated neighbor who was moved to a rest home. . . .

The only book I ever truly read from that stack, called *Paradise Below the Stairs,* fascinated me in a way all writers hope to engross readers. The novel was translated from the French and described sex among a group of teenagers. If I recall the plot correctly, one scene described a girl excusing herself from a *lycée* Latin class and returning to her desk, where she wrapped a single strand of her pubic hair in a piece of paper and passed it to the boy sitting behind her.

I entered that novel as if transported by light into heaven. And ever since then my idea of heaven has been to write the kind of stories that sweep people beyond the gray walls of their parents' living room, the blare of the TV, and the that's-life-so-what-are-you-gonna-do-about-it? attitude that made my relatives seem bitter and shriveled as dark black olives. I write for the girl I once was, who found paradise in the pages of a book and pure music in the characters' voices, which were strong enough to drown the summer-long drone of Phil Rizzuto calling out line drives to left field on my father's ancient, crackling table radio.

—from "Paradise Below the Stairs"

Clarice Lispector

(1925–1977)

At seven, Clarice Lispector realized for the first time that books were written: "I thought a book was like a tree, an animal, something that grows. I had no idea there was an author standing in the wings." This was the beginning of a distinguished career as one of Brazil's best modern novelists.

Someone once asked me which was the first book of my life. I prefer to speak of the first book of each of my lives. As I search in my memory, I have the physical sensation of clutching that treasure in my hands: a slim little volume which included the story of "The Ugly Duckling" and "The Tale of Aladdin and his Magic Lamp". As a child, I would read those stories over and over again. Children, unlike adults, do not have this foible of only reading books once: a child learns things almost by rote, and even when he has memorized it word for word, the child is capable of rereading the book with almost the same excitement experienced the first time. The story of the little duckling who was so ugly that he stood out amongst all the others who were pretty, but when he grew up the mystery was solved: he was not a duck but a beautiful swan. This story gave me much food for thought and I identified with the suffering of the ugly little duckling. Who knows, perhaps I, too, was a swan?

As for Aladdin, he sent my imagination into the realms of the impossible, I was so credulous. And at that age, I could still believe in the impossible. The idea of the Genie who said: "Ask of me what you will for I am here to serve you," made me feel quite faint. Sitting quietly in my corner, I wondered if the Genie would say to me one day: "Ask of me what you will." But even as a child, I somehow realized that I am one of those people who must rely on their own resources in order to get what they want, if and when the opportunity arises.

. . . In another of my lives, I became a member of a public library. I tended to choose books at random and usually by their title. And one day I picked out *Steppenwolf* by Hermann Hesse. I found the title appealing and somehow reminiscent of an adventure story such as Jack London's *The Call of the Wild*. With every reading, Hesse's novel continued to amaze me. This book contained more than one adventure. I had been writing short stories since my early teens but Hesse's influence opened up a new chapter of inspiration and I set about writing a long story in imitation of his style: this inner voyage was one of endless fascination. I had come into contact with great literature.

In yet another of my lives I was fifteen and earning money for the very first time. Feeling very pleased with myself, I went into a bookshop with money to spend and thought to myself that this was a world in which I could live quite happily. I leafed through most of the books displayed on the counters and read a few lines in each book before passing on to the next one. Until I opened a book which contained phrases so different from anything I had ever read before that I remained there, my eyes glued to the page. In my excitement I thought to myself: but this book is me! And struggling to control my emotions, I bought it. It was only later that I discovered that the author, far from being unknown, was considered to be one of the best writers of her age: none other than Katherine Mansfield.

—from *Discovering the World*

Lispector had a speech defect so that she rolled her r's as if she were speaking French, and sounded foreign, not really Brazilian. In fact she was born in a tiny Ukrainian village where her parents stopped on their way to the seaport of Odessa, and she arrived in Brazil at the age of two months. She started writing stories as a child in the

*northeastern Brazilian city of Alagoas. Eventually her family moved
to Rio de Janeiro, but the particular language of northeastern Brazil
was crucial to her work. She completed a law degree but never
practiced, and worked as one of Brazil's first women journalists. She
was prolific in her all-too-short life, publishing nine novels, eight
collections of stories, four children's tales, and a Portuguese translation of Oscar Wilde's* The Picture of Dorian Gray. *For about six
years, Lispector wrote* crônicas—*a form of diary, story, interview,
travel notes, and miscellany—for a Brazilian newspaper. Her* crônicas *have the same freshness and immediacy as Katherine Mansfield's
journals and letters, and it isn't surprising that she was drawn to
Mansfield's work. Among her favorite writers were Hermann Hesse,
Machado de Assis, and Jorge Amado.*

She was fat, short, and freckled and her hair was much too
frizzy. Her bust had become enormous while all the rest of us
were flat-chested. And as if this were not bad enough, she
would fill the top pockets of her blouse with toffees. But she
had what any little girl who adored stories would like to have: a
father who owned a bookshop.

She did not appear to benefit much from this good fortune;
the rest of us even less so. Instead of giving us a little book for
our birthday, she would hand us a postcard from her father's
shop. And what is more, with a view of Recife and its bridges,
the city where we ourselves lived. On the back she would write
words like *happy birthday* and *greetings* in fancy lettering.

But there was such a cruel streak in her nature. Making loud
noises as she sucked her toffees, she found ways and means of
being vindictive. How this little girl must have hated us, we
who were unforgivably pretty, slender, and tall, with long,
smooth hair. She practised her sadism on me with calm ferocity.
I was so anxious to borrow books that I did not even notice the
humiliations to which she subjected me: I kept on begging her
to lend me the books she never bothered to read. Until that
glorious day for her when she began to subject me to Chinese

torture. She casually informed me that she possessed a copy of
As reinações de Narizinho [The Adventures of Little Snotty].

It was a big book, dear God, a book one could live with, eat
and sleep with. And well beyond my means. She told me to call
at her house the next day and she would lend me the book.
Waiting for the following day to come, I became transformed
into the very promise of happiness: I was not living, but swimming slowly in tranquil waters.

Next day I went to her house, running all the way. She lived
in a house, not in a first-floor apartment like me. She did not
ask me in. Looking me straight in the eye, she told me she had
loaned the book to another girl and to come back the day after
to collect it. Dumbfounded, I slowly walked away, but hope
soon returned and I began skipping again, a strange habit of
mine, as I went through the streets of Recife. This time I did
not stumble once: the promise of that book guided me: the next
day would soon be here, the following days were to be my
whole life and I went skipping through the streets as usual
without stumbling even once.

Fine, but there was more to come. The secret plan of the
bookseller's daughter was calculated and diabolical. Next day I
was back on her doorstep with a smile, my heart pounding with
excitement. Only to hear the calm reply: the book had still not
been returned and I was to return the following day. Little did I
suspect that, for the rest of my life, this drama of waiting until
the following day would recur time and time again while my
heart went on pounding.

And so it continued. For how long? I could not say. She
knew there could be no definite time before the hatred drained
from that thick body of hers. I had already become aware that I
was her chosen victim. Sometimes I can sense such things. Yet
even though perceiving them, I often resign myself, as if the
person who wishes to cause me suffering needs to see me suffer.

For how long? I went to her house every day without fail.
Sometimes she would say: I had the book here yesterday but
you didn't come so I loaned it to another girl. And, unusual for
me, I began to feel dark circles forming round my startled eyes.

Until finally one day, as I was standing at her door, listening humbly and in silence to her excuses, the girl's mother appeared. She was obviously puzzled by the strange appearance of this girl who turned up day after day. She questioned both of us. There was silent confusion, interrupted by words which explained little or nothing. The girl's mother became more and more exasperated. Until the truth finally dawned on her. She turned to her daughter and exclaimed with great surprise: But that book has never left the house and you have shown no interest in reading it! This discovery was bad enough but not nearly as bad as discovering the kind of daughter she had. She looked at us in horror: this perverse daughter whom she scarcely recognized and the little girl standing at the door, weary and exposed to the wind-blown streets of Recife. Then, pulling herself together, she spoke firmly to her daughter without raising her voice: "You will lend *The Adventures of Narizinho* to this child at once." And to me she said the one thing I had never dared hope to hear: "And you must keep the book for as long as you like. Is that clear?" Those words meant more to me than being given the book: for as long as you like is all that anyone, young or old, could possibly wish for.

How can I describe what followed? I was in a daze as I took the book. No, no, I did not go skipping off as usual. I went off, walking very slowly. I know that I was clutching the book in both hands, pressing it to my bosom. How long it took me to reach home is of no consequence. My breast was warm, my mood troubled and pensive.

On arriving home I did not start to read. I pretended not to have the book, so as to postpone the pleasure of discovering I had it. I opened the book some hours later and read some lines, I closed it once more, went wandering through the house, ate some bread and butter to pass the time, pretended I could not remember where I had put the book, found it again, opened it for several moments. I invented the most absurd strategies to postpone that clandestine thing called happiness. I felt proud yet insecure. I was a vulnerable queen.

Sometimes I would sit in the hammock, swinging back and

forth in ecstasy, the book lying open on my lap, yet never touching it. I was no longer a little girl with a book: I was a woman with her lover.

—from *Discovering the World*

Hal Borland

(1900–1978)

If you manage to find a copy of High, Wide and Lonesome *(1956), Hal Borland's wonderful boyhood memoir of homesteading days in an isolated 14 × 20 cabin made of earth, a "soddy," in the high prairie of Colorado, you'll want to get out your U.S. atlas.*

Find the northeast corner of Colorado, south of the Platte River. You'll locate towns of Brush, Hillrose, Snyder, and Union but even today, there is a lot of blank space in that area of the map. This land was orginally deemed by President Rutherford B. Hayes "unsalable desert, unfit for human habitation" in 1877, the year after Colorado joined the union, and fifteen years after the Homestead Act of 1862.

Borland's people originally came to America from Scotland before the Revolution, and over generations followed the westward migration, some taking a gamble, as Borland's father did in 1910, on free land. As homesteaders, if settlers in northeastern Colorado could hold out without starving in that forbidding country, after three consecutive years of habitation the land was theirs. As Borland says in his introduction, High, Wide and Lonesome *was written when the Old West wasn't too far in the past.*

So remote was the Borland place, the nearest rail station was at Brush, often a daylong horseback ride. The nearest phone and post office were twelve miles away, a doctor was thirty miles away.

The Borlands finally gave up the homestead and Hal Borland's father took a job editing a newspaper in Flagler, Colorado. After college, Borland left Colorado, graduated from the Columbia School of Journalism, and settled in Connecticut. He often wrote about the West in novels and hundreds of magazine and newspaper pieces.

It was a glistening cold day and the snow hadn't melted. It lay soft and almost powdery, about five inches deep. I climbed the ridge back of the house and started west.

It's strange, when you're not out after rabbits you see dozens of them and when you are after them you can go five miles and not see one. That day, of course, they were lying close because of the cold. I saw the first jack. He was a big white-tail, and he jumped out of a clump of bunch grass twenty yards ahead of me. He ran like mad, quartering away from me, but I got a shot at him. I didn't lead him enough. The shot kicked up snow just behind him. Then he really ran.

I reloaded and took after him, hoping he would settle in and give me a chance for another shot. But he wasn't settling. I trailed him two miles and saw him twice, both times far out of range.

I was at least three miles from home when I saw a thread of smoke over the next rise half a mile away. It must be from the Bromley place, I thought. The Bromleys were the Chicago people who came out with the strange farm implements. Bromley was the man about whom people had joked, quoting his ridiculous questions and no doubt making up as many as he really asked. We still hadn't met them, because they had been using the road over west and doing their trading in Fort Morgan, which was eleven miles west of Brush.

I saw the thread of smoke and I remembered the funny stories. Then my rabbit jumped, just out of range, and I knew he was getting tired of running. Next time he might let me get close enough for a shot. I hurried on. Then, just as I topped the rise, another big white-tail lunged out of the snow right in front of me. I was lucky. I led him just right and he went end over end. I'd got my first rabbit with the new gun.

I was running down the slope to pick up my rabbit when I heard a man shouting. I looked up and there was the Bromley house just below me, a little white-painted house, and a tall, stooped man was standing in the doorway shouting, "Hello! Hello! Come on in! Merry Christmas!"

I picked up my rabbit, proud as a young Indian who had killed his first fat buffalo cow, and went down to the house.

Mr. Bromley had on a store-bought suit and a white shirt. I

left my rabbit in the snow outside the door and went inside. The house was as big as ours, but it looked smaller because the bedroom was partitioned off, not just curtained, and there was a rug on the floor and curtains at the windows. It was full of savory cooking smells. Mrs. Bromley, a tall, slender woman with gray in her hair, had on a city dress. Both of them were old folks; they must have been in their forties. She greeted me and took my mackinaw and she urged me to sit down.

I sat on the edge of a chair beside a bookcase and a few minutes later Mrs. Bromley brought a cup of hot cocoa and a plate of cookies. Then they both sat down and began to ask questions. I drank cocoa and ate cookies and told them who I was and that Father was a printer, and that we came from Nebraska. And I told them about my new gun and the rabbit.

"You are rather young, aren't you?" Mrs. Bromley asked, "to be out hunting alone. Aren't you afraid you will get lost?"

I smiled. I never got lost.

Mr. Bromley said, "You are talking to a young plainsman, Alice, not to a city boy. A direct descendant of Daniel Boone and Kit Carson." He smiled.

I don't know what she answered, but she didn't laugh. I wasn't paying much attention, because I had seen the books in that bookcase beside me. There must have been thirty or forty books. One group of them were all alike except their titles. They were large red books with figures of Indians and frontiersmen outlined on their covers.

Mrs. Bromley was talking to me, asking, "Do you read?" and I remembered my manners.

"Yes ma'am," I said. "I read everything. I've read hundreds of stories in magazines Jack Clothier gave me. He's a cowboy from over at the Lazy Four, but he's gone to Wyoming now."

"Have you ever read Cooper?" she asked. "James Fenimore Cooper."

"No ma'am." I wasn't sure whether that was the name of a book, a magazine, or an author.

"Or Scott? Or Dickens?"

"No ma'am."

"I think you might like them," she said. She took one of the large red volumes from the shelf and handed it to me. I opened it and began to read *The Last of the Mohicans.*

I don't know how long I read. At eleven a boy can immerse himself completely in Cooper newly discovered. Mr. and Mrs. Bromley, their house, the plains themselves, were completely forgotten. But at last, I heard Mr. Bromley saying, "Here's another cup of cocoa to warm you on your way. You must start home before dark or your mother will worry. And you might get lost."

I put down the book and drank the cocoa, still in the woods with Hawkeye and Uncas. Then I put on my mackinaw, and Mrs. Bromley gave me a little package of cookies for my pocket. And she asked, "Would you like to take a book with you?"

I didn't have to answer. She saw my face. She took the book I had been reading, wrapped it carefully, and said, "Put it inside your coat and keep it dry. When you've finished it, bring it back and get another."

I picked up my shotgun, remembered to say my thanks, and started for home over the hills where the purple shadows of early dusk already lay deep across the snow.

I was halfway home before I emerged from the story of Uncas and a land I had never seen or heard of, before I really saw the Colorado plains and felt the numbing cold of that Christmas evening. Then I remembered that I had left my rabbit beside the Bromley doorway. The first rabbit I had shot with my new gun.

The quick of a boy's being is close to the surface. I began to cry, excusing the tears because my hands were cold and I was bitterly disappointed. I wanted so desperately to be a man and a provider. Father had given me the gun so we could have meat for the table.

The thoughts of boyhood are at once so simple and so complex, and the feelings can be so deep, so immediate. He hasn't yet calloused himself with adulthood. The world is at once close about him and remote as the stars; it is friendly, and intimate, and hopelessly baffling. He hasn't yet made his compromises with it.

I had just discovered a world of horizons beyond horizons, a world I couldn't see even from the top of the hay stack on a clear day. I had found something that would shape my whole life. It was too late now to go back for the rabbit, and as I trudged on I began to sense my discovery, a discovery even bigger than the plains. The tears stopped and I hurried on home, hugging both the gun and the book.

—from *High, Wide and Lonesome*

Phil O'Keeffe

(b. 1928)

Phil (Philomena) O'Keeffe grew up in the Liberties section of Dublin, bordered by the head of the Grand Canal, Heuston Station, the Guinness Brewery, St. Patrick's Cathedral, and the quays of the River Liffey. Many old European commercial cities had sections called Liberties. *There, by royal grant, the broader laws of the land might not apply: a debtor, for example, might find safe haven within The Liberties.*

In her memoir, Down Cobbled Streets *(1995), writer, poet, and teacher Phil O'Keeffe evokes the streets and lanes of the Liberties in Dublin before World War II, a time when draymen carted barrels of Guinness from the brewery at St. James Gate; when bread was delivered on steaming trays from the bakery; when the doctor from the Coombe made housecalls carrying his heavy, brass-bound bag. On market day, drovers urged their cattle across the Quays and up Cork Street.*

Reading was important in our house. Comics were considered a luxury—money was needed for more important things than buying the *Dandy* and the *Beano,* though we traded marbles, sweets, and help with homework with those who seemed to have comics as if by right. My father and mother encouraged us to read the newspapers out loud to them. My father would scan the *Evening Mail* or the *Herald* for an appropriate piece and sit back with his eyes closed while we struggled through the report.

My eldest sister, Madge, was top of her class at sums and geography, and her practical common sense was a great help to my mother. Babs was a reader and a dreamer. In the nuns' eyes, being a reader was the more important of the two. It set you apart, and it had to mean that you were good at everything else;

32

if you were good at reading English, you must be good at reading Irish, and Latin would come easily too. As a result, Babs got away with murder. The readers, because of their supposed intelligence, were sent to take charge of a class when a teacher was absent or, as in Babs's case, as a way of grooming a senior to set her sights on becoming a teacher. But I became a reader simply because I was inquisitive. I was not a dreamer; I just liked reading books.

My appetite for books had been sharpened in fourth class. Our new English reader was the story of a lone Indian named Red Cloud. Up to this we had read stories about mythical Mammys and Daddys who worked in well-apppointed kitchens and had gardens full of beautiful flowers which bore no resemblance to my mother's wallflowers and pansies. We read poems by Joseph Mary Plunkett and learned how much William Butler Yeats loved the Irish peasantry. But *Red Cloud* was just one long story from cover to cover. I couldn't believe it. I flew home from school, raced through my homework, and curled up on the kitchen chair, my legs tucked under me. I had a whole book to read, with chapters and headings, a beginning, a middle, and an end, and I read until my mother took the book from me, declaring that I'd make myself blind. Even so, I had finished *Red Cloud* before the class got a third of the way through it in the reading-out-loud sessions where we all stood in a wide circle and took turns at reading.

Besides our textbooks we were given copies of *The Imeldist,* the *Sacred Heart Messenger,* and *Far East* to read, but we had no library in the school. I read everything I could lay my hands on from cover to cover, and in sixth class I was handed my card for the Public Library in Thomas Street.

Beyond the glass-panelled door with its huge notice—SILENCE—was a musty world of mysterious delight and adventure. With its closed blinds and dark interior, the library became a refuge from the heat of the city's pavements in summer, and in winter it was a place of warmth and security, its windows shuttered and an open fire sending shadows darting

among the brown bookcases. We tiptoed around as if on egg-
shells, and if we conferred too long or too loudly over our
books, Tim the librarian would stop indexing cards or stamping
books and warn us to be quiet.

We were allowed two tickets, one for fiction, the other nonfiction, but nobody used the nonfiction ticket. Who wanted to
read about somebody else's life or a journey up the Amazon or
Butler's *Lives of the Saints?* I thought it was time somebody took
this library system on, and I decided to try to borrow a second
storybook.

"*Dimsie—Headgirl!* That's not a work of nonfiction!" Tim
said scathingly. "Put it back!" he commanded in his strong
country accent, and he watched me as I put the coveted book
back on the shelves—there was no way I could sneak it out.

Row upon row of dull green- and brown-backed books were
arranged in strict alphabetical order, and we made our way
slowly along the bookshelves, searching for girls' books. It never
crossed our minds that we could take out boys' books, and in
turn any boy caught reading a girls' book would be branded a
sissy. My mother and father trusted the library to make sure we
read nothing unsuitable. There was no guidance from school;
the nuns were glad we were reading, but never suggested books
to us. So we learned from one another and ended up with the
Abbey Girls, the Chalet School, the Daphne and Dimsie
Maitland books. *What Katy Did* and did not do: all schoolgirl
adventure stories set in posh boarding schools somewhere in the
English countryside. We lapped up the paper chases and the
midnight feasts in the dorms and girls who adored their
prefects and aimed to become headgirls. There was always a
mamselle who was a dreadful French teacher and the Games
Mistress who stuck her chin out and loped along like an ante-
lope and was a jolly good sort. Later came the Pollyanna books,
and later still the light romances of Annie M.P. Smithson.

Not in our wildest imagination would we ever become like
the girls in the storybooks. Theirs was a different world. The
nearest we came to it was to see the girls in the college on the

Crumlin Road or the School for Young Ladies in the Coombe, where they wore smartly pressed gymslips, heavily pleated, with trailing sashes, startlingly white blouses, long blazers, and crested berets, and they carried tennis rackets and hockey sticks.

I was the only serious reader among my friends and so it was up to me to plan any unusual games which I might read about. I read a description of a paper chase in one of the Abbey Girls books and we laid our plans. Our first job was to gather as much newspaper as we could, but newspapers were a precious resource, carefully stored away and used for polishing windows, laying on the floor after it had been washed, or rolled up tightly to make fire-lighters. When we got past this first hurdle, I borrowed Tess's satchel, although she was unwilling to part with it, particularly as I told her that her legs were too short to join in the chase. We filled it with carefully torn scraps of paper and we drew lots as to who would be hares and who would be hounds.

"The hares will have to leg it as fast as they can up Cork Street," I said, and as organizer I intended to be one of the hares. "Give us odds of five minutes and then start after us."

Five minutes was three hundred seconds counted slowly— nobody owned a wrist watch. We hares set out, dribbling our bits of paper as we raced up Cork Street, along Dolphin's Barn, and back down the Pipes, making little detours to throw the hounds off the scent. How could they? Our scrappy bits of paper tangled with bigger scraps—cigarette packets, wrapping paper and all the flotsam of a busy street strewn about by horses' feet, bicycles, and buses. Sadly we trailed home. I had ignored the fact that in the storybooks the trail was set over acres of green parkland and rolling downs.

"That's a stupid game," my friends said.

I was nearly inclined to agree, but I was not beaten yet. "It's not. It's just that it's not right for our streets." In the books they had other trails which they laid, like making marks on trees and leaving arrows made of twigs, but that would not work either. Then I had a brainwave.

"Who's in charge of the chalk in school?"

This time nothing could go wrong. The hares set off, chalk-ing arrows on walls and doubling over in the middle of a quick run to mark one on the pavement, causing no end of obstruc-tion to innocent pedestrians who only saw flying pigtails, a flurry of dresses, and a huge chalked arrow, and wondered where the fire was. The game was a complete success.

One day, however, I decided that there must be more to literature than posh schoolgirl stories. I wandered along the aisles, starting right at the beginning and working through the alphabet. I came to M and fixed on Ethel Mannin. Her *Late Have I Loved Thee* gave me no end of problems. She continually referred to *The Confessions of Saint Augustine*, but Saint Augus-tine was a stranger to me. I searched under A again, but Augus-tine's *Confessions* were not to be found. I plucked up courage and approached Tim.

"Could you get me *The Confessions of Saint Augustine,* please?"

"The what?"

"*The Confessions of Saint Augustine,* the book is not on the shelves."

"To be sure it's not," he said. "What do ye want it for?" It wasn't every day in the week that Tim was asked by a twelve-year-old for such a ponderous title and he was entitled to be suspicious.

"This book," and I produced Ethel Mannin, "keeps referring to Saint Augustine, and I'd like to see what the author is talking about." He took the book and looked at it.

"I don't have time now," he said, "I'm busy. But I'll look for it when I have a chance." True to his word he did, and on my next visit he had a copy waiting for me, but not to take out. The book belonged to the adult library.

"Take it down to the table and look at it," he said, his boom-ing voice breaking the silence and causing everybody to stare. I felt important with this weighty volume under my arm, but *The Confessions of Saint Augustine* turned out to be most disap-pointing and uninteresting, and I didn't understand any of it.

"Well," the librarian said when I handed it back, "were you able to follow it?"

"No," I said.

"I didn't think you would be," he said. "Try something else."

Each week I toured the shelves, picking and choosing, trying out books of all kinds. We had to walk two miles to the library to get our precious fiction book, and two miles back home, so every title had to be given careful consideration before it was brought to the counter to be stamped. This meant reading the opening chapter, skipping through to the middle, and sneaking a look at the last page to make sure it had a happy ending. It must have lots of conversation—long chapters without any conversations were sure to be boring. My greatest find was a translation of the Greek legends which brought to life the wonderful adventures of Zeus, Hera, Athena, Aphrodite, and Heracles. I didn't understand all of it, though, and began to be afraid that maybe my mother would not approve of what I was reading, so I brought the book back pretty quickly.

The quickest way to the library was up by the canal and around by the grainstore, where if I was lucky there would be a horse and dray waiting to be loaded with grain and I could jump on as it moved away, the driver pretending not to see as I settled myself comfortably, my legs dangling over the back and my library book securely beside me. On the way home, I would settle the shopping bag on my arm, keep a wary eye ahead, and, stepping off and on the pavement, I walked home with my eyes glued to the pages. I usually had about a third of my library book read by the time I got there.

When we began to attend the lectures held in the library on winters' evenings, we poked fun at our fears as we headed home through the deserted streets. We walked along by the silent shape of Saint Catherine's church, the corners of the street dark and forbidding and the gas-lamps flickering uneasily. It was near here that Robert Emmet had been executed.

"Don't look now, you might see him."

"We should carry holy water with us—it wards off all the spirits."

"My father says it's only the ones who are not restin' who suddenly appear to people."

"You've lost me."

"Well, Robert Emmet might not be restin' easy. After all, nobody even knows where they buried him."

And with a fearful glance at the gray building we ran, gripping each other's hands, and didn't stop until we could see the lights of Thomas Court Bawn and the public house at the corner of South Earl Street and the twist of the street to Marrowbone Land and home.

—from *Down Cobbled Streets*

Linda Brodkey

(b. 1945)

Best known for her scholarly work on teaching writing and reading, Linda Brodkey here recalls her own early days as a reader in this excerpt from Writing on the Bias. *She says, "I wanted to document the experience of being my own informant as well as tell a story about a white working-class girl's sorties into white middle-class culture." She is an Associate Professor of Literature at University of California—San Diego where she directs the Warren College Writing Program and teaches graduate and undergraduate courses on writing and literacy.*

. . . I am sometimes reminded that I nearly became a reader rather than a writer in a vivid memory of myself as young girl slowly picking her way down the stairs of the Quincy Public Library. I know I am leaving the children's library and am en route to the rooms reserved below for adults. The scene is lit from above and behind by a window, through which the sun shines down on the child whose first trip to the adult library saddens me. On mornings when I wake with this memory, I am overcome by sorrow, even though I know the actual trip to have been a childish triumph of sorts. I literally read my way out of the children's library in the summer of the fifth grade.

This memory of myself is carefully staged. I can be looking only at the loss of innocence. A young girl. A descent. Away from the light. That I set the scene in a library suggests a loss specific to literacy. Yet here is a child who reads so much that the librarians have declared her an honorary adult and sent her to the adult library where there are even more books than in the children's library, some of them not suitable, she hopes, for children. She should be dancing down that stairway, as I may actually have done, full of herself and in full possession of the tangible proof and token of her recent enfranchisement—a card good for all the books in the adult library. Indeed there were more books there, so many more than the child imagined that she found she could not read her way out, not that summer, not soon, not ever. I can see the girl is on the brink of learning that the books are not hers, that books, even children's books, are copyrighted, someone's property. And, since she already knows that some properties are more valuable than others, before long she will confound their imputed value and her desire, and want only the best books.

I must have suspected even in the children's library that *someone* wrote the books I read. But they were my stories: I lifted them off the shelves, checked them out, took them home, read them, and returned them a few days later in exchange for more. In the child's economics of literacy, the cycle of exchange depended entirely on her reading. It is a childish and even a dangerous view of literacy, for it entirely ignores the labor of producing books (with the possible exception of the material facts of books themselves), and yet it is one that libraries and schools promote when they base children's experience of literacy solely on reading.

Finding out that every book belonged to an author made the adult books different from the children's books I had regarded as public property and treated as I did the equipment on the school playground or neighborhood park. I didn't think I owned the swings, but I believed they were mine while I used them. I read the children's books seriatim—fiction and nonfiction, off the shelves, one after the other, section by section, top to bottom, left to right. There must have been a card catalogue, but I remember no one suggesting I check the catalogue. Shelves rather than Dewey guided my reading, aided and limited by my height and what my mother called my "boarding house reach," since I was, as they say, tall for my age. What I could reach I read. And at some point, the librarians decided that I had read them all, or more likely that my grasp exceeded my reach, and sent me downstairs. Or more likely still, they probably ran out of prizes, having rewarded me for the most books read by a child in my school, my age, in a week, a month, over a summer, during a year.

Things were not the same in the adult library. Not just the books but the place. It smelled the same (of paste and glue and paper and must), but it neither looked nor felt the same. The books were tightly wedged on shelves, lined up like the aisles of supermarkets. There was just enough room between shelves to make a selection, but not enough to linger, and nothing like enough to stretch out on the floor and read. Truth to tell, I never felt I really belonged in the adult library, and I wonder now if that's because the loss of human space figured the even more important loss of books as stories. I was not ready to give up stories. If I didn't actually read all the children's books, I read every one I checked out—from the first word to the last. Today the only books I still read that way are mysteries.

It is only in the occasional glimpses of myself cautiously descending those library stairs that I realize that if I am uneasy about what I will learn in the adult library that may well be because I had yet to learn that *I* could write as well as read books. I am on the brink of believing instead that if I could not read them all, I could at least read the right ones. The right books are literature. Most of Shakespeare's plays and sonnets, some of Donne's lyrics, some of Wordsworth's, *The Canterbury Tales, Paradise Lost, Jane Eyre, David Copperfield,* and *The Scarlet Letter* are literature. I was working from a list. They were on it. It was only later that I learned that it's not that simple, that there is also *the literature,* as in the literature of a field or discipline, the right books *and* the right articles—about history, literature, physics, sociology, law, medicine. And it was much later still that I even thought to ask who made the lists, on which women rarely appear and people of color more rarely still, where America is a far-flung replica of an English village, and most of the rest of the world not even that.

The economics of literature is entirely different from that of stories. Frankly, one animal story was as good as the next as far as I was concerned, one biography, one mystery, one romance, one adventure. But the value of stories as measured against literature is very low indeed. Stories are a dime a dozen. Literature is scarce. Almost anyone can tell or write stories (even a child can do it). Not just anyone can write literature (most adults cannot), and not just anyone can read it. Literature is an acquired taste, it seems, and like a taste for martinis and caviar, it is acquired through associating with the right people, whose discernment guarantees a steady demand for a limited supply of literature. I used my adult card to check out *The House of Seven Gables,* which I probably chose on the recommendation of my fifth-grade teacher but which I read—with some difficulty. I read it not because I liked it, but because I wanted to be someone who liked literature, an experience not unlike that of wondering, while taking the first sip of martini or bite of caviar, if other people actually like the taste of turpentine or cat food, and immediately denying the thought.

Looking back, however, I would not want to have missed a single one of the stories dressed up as literature or, for that matter, all that many of those billed as *the* literature. But I do sometimes wish, on the mornings I wake to watch myself descending those stairs, that I understood why, when I realized I could not read all the books in the adult library, I took smug comfort in believing that only some of them were worth reading. What was my stake in the great books, the ones on the recommended lists distributed to honors students at my school? For years I read exclusively from those mimeographed lists, except for an occasional mistake like *Green Mansions* and some occasional lapses like *Gone with the Wind* and *Peyton Place,* and for many years I was comforted by the list, secure in my choices and certain that I was making progress. No sooner had I knocked off a great book than I had it recorded on a three-by-five card. One per book. Vital statistics on the front—author, title, main characters, and plot—a short memorable quote on the back.

My devotion to that card file bears a suspicious resemblance to my dedication to the barre, and I realize now that ballet and literature must be early tokens of my longing to replace the working-class fictions of my childhood with a middle-class fiction in which art transcends class. I see in that file, for instance, the evidence of my desire and struggle to acquire the middle-class habit of privileging authorship. That I remember novels I read in adolescence more readily by title than by author is probably evidence that I retained, despite my files, my earlier belief in stories, and possibly even the economic theory in which stories belong to the people who animate them in their reading. In the world of English professors whose ranks I sought to join, however, such mundane matters as the labor of literary production—the work of writing, placing, selecting, editing, printing, marketing, and distributing books—were thought to be distasteful, akin to asking the host how much the caviar cost. Only when I began studying and teaching writing did I finally remember that esthetics can be as effective a hermetic seal against the economic and political conditions of authorship as are industrial parks and affluent suburbs against the economic privation and desperation of the urban and rural poor.

Sometime during the second year of college I quit recording and filing my reading, probably around the time I began reading books that were banned, or that I believed were: *Tropic of Cancer, Lady Chatterley's Lover, Fanny Hill, The Story of O, The Hundred Dollar Misunderstanding.* But until then no one needed to monitor my reading. I policed myself. Worse, I set out to police my family, whose knowledge of and interest in literature I found sadly lacking. I had to write off my father, who read newspapers, automobile repair manuals, and union materials, but, to my knowledge, never read stories and only rarely told one. I had to write off my older sister as well, since she dismissed nearly everything I did as childish. I managed to impress the importance of literature on my younger sister, since she was accustomed to being bossed around by her older sisters. It was however my mother I literally harassed, for she read several books a week and each one provided me with an opportunity to

improve her taste. So caught up was I in the promise of literature that I chided unconscionably the same mother who first
took me to the library and walked me there until I was old
enough to go alone, who had the good sense not to tell the first-
grade teacher I could already read, so she could "teach" me,
who read *War and Peace* with me in the eleventh grade, just to
keep me company (I only read *Peace,* but she read both), and
who never issued any of those dire warnings—about ruining
my eyes, turning into a bookworm, or ending up a spinster—
that must have kept generations of female and male children
alike from reading much at all.

The list that identified some stories as literature also cast its
readers as superior to those who, like my mother, preferred
mysteries and romances. I suspect I desperately wanted her to
read literature because I believed that if she didn't have her own
passport to the middle class I would have to leave her behind
when I went away to college. There are times when I see each
great book I filed as also recording an inoculation against the
imputed ills of the working-class childhood that infected me
and that in turn threatened the middle-class children with
whom I studied. I do not think people in the 1950s believed
poverty was contagious. They had not yet been taught to see
poverty as something people bring on themselves and to spurn
the poor as people who didn't get and stay with the program.
But I probably did represent a threat to middle-class sensibility
that can be ascribed to growing up in a working-class house.

We were a family of five, my parents and three girls, in a
four-room house, a kitchen, a living room (known as the front
room), two bedrooms, and a bathroom. Attached to the back of
the house were an uninsulated and unheated enclosed porch (it
would have been a summer kitchen if it had been equipped
with a stove) and a storeroom (used as a playroom when the
weather was warm). In such small quarters, interior space is
social by definition, since to be in a room is to be in either the
company or the proximity of others. That I knew how to read
when I entered school can probably be attributed as much to

this social arrangement of space as to any unusual interest or precocity on my part. I would have been there while my mother checked my older sister's homework. My sister may even have taught me to read. But I would not have simply learned to read. I would have learned to read in the social space of the kitchen.

In a middle-class household, a child who insisted on reading in the kitchen during, say, meal preparation would probably be perceived as hostile, and would no doubt either be asked to set the table or be shunted off to another room, possibly even her own room. My mother was usually surrounded by her children. So, while I regularly read in the kitchen in the company of my mother and sisters and was often more attentive to what I was reading than what they were saying or doing, I can recall no one suggesting that the act itself was hostile or that I should read someplace else. It's not just that there was no place to send me. It's that I wasn't held literally responsible for my reading. Some kids sing, some cook, some read. It was a gift, like perfect pitch, not a skill I was honing or my mother nurturing. What was considered wonderful was my ability to read in the midst of conversation, what my mother called my "remarkable power of concentration." It was not cause for wonder, however, when I focused on grievances, for then my "remarkable power of concentration" became my "one-track mind."

My reading was not cause for wonder or concern at home because my mother believed she could always call me back if she wanted or needed me. But it was cause for concern at school, in fact, according to my mother, a source of considerable consternation for a beloved first-grade teacher who, exhibiting none of my mother's admiration for my unbridled reading, went to extraordinary lengths to break me of the habit. She took particular exception to my practice of "reading ahead," to find out what happened to the children and household pets in the Basal Reader. It seems strange to me now that I could have confused a primer with a story, but I took it very hard when the teacher taped the unread portion of the book closed to prevent me from "reading ahead" without her permission. I never untaped the book or directly challenged her right to regulate my reading. But in a rare act of childhood defiance, I remember promptly "reading ahead" when I happened on a copy of the reader in the children's library.

If my "reading ahead" concerned the teacher enough to justify taping the book closed, my habit of interrupting the other children while they were reading must have driven her to distraction, since I can still feel the heat of my humiliation and recall my terror as I stood alone and in tears in the cloakroom, where I had been sent for talking during reading. That happened only once that I can remember. The door that isolated me from the others may have terrified me more than it would have a child accustomed to closed doors. I was not in a dark or windowless room, but I could not hear what was being said in the classroom with the door closed. By some standards the punishment fit the crime. Yet it ignores the conflict that the middle-class practice of reading alone and in silence, only what is assigned when it is assigned, created in a working-class child whose reading had, until then, been part and parcel of the social fabric of home and whose choice of reading matter had been regulated by the holdings of the children's library and her reach.

I was not taught to read in the first grade, but was instead taught to unlearn how I already read by a well-meaning and dedicated teacher authorized by the state to regulate my reading. My father once complained that he never understood me after I went to school. I always thought he was referring to the speech lessons in the second grade that radically altered my dialect from the Southern Midland dialect spoken at home to the Northern Midland spoken by most of my teachers. But now I wonder whether it was a class rather than regional dialect that stood between us, whether the door that temporarily isolated me from the other children also threatened to closet me permanently from my family. That the ostensible autonomy of middle-class professionals depends on children internalizing the rules that regulate reading (and writing) seems obvious to me.

Less obvious, however, is what part reading and writing prac-
tices learned at home, and at variance with those learned at
school, continue to play in my intellectual life.

There is no denying that I recreate the cloakroom everywhere I live. It is not uncommon, of course, for academics to
furnish their homes with books. It is not even uncommon for
academics to read several at a time. But the inordinate pleasure
I take from littering all available surfaces with books makes it
seem unlikely that in my case books are indexing only my
academic enthusiasms. It seems more likely to me, now that I've
remembered and reflected on the cloakroom, that the books are
there to keep me company, that they are tokens of the absent
family and friends whose voices have been muted by time and
space. If so, it gives me a measure of satisfaction to believe that
this lifelong habit simulates reading as I learned it at home, that
even as I read the literature that took me so far from home I
have been protecting myself from total class annihilation.

As a young girl, I was not just reading about other people,
other places, and other lives. I was reading about people, places,
and lives utterly unlike mine. Virtually everything in the fiction
I read was fantastic: their houses, their families, their neighborhoods, their neighbors, their clothes, their food, their amuse-
ments, their feelings, their romances, their friendships, their
conversation, their desires, their problems, their prospects.
These things were different not just because literature is not
life, but because the drama in the books on the recommended
list, at least in the nineteenth-century novels I preferred, either
happened in middle-class houses—*Emma* and *Middlemarch*—
or, so I now realize, in defense of the middle class and their
houses—*Great Expectations* and *War and Peace*. I loved most
those novels that held literary open house, the ones that toured
prime literary real estate. I doted on the rooms reserved for
specific uses, parlors, drawing rooms, sitting rooms, libraries,
and only incidentally considered the heroines who retired there
to hold conversations, closeted from parents and siblings.

I skimmed descriptions of gardens or grounds, I skipped

altogether descriptions of cottages inhabited by tenant farmers, and I seem to have either ignored or forgotten descriptions of servants' quarters and kitchens. The uncertain course of romance and courtship, the tedium of manners, the ceaseless rounds of social obligations also went largely unnoticed. But not interior space, nor threats of its loss. The unheard-of privilege of privacy made palpable by the rooms middle-class heroines occupied made an immediate and lasting impression on me. I have no idea if many other children from working-class homes also acquired from their reading an appetite for privacy. But I am certain that the literature that fascinated me kindled and shaped a desire for privacy in me so acute that only hearing my mother's voice reminds me that not only I but an entire family paid the price of my replacing the sociality of my working-class home with the books that now keep me company at home.

—from *Writing on the Bias*

Zora Neale Hurston
(1901[?]–1960)

Just after the turn of the century, novelist Zora Neale Hurston attended a village school in Maitland, Florida, just north of Orlando, where she was noticed by two white ladies visiting from Minnesota. She was a regular visitor at their hotel while they were in Florida, and when they returned home they sent her a package of used clothing and books.

In that box were *Gulliver's Travels, Grimm's Fairy Tales, Dick Whittington, Greek and Roman Myths,* and best of all, *Norse Tales.* Why did the Norse tales strike so deeply into my soul? I do not know, but they did. I seemed to remember seeing Thor swing his mighty short-handled hammer as he sped across the sky in rumbling thunder, lightning flashing from the tread of his steeds and the wheels of his chariot. The great and good Odin, who went down to the well of knowledge to drink, and was told that the price of a drink from the fountain was an eye. Odin drank deeply, then plucked out one eye without a murmur and handed it to the grizzly keeper, and walked away. That held majesty for me.

Of the Greeks, Hercules moved me most. I followed him eagerly on his tasks. The story of the choice of Hercules as a boy when he met Pleasure and Duty, and put his hand in that of Duty and followed her steep way to the blue hills of fame and glory, which she pointed out at the end, moved me profoundly. I resolved to be like him. The tricks and turns of the other Gods and Goddesses left me cold. There were other thin books about this and that sweet and gentle little girl who gave up her heart to Christ and good works. Almost always they died from it, preaching as they passed. I was utterly indifferent to their deaths. In the first place I could not conceive of death, and in

49

the next place they never had any funerals that amounted to a hill of beans, so I didn't care how soon they rolled up their big, soulful, blue eyes and kicked the bucket. They had no meat on their bones.

But I also met Hans Andersen and Robert Louis Stevenson. They seemed to know what I wanted to hear and said it in a way that tingled me. Just a little below these friends was Rudyard Kipling in his *Jungle Books*. I loved his talking snakes as much as I did the hero.

I came to start reading the Bible through my mother. She gave me a licking one afternoon for repeating something I overheard a neighbor telling her. She locked me in her room after the whipping, and the Bible was the only thing in there for me to read. I happened to open to the place where David was doing some mighty smiting, and I got interested. David went here and he went there, and no matter where he went, he smote 'em hip and thigh. Then he sung songs to his harp awhile, and went out and smote some more. Not one time did David stop and preach about sins and things. All David wanted to know from God was who to kill and when. He took care of the other details himself. Never a quiet moment. I liked him a lot. So I read a good deal more in the Bible, hunting for some more active people like David. Except for the beautiful language of Luke and Paul, the New Testament still plays a poor second to the Old Testament for me. The Jews had a God who laid about him when they needed Him. . . .

In searching for more Davids, I came upon Leviticus. There were exciting things in there to a child eager to know the facts of life. I told Carrie Roberts about it, and we spent long afternoons reading what Moses told the Hebrews not to do in Leviticus. In that way I found out a number of things the old folks would not have told me. Not knowing what we were actually reading, we got a lot of praise from our elders for our devotion to the Bible.

Having finished that and scanned the Doctor Book, which my mother thought she had hidden securely from my eyes, I read all the things which children write on privy-house walls. Therefore, I lost my taste for pornographic literature. I think that the people who love it got cheated in the matter of privy houses when they were children.

In a way this early reading gave me great anguish through all my childhood and early adolescence. My soul was with the gods and my body in the village. People just would not act like gods. Stew beef, fried fat-back and morning grits were no ambrosia from Valhalla. Raking back yards and carrying out chamber pots were not the tasks of Thor. I wanted to be away from drabness and to stretch my limbs in some mighty struggle. I was only happy in the woods, and when the ecstatic Florida spring-time came strolling from the sea, trance-glorifying the world with its aura.

After her mother's death and father's remarriage, Hurston left home.

. . . So I went off to another town to find work. It was the same as at home so far as dreariness and lack of hope and blunted impulses were concerned. But one thing did happen that lifted me up. In a pile of rubbish I found a copy of Milton's complete works. The back was gone and the book was yellowed. But it was all there. So I read *Paradise Lost* and luxuriated in Milton's syllables and rhythms without ever having heard that Milton was one of the greatest poets of the world. I read it because I liked it.

—from *Dust Tracks on a Road*

Richard Rodriguez

(b. 1944)

Richard Rodriguez grew up in Sacramento in the 1950s "among gringos" in a primarily Spanish-speaking household.

"The boy who first entered a classroom barely able to speak English, twenty years later concluded his studies in the stately quiet of the reading room in the British Museum," says Rodriguez. One day, leafing through Richard Hoggart's The Uses of Literacy, *Rodriguez found a description of a "scholarship boy" in which he immediately recognized himself.*

In the life of such a boy, Hoggart sees an intense family intimacy that is a consolation for the boy's feelings of alienation in public and at school. Hoggart's scholarship boy seldom has a room of his own so he must isolate himself mentally as he tries to study at home. He hears his family talking in ways his teachers discourage. The scholarship boy is obedient and determined. With each academic success he leaves his family farther behind, at least for a while.

The eloquent essays of Richard Rodriguez have been collected in Hunger of Memory, Days of Obligation, *and* Mexico's Children.

From an early age I knew that my mother and father could read and write both Spanish and English. I had observed my father making his way through what, I now suppose, must have been income tax forms. On other occasions I waited apprehensively while my mother read onion-paper letters air-mailed from Mexico with news of a relative's illness or death. For both my parents, however, reading was something done out of necessity and as quickly as possible. Never did I see either of them read an entire book. Nor did I see them read for pleasure; their reading consisted of work manuals, prayer books . . .

Richard Hoggart imagines how, at home,

> . . . [The scholarship boy] sees strewn around, and
> reads regularly himself, magazines which are never
> mentioned at school, which seem not to belong to the
> world to which the school introduces him; at school
> he hears about and reads books never mentioned at
> home. When he brings those books into the house
> they do not take their place with other books which
> the family are reading, for often there are none or
> almost none; his books look, rather, like strange tools.

In our house each school year would begin with my mother's
careful instruction: "Don't write in your books so we can sell
them at the end of the year." The remark was echoed in public
by my teachers, but only in part: "Boys and girls, don't write in
your books. You must learn to treat them with great care and
respect."

OPEN THE DOORS OF YOUR MIND WITH BOOKS,
read the red and white poster over the nun's desk in early
September. It soon was apparent to me that reading was the
classroom's central activity. Each course had its own book. And
the information gathered from a book was unquestioned.
READ TO LEARN, the sign on the wall advised in December.
I privately wondered: What was the connection between reading and learning? Did one learn something only by reading it?
Was an idea only an idea if it could be written down? In June,
CONSIDER BOOKS YOUR BEST FRIENDS. Friends?
Reading was, at best, only a chore. I needed to look up whole
paragraphs of words in a dictionary. Lines of type were dizzy-
ing, the eye having to move slowly across the page, then down,
and across . . . The sentences of the first books I read were
coolly impersonal. Toned hard. What most bothered me, however, was the isolation reading required. To console myself for
the loneliness I'd feel when I read, I tried reading in a very soft
voice. Until: "Who is doing all that talking to his neighbor?"
Shortly after, remedial reading classes were arranged for me
with a very old nun.

At the end of each school day, for nearly six months, I would meet with her in the tiny room that served as the school's library but was actually only a storeroom for used textbooks and a vast collection of *National Geographic*s. Everything about our sessions pleased me: the smallness of the room; the noise of the janitor's broom hitting the edge of the long hallway outside the door; the green of the sun, lighting the wall; and the old woman's face blurred white with a beard. Most of the time we took turns. I began with my elementary text. Sentences of astonishing simplicity seemed to me lifeless and drab: "The boys ran from the rain . . . She wanted to sing . . . The kite rose in the blue." Then the old nun would read from her favorite books, usually biographies of early American presidents. Playfully she ran through complex sentences, calling the words alive with her voice, making it seem that the author somehow was speaking directly to me. I smiled just to listen to her. I sat there and sensed for the very first time some possibility of fellowship between a reader and a writer, a communication, never *intimate* like that I heard spoken words at home convey, but one nonetheless *personal*.

One day the nun concluded a session by asking me why I was so reluctant to read by myself. I tried to explain; said something about the way written words made me feel all alone—almost, I wanted to add but didn't, as when I spoke to myself in a room just emptied of furniture. She studied my face as I spoke; she seemed to be watching more than listening. In an uneventful voice she replied that I had nothing to fear. Didn't I realize that reading would open up whole new worlds? A book could open doors for me. It could introduce me to people and show me places I never imagined existed. She gestured toward the bookshelves. (Bare-breasted African women danced, and the shiny hubcaps of automobiles on the back covers of the *Geographic* gleamed in my mind.) I listened with respect. But her words were not very influential. I was thinking then of another consequence of literacy, one I was too shy to admit but nonetheless trusted. Books were going to make me "educated." *That* confidence enabled me, several months later, to overcome my fear of the silence.

In fourth grade I embarked upon a grandiose reading program. "Give me the names of important books," I would say to startled teachers. They soon found out that I had in mind "adult books." I ignored their suggestion of anything I suspected was written for children. (Not until I was in college, as a result, did I read *Huckleberry Finn* or *Alice's Adventures in Wonderland*.) Instead I read *The Scarlet Letter* and Franklin's *Autobiography*. And whatever I read I read for extra credit. Each time I finished a book, I reported the achievement to a teacher and basked in the praise my effort earned. Despite my best efforts, however, there seemed to be more and more books I needed to read. At the library I would literally tremble as I came upon whole shelves of books I hadn't read. So I read and I read and I read: *Great Expectations;* all the short stories of Kipling; *The Babe Ruth Story*; the entire first volume of the *Encyclopaedia Britannica* (A-ANSTEY); the *Iliad; Moby Dick; Gone with the Wind; The Good Earth; Ramona; Forever Amber; The Lives of the Saints; Crime and Punishment; The Pearl*. . . . Librarians who initially frowned when I checked out the maximum ten books at a time started saving books they thought I might like. Teachers would say to the rest of the class, "I only wish the rest of you took reading as seriously as Richard obviously does."

But at home I would hear my mother wondering, "What do you see in your books?" (Was reading a hobby like her knitting? Was so much reading even healthy for a boy? Was it the sign of "brains"? Or was it just a convenient excuse for not helping around the house on Saturday mornings?) Always, "What do you see . . . ?"

What *did* I see in my books? I had the idea that they were crucial for my academic success, though I couldn't have said exactly how or why. In the sixth grade I simply concluded that what gave a book its value was some major idea or theme it contained. If that core essence could be mined and memorized, I would become learned like my teachers. I decided to record in a notebook the themes of the books that I read. After reading *Robinson Crusoe*, I wrote that its theme was "the value of learning to live by oneself." When I completed *Wuthering Heights*, I noted the danger of "letting emotions get out of control." Rereading these brief moralistic appraisals usually left me disheartened. I couldn't believe that they were really the source of reading's value. But for many more years, they constituted the only means I had of describing to myself the educational value of books.

In spite of my earnestness, I found reading a pleasurable activity. I came to enjoy the lonely good company of books. Early on weekday mornings, I'd read in my bed. I'd feel a mysterious comfort then, reading in the dawn quiet—the blue-gray silence interrupted by the occasional churning of the refrigerator motor a few rooms away or the more distant sounds of a city bus beginning its run. On weekends I'd go to the public library to read, surrounded by old men and women. Or, if the weather was fine, I would take my books to the park and read in the shade of a tree. A warm summer evening was my favorite reading time. Neighbors would leave for vacation and I would water their lawns. I would sit through the twilight on the front porches or in backyards, reading to the cool, whirling sounds of the sprinklers.

I also had favorite writers. But often those writers I enjoyed most I was least able to value. When I read William Saroyan's *The Human Comedy,* I was immediately pleased by the narrator's warmth and the charm of his story. But as quickly I became suspicious. A book so enjoyable to read couldn't be very "important." Another summer I determined to read all the novels of Dickens. Reading his fat novels, I loved the feeling I got—after the first hundred pages—of being at home in a fictional world where I knew the names of the characters and cared about what was going to happen to them. And it bothered me that I was forced away at the conclusion, when the fiction closed tight, like a fortune-teller's fist—the futures of all the major characters nearly resolved. I never knew how to take such feelings seriously, however. Nor did I suspect that these experiences could be part of a novel's meaning. Still, there were pleasures to sustain me after I'd finish my books. Carrying a volume back to the library, I would be pleased by its weight. I'd run my fingers along the edge of the pages and marvel at the breadth of my achievement. Around my room, growing stacks of paperback books reinforced my assurance.

I entered high school having read hundreds of books. My habit of reading made me a confident speaker and writer of English. Reading also enabled me to sense something of the shape, the major concerns, of Western thought. (I was able to say something about Dante and Descartes and Engels and James Baldwin in my high-school term papers.) In these various ways, books brought me academic success as I hoped that they would. But I was not a good reader. Merely bookish, I lacked a point of view when I read. Rather, I read in order to acquire a point of view. I vacuumed books for epigrams, scraps of information, ideas, themes—anything to fill the hollow within me and make me feel educated. When one of my teachers suggested to his drowsy tenth-grade English class that a person could not have "complicated ideas" until he had read at least two thousand books, I heard the remark without detecting either its irony or its very complicated truth. I merely determined to compile a list of all the books I had ever read. Harsh with myself, I included only once a title I might have read several times. (How, after all, could one read a book more than once?) And I included only those books over a hundred pages in length. (Could anything shorter be a book?)

There was yet another high-school list I compiled. One day I came across a newspaper article about the retirement of an English professor at a nearby state college. The article was accompanied by a list of the "hundred most important books of Western Civilization." "More than anything else in my life," the professor told the reporter with finality, "these books have made me all that I am." That was the kind of remark I couldn't ignore. I clipped out the list and kept it for the several months it took me to read all of the titles. Most books, of course, I barely understood. While reading Plato's *Republic,* for instance, I needed to keep looking at the book jacket comments to remind myself what the text was about. Nevertheless, with the special patience and superstition of a scholarship boy, I looked at every word of the text. And by the time I reached the last word, relieved, I convinced myself that I had read *The Republic.* In a ceremony of great pride, I solemnly crossed Plato off my list.

—from *Hunger of Memory*

Penelope Lively

(b. 1933)

Oleander, Jacaranda *is novelist Penelope Lively's account of growing up English during the 1930s and 1940s in Egypt, which had
been accorded an ambivalent independence from Britain. Her parents spent little time with her and she was raised mainly by an
English nanny named Lucy.*

*Instead of being sent to English schools in Cairo, Penelope Lively
was taught at home with materials provided by an organization
named Parents National Education Union (PNEU). The PNEU
was and still is a home-schooling system and philosophy of education
which provides books, timetables, and instruction manuals. Together, Penelope Lively and Lucy applied themselves to the requirements of the PNEU.*

*The PNEU schedule was chopped up into 20-minute periods, six
half-days a week, and included the Bible, Science, Latin, French,
Picture Study, Mathematics, Citizenship, and Reading. Character-
ized by endless repetition; virtually everything was learned by heart.*

*Sometimes the rigid PNEU program was altered to suit the apti-
tudes of young Penelope and of Lucy who was neither educated nor
a teacher. Reading was what they were both good at and read is
mostly what they did. The PNEU books, sent by sea from wartime
England, often failed to arrive and they fell back on whatever was
around—Somerset Maugham, Noël Coward, and so on.*

*Penelope Lively is the author of many distinguished books includ-
ing the Booker Prize-winning* Moon Tiger.

Geography meant Bartholomew's atlas, of course, and the
global rash of pink. Latin we played about with, insincerely.
Mensa. Puella. Amo, amas, amat. Lucy did not take Latin seriously, and her contempt spilled over to me. I was still having
trouble with Latin at eighteen, confronted with Oxford Prelims.

For French we enjoyed ourselves with the Pèfre Castor story-
books and another series, about a splendid bourgeois rodent
called Madame Souris, who went shopping and nagged her
husband and batted her children around. There was also
Perlette: L'Histoire d'une goutte d'eau, a wonderfully surreal tale
about a drop of rain which falls into a stream and ends up in the
ocean. The amorphous areas of Literature and Composition we
simply included in the great untrammeled indulgence of Reading.

   For Reading was what we were best at, and we knew it. We
were happy to read till the cows came home, and did so. Lucy
read; I read. I told back; I wrote back. We read everything the
PNEU suggested: Greek and Roman mythology, Norse mythology, stories from Chaucer and Piers Plowman, the *Arabian
Nights.* And then we read it all again, and when we were
saturated in it we turned to whatever else we could find. *Nicholas Nickleby. The Talisman. The Rose and the Ring.* Somerset
Maugham and Oscar Wilde and Noël Coward and Mary Webb,
who was responsible for the concept of rural English society
which was to cause me much perplexity when eventually I
arrived at my grandmother's home in Somerset after the war.
Some of this reading would have been shared with Lucy, much
of it I did on my own, the compulsive retreat of a solitary child.

   I had children's books too, as such, though not a wealth of
them. *Alice, The Wind in the Willows,* the *Just So Stories,* the
Jungle Books. All of them read and reread because there was no
library available from which to ring the changes. And when the
Arthur Ransome books found their way to the Express Bookshop in Cairo I became infatuated, addicted. I saved up my
pocket money to buy them as they arrived—objects so covetable
as to be awesome, those green bindings with the gold lettering,
and the distinctive dust jackets. I read them like some awe-
struck peasant, gawping at the goings-on of these incredible
children: their airy confidence, their sophistication, their independence. The narratives patently bore no relation to real life
but were enthralling as pure fantasy. And then there was the
matter of the ambience, this exotic landscape of hills and lakes

and greenery and rain and boats and peculiar birds and animals. From time to time I would lift my eyes from the page to look out at my own humdrum environment of palms and donkeys and camels and the hoopoe stabbing the lawn.

Greek mythology was another matter—altogether more accessible. Here, I was without inhibitions. I could march in and make it mine, manipulate the resources to my own convenience. Of course, I was right in there anyway—Penelope—but saddled with a thoroughly unsatisfying role. All that daft weaving, and it was not even clear that she was particularly beautiful. So I would usurp other parts, wallowing in vicarious experience, hidden away in my secret place—the hammock of creepers behind the swimming pool. I would reenact it all, amending the script, starring in every episode. I was Helen, languishing in the arms of Paris. I was Achilles, nobly dying. I was Nausicaä, nude and distinctly sexy on a beach. The erotic overtones had not escaped me—or rather, they had reached mysterious levels of my own nature. I perceived that there was something going on here that I found distinctly exciting, and reacted accordingly. I ceased to be a podgy child daydreaming in a hedge, and shot up and away into a more vivid place where I controlled everything, where I was the heroine and the creator all at once, where I set the scene and furnished the dialogue and called the shots. I dressed myself in wonderful clothes and felt the drapery slide across my adult limbs. I fled, as Daphne, sensing the wind in my hair and my own speed and then the strange insidious shiver as I began to turn into a tree. I walked the ramparts of Troy, I was rescued from the Minotaur, I listened for Orpheus. I became adept. I could slide off into this other world at will, trudging along the canal path behind Lucy, so busy in the head that I saw and heard nothing.

It cannot be done now. Perhaps the next best thing is writing fiction, but that, alas, has not the transforming element of identification. You may create, but you do not become. Reading Greek mythology today, I get an occasional emotive whiff of lost capacity.

I believe that the experience of childhood reading is as irretrievable as any other area of childhood experience. It is extinguished by the subsequent experience of reading with detachment, with objectivity, with critical judgment. That ability to fuse with the narrative and the characters is gone. It is an ability that seems now both miraculous and enviable. And anyone who has had the temerity to write for children must be forever reminded of it.

But children are distinctly selective in their acts of identification and their abandoned fusion with a text. Some sort of judgment is indeed exercised. Norse mythology never engaged me in the same way. All that fire and ice was off-putting, somehow. And who would want to be Brynhild, who gave an impression of being overweight and had plaits, which were not glamourous at all, in my view. Involvement could take other forms too. Lucy and I read *Nicholas Nickleby* together, on the pansy-strewn sofa in the nursery, taking a paragraph each, Lucy resuming sewing when it was my turn to read, both of us openly weeping at the sad bits. We exercised our objectivity and our critical capacities, all right, but in the immediate sense of outrage at this display of inhumanity. We discussed exactly what we would do to the Squeers family if we got the chance. If we could take Smike in, we would feed him up with Lucy's porridge and he would have the small spare room. We responded as though to an account of things happening to people we knew, with the intensity of personal involvement. The context of the book, its nineteenth-century setting, was neither here nor there. We read as literary innocents, and I realize now that there is an eerie advantage to be had in this.

I never acquired a comic but at some point came across cartoon strips in newspapers or magazines and was hooked though also baffled by the evident sophistication. Popeye was an especial challenge: I couldn't understand the running joke about spinach, which we did not have. And then there was Jane, the peroxide blonde with gargantuan bust and cleavage; I thought her immensely appealing but could not work out exactly why. *The New Yorker* sometimes found its way into the house, and I pored over it, trying to decode the advertisements. Nylon stockings? Waffle makers? Coca-Cola? Again, something was awry with my own language. This was English, but not an English I recognized. I saw that this rich, glib prose and these jaunty pictures reflected some complex and confident other world of which I knew nothing whatsoever, more unreachable even than the England I could barely remember but whose icons and mythologies were all around me. Pondering the teasing terminology of the *New Yorker* advertisements, I came up once more against the opaque screen of culture and identified a difficulty over and beyond the familiar difficulties of words you did not understand. Here was a world far more inaccessible than the worlds of Greek mythology or of *Nicholas Nickleby*.

—from *Oleander, Jacaranda*

Tobias Wolff

(b. 1945)

This Boy's Life *(1989), Tobias Wolff's story of growing up in the 1950s, reads like a boy's adventure tale.*

The child of an amazingly crooked father (see The Duke of Deception: Memories of My Father *by brother Geoffrey Wolff), Tobias Wolff managed—through guile, imagination, and an innate toughness—to survive his turbulent boyhood. Wolff later became an acclaimed writer of fiction and short stories, and has won fellowships and awards, among them the PEN/Faulkner Award, and the Lila Acheson Wallace/Readers Digest Writers' Award.*

Preceding the following passage about reading a hand-me-down Scout Handbook, *his mother's boyfriend, Dwight, has made Tobias join the Boy Scouts because he thought he had too much spare time.*

Dwight gave me Skipper's old Scout manual, *Handbook for Boys,* outdated even when Skipper had it, a 1942 edition full of pictures of "Fighting Scouts" keeping a lookout for Nazi subs and Jap bombers. I read the *Handbook* almost every night, cruising for easy merit badges like Indian Lore, Bookbinding, Reptile Study, and Personal Health ("Show proper method of brushing teeth and discuss the importance of dental care. . . ."). The merit-badge index was followed by advertisements for official Scout gear, and then a list of The Firms That Make the Things You Want, among them Coca-Cola, Eastman Kodak, Evinrude, and Nestle's ("The Boy Scout Emergency Ration"), and finally by a section called Where to Go to School. The schools were mostly military academies with sonorous double-barreled names. Carson Long, Morgan Park, Cochran-Byran, Valley Forge, Castle Heights.

I liked reading all these advertisements. They were a natural part of the *Handbook,* in whose pages the Scout Spirit and the spirit of commerce mingled freely, and often indistinguishably. "What the Scout *Is* determines his progress in whatever line of business he may seek success—and Scout Ideals mean progress in business." Suggested good turns were enumerated on a ledger, so the Scout could check them off as he performed them: *Assisted a foreign boy with some English grammar. Helped put out a burning field. Gave water to crippled dog.* Here, even the murky enterprise of self-examination could be expressed as a problem in accounting. "On a scale of 100, what all-around rating would I be justified in giving myself?"

I liked all these numbers and lists, because they offered the clear possibility of mastery. But what I liked best about the *Handbook* was its voice, the bluff hail-fellow language by which it tried to make being a good boy seem adventurous, even romantic. The Scout Spirit was traced to King Arthur's Round Table, and from there to the explorers and pioneers and warriors whose conquests had been achieved through fair play and clean living. "No man given over to dissipation can stand the gaff. He quickly tires. He is the type who usually lacks courage at the crucial moment. He cannot take punishment and come back smiling."

I yielded easily to this comradely tone, forgetting while I did so that I was not the boy it supposed I was.

Boy's Life, the official Scout magazine, worked on me in the same way. I read it in a trance, accepting without question its narcotic invitation to believe that I was really no different from the boys whose hustle and pluck it celebrated. Boys who raised treasure from Spanish galleons, and put empty barns to use by building operational airplanes in them. Boys who skied to the North Pole. Boys who sailed around the Horn, solo. Boys who saved lives, and were accepted into savage tribes, and sent themselves to college by running traplines in the wilderness. Reading about these boys made me restless, feverish with schemes.

—from *This Boy's Life*

V.S. Pritchett

(b. 1900)

V.S. Pritchett (Sir Victor Pritchett C.B.E.) moved eighteen times before he was twelve, caught between his "cocksparrow" salesman father and his high-strung Cockney mother.

During his long life, he has written short stories, novels, plays, and criticism and is known as a broadcaster, lecturer, and teacher.

The passage below is from A Cab at the Door *(1968), the first part of his autobiography. He is about 11 here, attending a working-class London school with fifty or sixty students in a class, where general order is kept with a cane. Into this class comes a teacher sent by the Education Office to introduce new methods and through him, Pritchett finds literature and poetry a revelation.*

"I was caught," he says, "by the passion for print as an alcoholic is caught by the bottle."

On the lowest shelf of my father's bookcase were several new ornate and large volumes of a series called the International Library of Famous Literature. They were bound in red and had gold lettering. They had never been opened and we were forbidden to touch them. I think Father must have had the job of selling the series, on commission, at one time. I started to look at them. There were photographs of busts of Sophocles and Shakespeare. There were photographs of Dickens, Thomas Hardy, of Sir James Barrie and Sir Edmund Gosse in deep, starched wing collars, of Kipling rooting like a dog at his desk, and of G.K. Chesterton with his walking-stick. There was Tolstoy behind his beard. The volumes contained long extracts from the works of these writers. I found at once a chapter from Hardy's *Under the Green-*

wood Tree; and discovered a lasting taste for the wry and ironical. I moved on to *Longinus on the Sublime* and could not understand it. I was gripped by Tolstoy and a chapter from *Don Quixote.* In the next two or three years I read the whole of the International Library on the quiet. These volumes converted me to prose. I had never really enjoyed poetry for it was concerned with inner experience and I was very much an extrovert and I fancy I have remained so; the moodiness and melancholy which fell on me in Dulwich and have been with me ever since, must have come from the disappointments of an active and romantic nature; the forms of Protestantism among which I was brought up taught one to think of life rigidly in terms of right and wrong and that is not likely to fertilize the sensibilities or the poetic imagination. The poet, above all, abandons the will; people like ourselves who were nearly all will, burned up the inner life, had no sense of its daring serenity and were either rapt by our active dramas or tormented by them; but in prose I found the common experience and the solid worlds where judgments were made and which one could firmly tread.

An extract from *Oliver Twist* made me ask for a copy for Christmas. I put it in one green armchair and knelt there reading it in a state of hot horror. It seized me because it was about London and the fears of the London streets. There were big boys at school who could grow up to be the Artful Dodger; many of us could have been Oliver; but the decisive thing must have been that Dickens had the excited mind, the terrors, the comic sense of a boy and one who can never have grown emotionally older than a boy is at the age of ten. One saw people going about the streets of London who could have been any of his characters; and right and wrong were meat to him. In all of Dickens, as I went on from book to book, I saw myself and my life in London. In Thackeray I found the gentler life of better-off people and the irony I now loved. To have been the young man in *The Virginians,* to have travelled as he did and to find oneself among affectionate, genial, and cultivated families who enjoyed their fortunes, instead of struggling for them, must be heaven. And I had seen enough in our family to be on the way to acquiring a taste for disillusion.

—from *A Cab at the Door*

Eva Hoffman

(b. 1946)

Eva Hoffman was born in Cracow and moved to Vancouver when she was thirteen.

Trying to fit in while preserving one's identity is a tricky proposition for any adolescent. Being caught between two languages, gradually releasing one and assimilating the other, requires a unique coming to terms.

At Rice University, she found herself in an English department "firmly in the grip of the New Criticism," which relies on close textual reading without reference to cultural or historical sources.

But my particular kind of alienness serves me well too, for I soon discover that triangulation is a more useful tool in literary criticism than it is in life. As I read, I triangulate to my private criteria and my private passions, and from the oblique angle of my estrangement, I notice what's often invisible to my fellow students. When I read *The Catcher in the Rye,* it's Holden Caulfield's immaturity that strikes me, and I write a paper upbraiding him for his false and coy naïveté—my old, Polish terms of opprobrium. Reading *The Ambassadors* requires a torture of concentration, but a glimpse of Strether coming ashore in France and registering the ever-so-minute changes of light and smell and facial expressions and angle of objects delivers a thrill of recognition: that's just what it's like to land on a foreign shore, and I want to write Henry James a thank-you note for capturing the ineffable with such exactitude. In Malamud's *The Assistant,* it's not the religious parable that fixes my attention but the dingy, dark little store in which the Jewish shopkeeper ekes out his hopeless living; I'm grateful again, that someone has made literature of such a condition.

—from *Lost in Translation*

Anne Lamott

(b. 1954)

California writer Anne Lamott is the author of Operating Instructions: A Journal of My Son's First Year *(1993) and* Bird by Bird *(1994), her observations on writing.*

I grew up around a father and a mother who read every chance they got, who took us to the library every Thursday night to load up on books for the coming week. Most nights after dinner my father stretched out on the couch to read, while my mother sat with her book in the easy chair and the three of us kids each retired to our own private reading stations. Our house was very quiet after dinner—unless, that is, some of my father's writer friends were over. My father was a writer, as were most of the men with whom he hung out. They were not the quietest people on earth, but they were mostly very masculine and kind. Usually in the afternoons, when that day's work was done, they hung out at the no-name bar in Sausalito, but sometimes they came to our house for drinks and ended up staying for supper. I loved them, but every so often one of them would pass out at the dinner table. I was an anxious child to begin with, and I found this unnerving.

—from *Bird by Bird*

II
Sorts of Readers

Our writers may help you understand not only what your reading style is, but—perhaps—why. One reader of our acquaintance used to commute to graduate school from Kingston, New York, to the middle of Long Island, and his books were filled with almost illegible scrawlings, the result of writing while reading while driving. Those who eat while reading, by the way, would do better not to borrow books.

Samuel Taylor Coleridge

(1772–1834)

By way of John Donne, Samuel Taylor Coleridge defined various styles of reading. We all would like to be "diamond sieves"—capable of finding and keeping the purest nuggets of literary treasure. We have left Coleridge's spelling in its original 1808 glory.

4 Sorts of Readers. 1. Spunges that suck up every thing and, when pressed give it out in the same state, only perhaps somewhat dirtier—. 2. Sand Glasses—or rather the upper Half of the Sand Glass, which in a brief hour assuredly lets out what it has received—& whose reading is only a profitless measurement and dozeing away of Time—. 3. Straining Bags, who get rid of whatever is good & pure, and retain the Dregs.—and this Straining-bag class is again subdivided into Species of the Sensual, who retain evil for the gratification of their own base Imagination, & the calumnious, who judge only by defects, & to whose envy a beauty is an eye-sore, a fervent praise respecting another a near-grievance, and the more virulent in its action because the miserable man does not dare confess the Truth to his own Heart—. 4. and lastly, the Great-Moguls Diamond Sieves—which is perhaps going farther for a Simile than its superior Dignity can repay, inasmuch as a common Cullender would have been equally symbolic/but imperial or culinary, these are the only good, & I fear the least numerous, who assuredly retain the good, while the superfluous or impure passes away and leaves no trace.

—from *1808 Lectures on Principles of Poetry (Lecture 3)*

Joseph Epstein

(b. 1937)

The reader as a kitchen utensil: sponge, egg timer, strainer, colander? We like the idea of the reader as a grazing animal, a horse or a cow. Ideally, years of directed reading called education prepare one for a life of happy grazing in which no one else has control over what, when, or why you read.

Joseph Epstein had an "extremely happy childhood in which books played almost no part"; not until he was twenty did he became a first-class desultory reader. He is a keen observer of his own reading habits, which are shared by many others, in fact.

My passion for reading showed up in the dark winter of my junior year at the University of Chicago. That winter, because all my classes met in the morning hours, I decided to sleep days and stay up nights, on the model, I subsequently learned, of George Sand. I would return from class at eleven A.M. and sleep until dinner at six or so. After dinner I played poker or gin, watched television, went to the movies, schmoozed, and engaged in other such character-building activities until nearly midnight. Then, when everyone else had turned in, I spent three or so hours doing my various school assignments. That left four or five utterly quiet, altogether solitary, absolutely delicious hours for reading exactly what I pleased.

What I pleased to read was not all that elevated. Elevation to heights where oxygen equipment came in handy was already available in the classroom, for the curriculum at the University of Chicago offered only great books for study. I had no argument with that; I still don't. But I, for my own personal reasons, had a simultaneous hunger for merely good books and even for a few rubbishy ones. So there I sat, in a small but immensely comfortable armchair purchased for five bucks from the Salva-

76

tion Army, in my robe, a blanket over my lap, smoking cigarettes and drinking coffee, or Pepsi-Cola, reading the novels of
John O'Hara, Christopher Isherwood, Aldous Huxley, Henry
Miller (in the plain green paperback covers provided by the
Olympia Press), J. D. Salinger, Truman Capote, and I forget
what others, awaiting the sunrise, feeling flat out, deliriously,
pig-heaven happy. The hook was in, deep down, permanently
planted. Henceforth one of my life's perennial problems was
how to clear a decent bit of time for that lovely, anti-social,
splendidly selfish habit known as reading. In *The Principles of
Psychology*, William James remarks that "the period between
twenty and thirty is the critical one for the formation of intellectual and professional habits," which certainly proved true in my
case. I was fortunate in being able to indulge my newfound
habit in a big-time way by being drafted for two years in the
peacetime army, where reading, in the fastnesses of army posts
in Texas and Arkansas, seemed far and away the best if not the
only game in town. Early in my time in the army—in, specifi-
cally, basic training—no books, magazines, even newspapers
were allowed, and, though this lasted only eight weeks, I can
distinctly recall feeling it as a genuine deprivation, like with-
drawal from cigarettes or sweets. Later in the army I found
myself living alone with occasional stretches of seventy-two
hours with no responsibilities and no money for sporting diver-
sions and nothing else to do but read, which I did, at three- and
four-hour uninterrupted clips. William James, in his chapter on
habit . . . , suggests that "even the habit of excessive indulgence in music, for those who are neither performers themselves nor musically gifted enough to take it in a purely intellectual way, has probably a relaxing [by which James meant a *bad]*
effect upon the character." But I took care of this little problem
by determining to become a writer. . . .

Not long after this decision, I moved to New York. . . .
While living in New York, I acquired the habit of rarely going
out without tucking a book or magazine under my arm. Vi-
brant and fascinating though New York can be, it has so many

parts and patches that are best read through: riding subways, standing in bank lines, arranging any sort of bureaucratic business, sitting through traffic jams. New York probably offers more good reasons to avert one's eyes than any other city in America, and where better to avert them than into a book? To this day, though long removed from New York, I still usually walk about with a book in hand, and I keep a book or two in my car, often getting in a quick paragraph at a stoplight. If you happen to be behind me, please don't honk when the light turns green, for I could be coming to the end of a paragraph.

Sometime in my middle twenties I began to review books, which, as a reader, I looked upon as the equivalent in sports of turning pro. The notion of being paid for reading was exhilarating. To be sure, the money was poor, but the hours were long and the fame almost yet not quite fleeting. As a youthful book reviewer, I was apparently able to do a convincing impression of an intelligent and cultivated fellow, and so I was soon asked to review books intrinsically much more serious than I was. Would I care to review the most recent volume of Bertrand Russell's autobiography? Yes, I rather should. An English translation of Thomas Mann's letters is about to be published, and would I be interested in writing about it? Actually, I would. The memoirs in four volumes of Alexander Herzen have appeared, and did I have time to read and write about them? Not, I allowed, a problem. (Who, exactly, was Alexander Herzen, I recall thinking after agreeing to write about him, and I rushed to an encyclopedia to find out.) Yet I worked hard on these reviews, reading lots of other books in connection with them, in no small measure because I was fearful of making a jackass of myself by committing some horrendous error. This, I believe, is what's known as getting one's education in public. Whether it is also known as fraud is a question I prefer to let pass.

As a reviewer, I took notes on my reading and made light vertical pencil markings alongside pertinent passages that I wanted either to quote or to reread. It was all a bit like being a student again, which was not my idea of a jolly good time. One of the reasons I was so eager to be out of school—and knew with a certainty that graduate school was not for me—was my ardor to read what I wished and precisely the way I wished to read it: not to read for examination or to acquire someone else's sense of a book. My temperament led me away from concentrated study. An expert—on anything—was the last thing I wished to become. If not in life then at least among books, I was a born roamer. Boswell reports that Samuel Johnson's mind was "more enriched by roaming at large in the fields of literature, than if it had been confined to any single spot," adding that "the flesh of animals who feed excursively, is allowed to have a higher flavor than that of those who are cooped up." If desultory reading was good enough for the Doc, I figure it is plenty good enough for me.

But to read desultorily, to be an intellectual romancer and grazer, luxurious though the freedom of it is, carries its own complications. Certain reading habits require a commensurate reading habitat. Multiple have been the definitions of the intellectual, that professional dilettante, but any realistic definition should include the unfailing identifying mark of his living amidst a vast welter of paper. In the abode of the intellectual, books, magazines, newspapers are everywhere. The splendidly sensible Sydney Smith, in composing a sketch for a cheerful room, suggests that tables "should be strewn with books and pamphlets," but he elsewhere warned that, to preserve oneself from becoming completely swamped by books, one should never "auffer a single shelf to be placed in [a room]; for they will creep around you like an erisypelas till they have covered the whole."

The home of any serious desultory reader has to be a shambles of odd reading matter, chiefly because such a reader has no useful principle of exclusion. By the very nature of his reading, his interests tend to widen not to narrow, to exfoliate endlessly, like a magical rose. Ten or so years ago I could have confidently said that I had no interest, as a reader, in space travel. I have since taken a very elementary course in astronomy, and so books on space and astronomy come into our apartment as does a subscription to *Astronomy Magazine*. A recent trip to Italy has brought modern Italy into the already crowded list of subjects I now read about regularly. An essay in the British magazine *Encounter* on a writer I had not hitherto heard of named Julian Jaynes caused me to acquire a copy of Jaynes's book, *The Origin of Consciousness in the Breakdown of the Bicameral Mind*. It begins brilliantly. Another bookmark in yet another book; another book atop yet another pile of books—one of several—with bookmarks in them. It is endless, absolutely endless—and I must confess that I wouldn't have it any other way.

Katherine Mansfield
(1888–1923)

Sunday 16 May Paris . . . I bought a book by Henry James yesterday and read it, as they say, "until far into the night". It was not very interesting or very good, but I can wade through pages and pages of dull, turgid James for the sake of that sudden sweet shock, that violent throb of delight that he gives me at times.

JOURNAL (1915)

Having too much to read isn't a worry; having too little to read has been on occasion. In paucity, never profligacy, lies fear. Sir James Mackintosh, a journalist and jurist who wrote for the *Edinburgh Review*, used to travel around the country with so many books in his carriage that he couldn't pull down the windows. S. N. Behrman, the American playwright and memoirist, used to travel with a portable library, a smallish leather case that contained twenty-five or thirty books. To people who do not require ample dosages of print, taken daily, this will seem excessive, even foolish. I myself think it shows eminent good sense. Abroad, in the town of Ravenna, I had read my way through the books in English that I had brought along. Sheer panic set in. I discovered a shop off the Piazza del Popolo that sold British paperbacks. I bought two novels of the insufficiently amusing British novelist Simon Raven, at the scandalous price of ten dollars a shot, which at least calmed me down until I returned home.

I don't mean to imply that anything at all satisfies my hunger for reading. I have never, for example, been able to read detective stories or spy thrillers, no matter how elegantly composed, though I enjoy both kinds of stories in the movies or on television. . . . Whenever possible I prefer books that amuse me; this comes down to meaning books that were written with style. I would rather read a stylish book than a style-less more scholarly book on the same subject. I have of late been reading Sacheverell Sitwell's *Liszt*. Doubtless more serious books on Liszt have been written; it is doubtful that I shall read another full book on Liszt in my lifetime. Yet Sachie, as Sitwell's friends called him, seems to me to have written a fine book because he knew what was interesting in life, knew how to tell an anecdote well, knew how to put a lot of spin on his sentences. He was, in two words, no dope. I prefer not to read dopes. I prefer to read writers who know more about the world than I do, and to steer clear of those who know less. I discover more of the latter as I grow older, but the growth of my own wisdom is not proceeding at so alarming a rate that I fear running out of things to read.

Although reading is a solitary act, it need not be done in isolation from other acts. In his chapter on habit, William James cites a man named Robert Houdin who could read while juggling four balls. (I assume he wasn't reading Immanuel Kant.) A husband and wife conversing behind their separate sections of newspaper over breakfast is an old cartoon set piece. Lots of people—I am among them—read while watching television, sometimes during commercials or through the more trivial news items or awaiting a weather report or sport scores. Reading while watching baseball on television is especially fine and, given light reading, is easily brought off with the help of the instant replay. Why do one thing at a time when you can do two? And between the two done simultaneously, light reading and watching television, the former almost always wins out.

Reading . . . in the bathroom is a subject that, in any earnest survey of reading habits, cannot be avoided. ("It's alimentary, my dear Watson.")

Books for bathroom reading oughtn't be too heavy, in any sense of the word—neither too large nor too densely argued. What is wanted is writing that can be read in short takes, easily abandoned and returned to at a later time without losing the thread. Diaries and journals and collections of letters fill the bill nicely; so do wittily written novels of modest length. I read a volume of Tocqueville's letters in the bathroom; I am currently reading selections from James Agate's amusing diary (*The Selective Ego*); and some years ago, over a two-year stretch, I read through the twelve slender novels that comprise Anthony Powell's *Dance to the Music of Time*. More recently, I read three volumes of Frank Sullivan's humorous writings, and I continue to read, intermittently, two books by Arthur Koestler on scientific subjects: *The Case of the Midwife Toad* and *The Watershed*, a biography of Johannes Kepler. But then everyone will have his own notions about what makes for the most commodious reading.

Reading while eating has its own complexities. Eating alone, especially in a restaurant, one's solitude seems redoubled. One notices, as one rarely does when dining in company, the lengthiness and noisiness of one's chewing, the slight awkwardness with which one handles one's cutlery, one's ineptitude with lettuce. Dining in solitude renews one's sense of the necessity of company to the enjoyment of food. A book at the side or in front of one's plate takes one's mind off all that, serving as a screen against the public when dining out, as a companion when dining alone in one's own home. . . .

If I were a fast reader, I have sometimes thought, it might only be the worse for me. My reading ambitions might have doubled. I might have been unhappy—felt guilty—if I didn't read at least a book a day, as the literary critic Stanley Edgar Hyman once told me that he did. As a fast reader, too, I should have often been tempted to stay up all night to finish a stirring book—a thing I have done only twice in my life, both times with novels: once, in my adolescence, with Willard Motley's *Knock on Any Door,* and a second time, in my twenties, with I. J. Singer's *The Brothers Ashkenazi.* H. L. Mencken is said to have been a blazingly fast reader. Samuel Johnson may have been, if not faster, more efficient, for according to Adam Smith's account as retold through James Boswell, Johnson "had a peculiar facility in seizing at once what was valuable in any book, without submitting to the labor of perusing it from beginning to end." . . . Johnson's own method was to begin a book in the middle and if he felt the inclination to read more to go back to the beginning.

My own present modus operandi is to begin a book at the beginning and, for one reason or another, often to bog down somewhere near the middle. On a quick search of our apartment, I find twenty-three books with bookmarks in them, and this does not count books I am reading for professional reasons. Jumping from one book to another, reading lots of magazines in between, sometimes I go a week or two without actually finishing a book. Every once in a while, out of sheer frustration, I sit down and finish reading two or three books, if only to get some minor sensation of completion in my life. All these half-read books, taken together, form no pattern, show no evidence of anything resembling coherence. . . . If I had to extrapolate the personality of the man from this pile of his half-read books, I would posit a man without much discipline, an intellectual clearly, but also a hedonist of the intellect, who gives way to his every whimsical interest. He may be a man who has come to feel that not only is reading a significant form of experience but in some respects it is rather more efficient and pleasurable than actual experience.

Repose ought, in some part, to be the intention of all readers. Some reading, of course, is more reposeful than others. The least reposeful for me is that provided by the newspapers. Many people make a meal out of a newspaper, chewing and swallowing every morsel; I can't find the makings for the lightest of snacks. I read only one, the *New York Times,* and that only six days a week, and never, never, like the prostitutes in Athens, on Sunday. A wise man whose name I cannot recall said that one picks up newspapers in anticipation and inevitably sets them down in disappointment. I no longer feel the anticipation. I chiefly consult the newspaper to get a feeling for the heft and slant of current political opinion and to discover—the only real news—who has died. I scan the letters column in the (usually) vain hope of finding a man or woman after my own heart. I take a pass on the editorials, unless they promise to be especially cowardly, and quickly check the sports. I glance at the reviews and absurdities on display in the pages given over to the arts. I merely glimpse the general news, and read only to the end articles about scandals. I prefer to have the whole deal out of the way in something under twenty minutes, and generally do.

As one grows older, reading becomes an ever keener pleasure and an ever greater comedy. Part of the pleasure derives intrinsically from the activity itself; and part from its extrinsic rewards, not the least of which is knowing that there will always be plenty to read and so superannuation presents no real fear. (Great readers have this advantage over great lovers.) The comedy of reading is owing in part to one's memory, which in the natural course of things retains less and less of what one reads; and in part to that oldest joke of all, which Dostoevsky insists comes to each of us afresh, I speak—hushed tones please—of death, which among other erasures rubs out all that one has read over a lifetime.

—from "Waiter, There's a Paragraph in My Soup!"

Ralph Waldo Emerson
(1803–1882)

It is no wonder that Ralph Waldo Emerson, who valued direct experience, should have protested the intermediary nature of reading, in which the book stands between the reader and the life the text describes.

What are books? They can have no permanent value. . . . When we are aroused to a life in ourselves, these traditional splendors of letters grow very pale and cold. Literature is made up of a heap of nouns and verbs enclosing an intuition or two. . . . Why should I quit the task however narrow and mean assigned to me by the Soul of Nature, to go gazing after the tasks of others or listening to the rumor of their performance? There is other peeping beside setting the eye to chinks and keyholes. This everlasting reading, for example, of what others have done. . . . Let us think more nobly. Let us, if we must have great actions, make our own so. . . . Let us do our own duties. Why need I go gadding into the scenes and philosophy of Greek or Italian History, before I have built my own house and justified myself to my own benefactors? . . . Is not that a just objection to much of our reading? . . . It is peeping. By- ron says of Jack Bunting,

He knew not what to say and so he swore.

I may say of our preposterous use of books,

He knew not what to do and so he read.

In defending the reader against the book in this way, Emerson expressed an extreme, and modern, view of the reader's relation to reading matter:

What can we see, read, acquire, but ourselves? Take the book, my friend, and read your eyes out; you will never find there what I find. . . . To introduce a man to a good book is like introducing him to fine company. It is nothing if he is nothing.

He repeated this belief with variations throughout his life. Emerson meant that we each bring to our reading the images, sensations, emotions, and experiences that constitute us as individuals; we populate the world of the book with our unique selves. No matter how carefully the writer might describe a place or a character, we each envision a different place and see a different character. If a writer leaves us cold, we see and hear nothing, though the same writer might touch another reader's intimate imagination.

Emerson noticed the uncanny way in which what we pick up randomly and read is often piercingly relevant to our interests, however passing. Books connect with one another in our minds, and these connections bring us new understanding. When a book amazes us with its personal relevance we glimpse the hallucinatory quality of reading; a sentence that has spent hundreds of years waiting for us. Our reading matter, of course, changes as we do; sometimes fiction absorbs us and sometimes seems false. In times of crisis poetry helps, and in exhaustion, cookbooks relax us. Biography and history keep us in touch with a larger world than our personal one. More than subject matter changes. As we change we may find far less in a favorite book on rereading. We may even wonder what it was we saw in it to start with. Then again, we may find the self we used to be.

Emerson read widely and randomly, as his biographer Robert D. Richardson, Jr., eloquently notes, ". . . with the contented nonchalance of one who never knows from what direction inspiration will appear but who knows that it will appear." Emerson advised Charles Woodbury, then a Williams College student:

. . . learn how to tell from the beginnings of chapters and from glimpses of the sentences whether you need to read them entirely through. So turn page after page, keeping the writer's thoughts before you, but not tarrying with him, until he has brought you the thing you are in search of. . . .

If Emerson was an inspired skipper, he was also an orderly one. He indexed his journals and kept track of the books he read. He might have grazed but he made sure he knew where to go if he wanted to revisit a particular spot.

A certain amount of skipping comes, of course, with age and bifocals. When we lie down to read we have to adjust head and glasses to line up the right focus on the page. At times our eyes slip over the sentence from beginning to end, bounding from word to word several times until the meaning assembles itself or not. This was probably not what Emerson meant, but intentional reading method or not, it happens.

Charles Lamb

(1775–1834)

A serious stammerer, Charles Lamb wrote prose that is clear, un-fussy, and direct. Generations of children have read the plots of Shakespeare's plays in the famous Tales from Shakespeare *(1806) by Charles Lamb and his sister Mary. Usually known as "Lamb's Tales of Shakespeare," this classic has finally fallen out of use.*

Such an innocent name, Lamb, yet the Lamb family was men-tally unsound and at times violent. The father had a disabling mental disease, and Charles Lamb spent a short time in an asylum. Mary Lamb—years before she collaborated with her brother on the Tales—*stabbed her father nearly to death and had better success with her mother.*

After the attack on her parents, Mary was sent to the asylum. Later Charles obtained her release and undertook a lifetime of her care. She outlived him by about ten years.

His devotion and self-sacrifice did not keep Charles Lamb from holding a job and from writing essays and poems on such timeless topics as giving up tobacco, acting on the stage, and going to a wedding for The London *and other magazines. He inspired great loyalty to himself and was friends with the Wordsworths, Coleridge, Robert Southey, and the painter William Hazlitt.*

. . . . I dream away my life in others' speculations. I love to lose myself in other men's minds. When I am not walking, I am reading; I cannot sit and think. Books think for me.

I have no repugnances. Shaftesbury is not too genteel for me, nor Jonathan Wild too low. I can read anything which I call *a book*. There are things in that shape which I cannot allow for such.

In this catalogue of *books which are no books—biblia a-bib-*

lia— I reckon Court Calenders, Directories, Pocket Books, Draught Boards, bound and lettered on the back, Scientific Treatises, Almanacs, Statutes at large; the works of Hume, Gibbon, Robertson, Beattie, Soames Jenyns, and generally, all those volumes which "no gentleman's library should be without" . . . With these exceptions, I can read almost anything. I bless my stars for a taste so catholic, so unexcluding. . . .

Much depends upon *when* and *where* you read a book. In the five or six impatient minutes, before dinner is quite ready, who would think of taking up the Faëry Queen for a stopgap, or a volume of Bishop Andrewes' sermons?

Milton almost requires a solemn service of music to be played before you enter upon him. But he brings his music, to which, who listens, had need bring docile thoughts, and purged ears.

Winter evenings—the world shut out—with less of ceremony the gentle Shakespeare enters. At such a season the *Tempest,* or his own *Winter's Tale*—

E. M. Forster
(1879–1970)

1926: *Clarissa Harlowe.* Have read 1/3 of. Long books, when read, are usually overpraised, because the reader wants to convince others and himself that he has not wasted his time. cf. St. Paul's argument for immortality. Certainly I am bored. . . .

THE COMMONPLACE BOOK

These two poets you cannot avoid reading aloud—to yourself, or (as it chances) to some single person listening. More than one—and it degenerates into an audience.

Books of quick interest, that hurry on for incidents, are for the eye to glide over only. It will not do to read them out. I could never listen to even the better kind of modern novels without extreme irksomeness.

A newspaper, read out, is intolerable. . . . Newspapers always excite curiosity. No one ever lays one down without a feeling of disappointment.

. . . Coming into an inn at night—having ordered your supper—what can be more delightful than to find lying in the window seat, left there time out of mind by the carelessness of some former guest—two or three numbers of the old *Town and Country Magazine*, with its amusing tête-à-tête pictures—"The Royal Lover and Lady G—"; "The Melting Platonic and the Old Beau"—and suchlike antiquated scandal? Would you exchange it—at that time, and in that place—for a better book?

Poor Tobin, who latterly fell blind, did not regret so much for the weightier kinds of reading—the *Paradise Lost,* or "Comus," he could have *read* to him—but he missed the pleasure of skimming over with his own eye a magazine, or a light pamphlet.

I should not care to be caught in the serious avenues of some cathedral alone, and reading *Candide*.

. . . I am not much a friend to out-of-doors reading. I cannot settle my spirits to it. I knew a Unitarian minister, who was generally to be seen upon Snow Hill (as yet Skinner's Street *was not*), between the hours of ten and eleven in the morning, studying a volume of Lardner. I own this to have been a strain of abstraction beyond my reach. I used to admire how he sidled along, keeping clear of secular contacts. An illiterate encounter with a porter's knot, or a breadbasket, would have quickly put to flight all the theology I am master of, and have left me worse than indifferent to the five points.

There is a class of street-readers, whom I never contemplate without affection—the poor gentry, who, not having the wherewithal to buy or hire a book, filch a little learning at the open stalls—the owner, with his hard eye, casting envious looks at them all the while, and thinking when they will have done. Venturing tenderly, page after page, expecting every moment he shall interpose his interdict, and yet unable to deny themselves the gratification, they "snatch a fearful joy."

—from *The Last Essays of Elia*

Eugène Delacroix

(1798–1863)

Eugène Delacroix, a man who was never idle, brings us a per-
spective on reading from the point of view of another kind of
seeing and perceiving. The great painter and diarist was ill and
confined at home for three months in 1857, and during that time
he plunged enthusiastically into the writing of a dictionary of the
fine arts.

The following was intended as part of the Preface. By his com-
parison between the experience of reading a book and seeing a
painting, Delacroix illuminates the temporal and jagged quality of
the reading experience, and points up the work a reader must do to
grasp a book as a unified whole.

A dictionary is not a book: it is an instrument, a tool for
making books or any other thing. The material, thus divided
into articles, is thus extended or restricted according to the
disposition of the author, and at times according to his lazi-
ness. It thus suppresses the transitions, the necessary connections among the parts, in order in which they should be disposed.

Although the author professes much respect for the book,
properly so called, he, like a pretty considerable number of
readers, has often experienced a kind of difficulty in giving
the necessary attention to all the deductions and all the link-
ing-together of a book, even one that has been well conceived and executed. We see a picture all at once, at least in
its ensemble and its principal parts: for a painter accustomed
to an impression like that, which is favorable to the understanding of the work, the book is like an edifice of which
the front is often a signboard behind which, once he is introduced there, he must again and again give equal attention to

the different rooms composing the monument he is visiting, not forgetting those which he has left behind him, and not without seeking in advance, through what he knows already, to determine what his impression will be at the end of his expedition.

It has been said that rivers are moving roads. It could be said that books are portions of pictures in movement, among which one follows the other without its being possible to grasp them at one time; to seize upon the connection among them demands from the reader almost as much intelligence as from the author. If the work is one of fantasy, addressing itself to the imagination alone, the attention demanded may become a pleasure; a well-composed history produces the same effect upon the mind: the necessary sequence of events and their consequences forms a natural chain which the mind follows without trouble. But in a didactic work, the same cannot be true. The merit of such a work residing in its utility, it is to an understanding of all its parts and to extracting the meaning of them that the reader applies himself. The more easily he deduces the doctrine of the book, the more fruitful his reading will have been: now is there a simpler means, one that is more the enemy of all rhetoric, than this division of the material? . . .

In what art does execution so intimately follow invention? In painting and in poetry, *form is inseparable from conception*, etc., etc. Among readers, it is for instruction that some read, while others do it for amusement.

Delacroix quotes from his journal entry, May 7, 1850:

"Montaigne writes by fits and starts. Those are the most interesting works. After the effort needed by the author to follow the thread of his idea, to keep that idea warm, etc., one must realize that there is also the work of the reader who, having opened his book for his recreation, finds himself insensibly caught, almost as a matter of honor, by the task of deciphering, etc."

Men of genius would not come to an understanding as to the production of a dictionary: on the other hand, if you had from each one a collection of their special observations, what a dictionary could be composed with such material!

—from *The Journal of Eugène Delacroix*

Elinore Standard

(b. 1933)

Are you a serial reader? Maybe you began with *Uncle Wiggily* and *Raggedy Ann* and *Winnie-the-Pooh*. Then you moved on to *The Five Little Peppers* and *The Boxcar Children*, *Mary Poppins* and *The Lion, The Witch and The Wardrobe*. After that, you immersed yourself in Nancy Drew and Judy Bolton or Jack London. You panicked if the library didn't have the next book in your series, and pouted if your mother wouldn't take you to a bookstore. You were called obsessed. You heard them say so much reading would ruin your eyes and your posture, and they made you go outside to get some fresh air.

Now you're the grown-up, and you can drive yourself and you will always drive your kids when they are desperate for a book because you remember. . . .

Come with us to those thrilling days of yesteryear! Yes, come to the parsonage in Barsetshire or into Parliament with Trollope's Pallisers! Step into the drawing room with Jeeves and Bertie Wooster. Come in from the smoggy streets of Victorian London and warm yourself by the fire at 221-B Baker Street. Sit back as a large cast of characters ages along with you in the twelve novels of Anthony Powell's *A Dance to the Music of Time*.

Stay at home, see the world!

Go to the Dublin horse show with Bartholomew Gill's Inspector McGarr or prowl the Bayou country with James Lee Burke's Dave Robicheaux, or perhaps you'd like to try raising orchids and eating anchovy fritters with Rex Stout's Nero Wolfe. You might roam the Outback with Arthur W. Upfield's Napoleon Bonaparte or cruise the South African *veldt* with Patrick McGinley's Bantu Sergeant Zondi. Track the Navajo country with Tony Hillerman's policemen Jim Chee and Joe Leaphorn. Observe the Paris skyline with stolid, well-fed Maigret. Get depressed during a Swedish winter with Maj

Sjöwall and Per Wahlöö, or get depressed during a Moscow winter with inspectors Arkady Renko and Porfiry Rostnikov.

Do some handicapping at Santa Anita with William Murray's Shifty Lou Anderson. You can live in Fort Lauderdale on Travis McGee's "Busted Flush." Join a 12-step program along with Lawrence Block's Matthew Scudder, do an autopsy with Patricia Cornwell's Kay Scarpetta, M.E., call on the vicar with Miss Marple, be a Mayfair lawyer along with Frances Fyfield's smart and quirky Sarah Fortune.

And doesn't it make you fume when the writer kills off your favorite hero as Nicholas Freeling did with Inspector Van der Valk? Sir Arthur Conan Doyle had to resurrect Holmes after he killed him. What do you do when the author dies in mid-series as Ian Fleming did, leaving you behind? And what about when the author finally puts an end to the entire series? Remember how you felt at the close of *Gaudy Night* when Lord Peter Wimsey asks, *"Placetne, magistra?"* and Harriet Vane replies, " *Placet.*" and that was it? Fine for them but you want more. You always want more. The writer could live to be a hundred and you'd still be hoping for a book a year.

I know a woman (she claims to know nothing whatever about anything nautical) who finished the seventeenth novel in Patrick O'Brian's seafaring saga and then turned around and began all over again. She may have the solution: read the series in a loop: that way you always have a backup book. Male or female, old or young, we consume these serial works because they take us deep into complete, sustained worlds where over time we grow to love or hate the characters. We think about the characters in these books; we hold little dialogues with them as we go about our everyday lives—they live a shadowy existence, right at the edge of our minds.

—from "My Reading Life"

Tamar Lewin

(date unknown)

Newspaperwoman Tamar Lewin gives us a gender-smashing look at books in series.

Bookstores and libraries can divide up their books however they want, but there are really only two important categories: boy books and girl books.

Boy books are biographies of dead presidents, books by almost any Eastern European intellectual ("How much Solzhenitsyn have you gotten through?" sneers a woman friend) or anything else in which the point is the ideas (Italo Calvino), the landscape (Cormac McCarthy), or the action (Robert Ludlum). It is generally guys who are in thrall to Pete Dexter or Tom Clancy.

Girl books are about relationships, families, feelings, and the details of daily life. Think Jane Austen, Margaret Drabble, Alice Hoffman, Toni Morrison, or Amy Tan, or the cross-writers, male authors like Henry James or Anthony Trollope who wrote girl books despite themselves.

While there are cross-readers—women who like boy books and men who like girl books—the difference between the sexes basically comes down to *Moby Dick* versus *Little Women*. So it has been something of a shock to find myself—an inveterate reader of girl books—obsessed with Patrick O'Brian's Napoleonic-era historical novels, with the pictures of ships on their covers and the diagrams of the various sails inside.

A woman friend whose taste I almost always share began pushing Patrick O'Brian more than a year ago. Put off by the thought of plowing through prose dense with studdingsails and carronades, I resisted for months. But now I dwell mostly in the world of Captain Jack Aubrey, a big, bluff British monarch of the sea, and Stephen Maturin, his Irish-Catalan ship surgeon, who is also a naturalist and intelligence agent. I read the first sixteen Aubrey-Maturin novels from January to March and spent April awaiting the moment the seventh would arrive in bookstores so I could plunge back into the realm of gunroom dinners and ships sighted, hull-up on the horizon.

Last week a friend who referred in passing to something as the tip of the iceberg had to endure my detailed description of how Jack and Stephen ran into an iceberg, the noise made by the crashing and, a few books later, their close call in a different ice-infested passage.

Another friend had the misfortune of wondering, in my earshot, about eighteenth-century English usage. True, the Aubrey-Maturin books don't start until 1800, but I had many things to say about how Stephen and Jack use expressions like "I am with child to know" when they are waiting for news and "Give you joy" instead of "Congratulations."

My husband is sick of hearing me chortle over the puns that come up, book after book, like "the lesser of two weevils." He was less than enthralled by the news that Jack not only wears his hat as his hero, Lord Nelson, does but actually met Lord Nelson—who asked him, in the most kindly way, to pass the salt. My son, usually engaged by animal facts, was only mildly interested in how Stephen was stung by a male duckbill platypus and nearly died. My daughter just wants me to put down the books and play.

It could be worse: I have not joined the O'Brian discussion group on the Internet. I don't have the Patrick O'Brian calendar or the Patrick O'Brian newsletter put out by his publisher, W. W. Norton.

But Jack and Stephen are always on my mind.

For even if the Aubrey-Maturin novels sound like quintessential boy books, what with all the detail about life on a British Navy man-of-war in the time of Napoleon Buonaparte (O'Brian's spelling, no doubt historically accurate) and the dense asides on Inca history (Stephen has a close call in

Peru), I read them as girl books, hurrying through the adventures to find out about Jack and Stephen and their feelings for the men who sail with them and the women they carry in their hearts.

Indeed, while men seem to read O'Brian largely for the battles and the facts, what keeps me hooked are the evolving relationships between Jack and Stephen and the women they love—who are stuck on land most of the time but ever present, in letters and thoughts, nonetheless.

Patrick O'Brian is not the only author who can serve both kinds of readers. Many mystery and detective authors have crossover series, too: Men love the action in Robert B. Parker's Spenser books, but women mostly hang in there for the relationship between Spenser and his sidekick, Hawk, and his girlfriend, Susan Silverman.

An obsession with boy books can drive a girl-book reader crazy, though. While O'Brian would never end a novel midbattle, he does go through several volumes dropping maddening hints that something is terribly wrong with Stephen's daughter, Brigid—born while he was at sea—without resolving the question.

Still, when O'Brian came to New York last spring to promote "The Commodore," the seventeenth in the Aubrey-Maturin series, the girl-book fans and the boy-book fans separated out. Yes, men and women alike laughed warmly when the president of the New York Public Library turned to O'Brian and said, "We give you joy of 'The Commodore.' " And with the author in his eighties, everyone applauded when O'Brian, on hearing that one reader had dreamed there would be eight more volumes out by Christmas, promised "I intend to go on as long as ever I can."

But while the men perked up when O'Brian mentioned his research on naval history and Linnaeus or the Nelson banquet on Trafalgar night, women nodded most happily when he expressed his debt to Jane Austen, whom he called "that excellent woman." And during the question period, men asked why guns

kick more when they're hot and how the opening of the Royal
Naval College had changed His Majesty's Navy. But women
wanted to talk about their favorite characters or to find out the
color of Stephen's colorless eyes. ("That indefinite palette,"
O'Brian answered, before being pinned down to "greenish.")

I already knew that men and women read O'Brian differently: on finding that we shared an Aubrey-Maturin obsession,
a colleague sent me an E-mail message, asking, "How did you
get interested in Napoleonic naval history?" A male colleague,
obviously, who did not understand that I have no interest whatsoever in Napoleonic naval history.

I just want to know everything I can about Stephen and Jack
and what's up with little Brigid. I am with child to know.

—from "Hooked on Boy Books"

Eric Gill

(1882–1940)

When Eric Gill was twenty-four, he wrote in his diary "Tried wood-engraving a little in the evening." By the end of his life as a typographer, sculptor, and engraver, he had produced a prolific body of work of the highest quality. He is considered one of the most interesting representatives of the Arts and Crafts Movement. His typefaces are still in use, and his lettering is studied by graphic designers everywhere.

The son of a parson, Gill became an ardent Catholic convert who held strong views on every subject. He was described by a contemporary as "the most chivalrous hater, the most generous and scrupulous of enemies."

In his Autobiography *(1941), Gill talks about being a day-boy at a grammar school near Brighton where the headmaster was "keener on games than on books. He sneered at books; but he never sneered at football." Gill says he was never a good speller—interesting for a person who chiseled words in wood and stone.*

I don't want to write all I could write about the teaching of English spelling. I only want to explain why, in my opinion, learning to read English must be of its nature boring to rational creatures and that it is only made more so by the irrational attempts of teachers to make rules and regulations for teaching it. The only way to learn to read English is by sight, and that's what we all do in the end. Every word makes a different sort of pattern and we have to learn these patterns by heart. I will only add this: that I don't believe there can be such a thing as correct or incorrect spelling, but only good spelling and bad, unless by "correct" you simply mean "standard."

—from *Autobiography*

Anthony Trollope

(1815–1882)

During the Blitz, London bookshops were sold out of Trollope's novels. People wanted a good, long book to take them away from the war, something that might see them through long hours in bomb shelters. And there was Trollope—many of his major novels originally were published in two or three volumes, nothing shorter than 600 pages, most longer than that. There was Trollope with two or three plots working at the same time, plenty of tension, characters you loved to hate, and always an enticing romance and a happy ending.

Today, Trollope is available in paperback—huge doorstops so thick they are hard to hold up, especially if you are trying to read in bed. If you adjust your bedclothes properly, you can fix it so the book balances nicely, until you fall asleep and the book clunks to the floor and wakes you up. A Trollope novel is just the thing for a long airplane trip. The waits and delays will mean nothing so long as you're lugging your book.

Anthony Trollope says in his autobiography that the first twenty-six years of his life were "years of suffering, disgrace, and inward remorse." He worked at the General Post Office in London where he hated his work and hated wasting his life. He was always in trouble, always "on the eve of being dismissed." He was broke and on the run from bill collectors and desperate about what was to become of him.

He lived in dismal lodgings, and describes casting about for alternatives:

Parliament was out of the question. I had not the means to go to the Bar. In official life, such as that to which I had been introduced, there did not seem to be any opening for real success. Pens and paper I could command. Poetry I did not believe to be within my grasp. The drama, too, which I would fain have chosen, I believed to be above me. For history, biography, or essay writing I had not sufficient erudition. But I thought it possible that I might write a novel.

In those days I read a little, and did learn to read French and Latin. I made myself very familiar with Horace, and became acquainted with the works of our own greatest poets. I had my strong enthusiasms, and remember throwing out of the window in Northumberland Street, where I lived, a volume of Johnson's *Lives of the Poets,* because he spoke sneeringly of *Lycidas.* That was Northumberland Street by the Marylebone Workhouse, on to the back-door of which establishment my room looked out— a most dreary abode, at which I fancy I must have almost ruined the good-natured lodging-house keeper by my contin- ued inability to pay her what I owed.

Trollope's luck changed when he left London, went to work for the Irish Post Office, bought a horse, began to ride to hounds, married an Irish woman in 1844, and produced his first novel a year later. Increasing success, recognition, and happiness followed throughout the years, and toward the end of his life he compiled a record of his "literary performances," totaling 65 books and novels. "If any English authors not living have written more—I do not know who they are." In closing the Autobiography, *which was published soon after his death in 1882, Trollope writes:*

That I can read and be happy while I am reading, is a great blessing. Could I have remembered, as some men do, what I read, I should have been able to call myself an educated man. But that power I have never possessed. Something is always left—something dim and inaccurate—but still something suffi- cient to preserve the taste for more. I am inclined to think that it is so with most readers.

—from *Autobiography*

W. H. Auden

(1907–1973)

The poet and critic begins "The Guilty Vicarage," his analysis of the detective story and its reader, by quoting Rom. 7:7 "I had not known sin, but by the law."

For me, as for many others, the reading of detective stories is an addiction like tobacco or alcohol. The symptoms of this are: firstly, the intensity of the craving—if I have any work to do, I must be careful not to get hold of a detective story for, once I begin one, I cannot work or sleep till I have finished it. Secondly, its specificity—the story must conform to certain formulas (I find it very difficult, for example, to read one that is not set in rural England). And, thirdly, its immediacy. I forget the story as soon as I have finished it, and have no wish to read it again. If, as sometimes happens, I start reading one and find after a few pages that I have read it before, I cannot go on.

Such reactions convince me that, in my case at least, detective stories have nothing to do with works of art. It is possible, however, that an analysis of the detective story, i.e., of the kind of detective story I enjoy, may throw light, not only on its magical function, but also, by contrast, on the function of art.

The Reader

The most curious fact about the detective story is that it makes its greatest appeal precisely to those classes of people who are most immune to other forms of daydream literature. The typical detective-story addict is a doctor or clergyman or scientist or artist, i.e., a fairly successful professional man with intellectual interests and well-read in his own field, who could never stomach the *Saturday Evening Post* or *True Confessions* or movie magazines or comics. If I ask myself why I cannot enjoy stories about strong silent men and lovely girls who make love in a beautiful landscape and come into millions of dollars, I cannot answer that I have no fantasies of being handsome and loved and rich, because of course I have (though my life is, perhaps, sufficiently fortunate to make me less envious in a naïve way than some). No, I can only say that I am too conscious of the absurdity of such wishes to enjoy seeing them reflected in print.

Frank Tuohy (b. 1925) about
William Butler Yeats (1865–1939)

Western tales, together with detective stories, were something of an addiction. [Yeats's daughter] remembered how once in a delirious fever he shouted out, "Send for the Sheriff!"

YEATS

I can, to some degree, resist yielding to these or similar desires which tempt me, but I cannot prevent myself from having them to resist; and it is the fact that I have them which makes me feel guilty, so that instead of dreaming about indulging my desires, I dream about the removal of the guilt which I feel at their existence. This I still do, and must do, because guilt is a subjective feeling where any further step is only a reduplication—feeling guilty about guilt. I suspect that the typical reader of detective stories is like myself, a person who suffers from a sense of sin. From the point of view of ethics, desires and acts are good and bad, and I must choose the good and reject the bad, but the I which makes this choice is ethically neutral; it only becomes good or bad in its choice. To have a sense of sin means to feel guilty at there being an ethical choice to make, a guilt which, however "good" I may become, remains unchanged. It is sometimes said that detective stories are read by respectable law-abiding citizens in order to gratify in fantasy the violent or murderous wishes they dare not, or are ashamed to, translate into action. This may be true for the reader of thrillers (which I rarely enjoy), but it is quite false for readers of detective stories. On the contrary, the magical satisfaction the latter provide (which makes them escape literature, not works of art) is the illusion of being dissociated from the murderer.

The magic formula is an innocence which is discovered to contain guilt; then a suspicion of being the guilty one; and finally a real innocence from which the guilty other has been expelled, a cure effected, not by me or my neighbors, but by the miraculous intervention by a genius from the outside who removes guilt by giving knowledge of guilt. (The detective story subscribes, in fact, to the Socratic daydream: "Sin is ignorance.")

If one thinks of a work of art which deals with murder, *Crime and Punishment* for example, its effect on the reader is to compel an identification with the murderer which he would prefer not to recognize. The identification of fantasy is always an attempt to avoid one's own suffering: the identification of art is a sharing in the suffering of another. In Kafka's *The Trial,* it is the guilt that is certain and the crime that is uncertain; the aim of the hero's investigation is not to prove his innocence (which would be impossible for he knows he is guilty), but to discover what, if anything, he has done to make himself guilty. K, the hero, is, in fact, a portrait of the kind of person who reads detective stories for escape.

The fantasy, then, which the detective-story addict indulges is the fantasy of being restored to the Garden of Eden, to a state of innocence, where he may know love as love and not as the law. The driving force behind this daydream is the feeling of guilt, the cause of which is unknown to the dreamer. The fantasy of course is the same, whether one explains the guilt in Christian, Freudian, or any other terms. One's way of trying to face the reality, on the other hand, will, of course, depend very much on one's creed.

—from *The Dyer's Hand and Other Essays*

David Plante (b. 1940) about Jean Rhys (1890[?]–1979)

Sometimes we talked about writers, and she admitted, with no sign of great regret, that she hadn't read Balzac, Proust, Fielding, Trollope, George Eliot, James, Conrad, Joyce. She couldn't read Austen, she had tried. She had read a lot of Dickens. She had read, and remembered in great patches, the English Romantic poets, and Shakespeare. Her favorite writer, she said, was Robert Hitchens, who wrote turn-of-the-century melodramas; she said his books took her away, especially *The Garden of Allah*. But when friends brought her his novels from second-hand bookshops she left them in a pile. She read, instead, thrillers, and in her late life she read almost nothing else but. In Chelsea, she read, over and over, a novel called *The Other Side of Midnight,* and she said, "It's trash, perfect trash, but it takes you away," and made a sign as of going away, far off, with her hand.

III
Reading Aloud

Reading teachers tell us that children who are read to, learn to read and to love reading, and we don't doubt the word of those who are in the trenches. Reading to a child is one of the pleasurable regularities of family life. However, once we are on our own, some of us would rather not be read to.

Jane Austen
(1775–1817)

During quiet evenings at Steventon parsonage, Jane Austen's father read aloud to his family. In a letter, Austen mentions him reading poetry by William Cowper (1731–1800) and comments, "I listen when I can." In her novels, characters read and are read to. In Chapter 3 of Sense and Sensibility *(1811), Marianne Dashwood criticizes Edward Ferrars for lack of sensibility in his reading of Cowper:*

". . . I could not be happy with a man whose taste did not in every point coincide with my own. He must enter into all my feelings; the same books, the same music must charm us both. Oh! Mama, how spiritless, how tame was Edward's manner in reading to us last night! I felt for my sister most severely. Yet she bore it with so much composure; she seemed scarcely to notice it. I could hardly keep my seat. To hear those beautiful lines which have frequently almost driven me wild, pronounced with such inpenetrable calmness, such dreadful indifference!"

In Mansfield Park *(1814) one of Fanny Price's main duties is to read to her languorous aunt. Fanny's cousin, Edmund Bertram, recommends books and encourages her taste. ". . . He made reading useful by talking to her of what she read." In a long passage in Chapter 34, reading aloud is discussed by the newly ordained Edmund and their friend, Mr. Crawford:*

The subject of reading aloud was farther discussed. The two young men were the only talkers, but they, standing by the fire, talked over the too-common neglect of the qualification, the total inattention to it, in the ordinary school-system for boys, the consequently natural—yet in some instances almost unnatural degree of ignorance and uncouthness of men, of sensible and well-informed men, when suddenly called to the necessity of reading aloud, which had fallen within their notice, giving instances of blunders, and failures with their secondary causes, the want of management of the voice, of proper modulation and emphasis, of foresight and judgment, all proceeding from the first cause, want of early attention and habit; and Fanny was listening again with great entertainment.

"Even in my profession"—said Edmund with a smile—"how little the art of reading has been studied! how little a clear manner, and good delivery, have been attended to! I speak rather of the past, however, than the present.—There is now a spirit of improvement abroad; but among those who were ordained twenty, thirty, forty years ago, the larger number, to judge by their performance, must have thought reading was reading, and preaching was preaching. It is different now. The subject is more justly considered. It is felt that distinctness and energy may have weight in recommending the most solid truths; and, besides, there is more general observation and taste, a more critical knowledge diffused, than formerly; in every congregation, there is a larger proportion who know a little of the matter, and who can judge and criticize."

There is no doubt Jane Austen felt strongly about reading, and her views emerge in the novels. She often presents characters favorably or unfavorably through what they like to read. For example, in the first sentence of Persuasion *(1818) we meet mean, dishonest Sir Walter Elliot who "never took up any book but the Baronetage." There is probably nothing accidental about the name of this unpleasant character; Austen envied (but grudgingly admired) Sir Walter Scott. In a letter to a niece, she says, "Walter Scott has no business to write novels, especially good ones. It is not fair. He has fame and profit enough as a poet, and should not be taking the bread out of the mouths of other people. I do not like him and do not mean to like 'Waverly' if I can help it, but fear I must."*

Later in Persuasion *we find Captain Benwick, a shy, abstracted young man who has limited his reading to romantic poetry. "His reading has done him no harm," says Charles Musgrove, making apologies for a man who reads poetry, "for he has fought as well as read. He is a brave fellow." In* Emma *(1815) we understand Harriet Smith's lowbrow taste when she mentions reading such popular sentimental novels as* The Romance of the Forest *(1791) by Anne Radcliffe and* The Children of the Abbey *(1798) by Regina Maria Roche.*

In Northanger Abbey *(1803), Jane Austen's satire on the Gothic novel, Catherine Morland is happy to discover Henry Tilney also enjoys Mrs. Radcliffe's* The Mysteries of Udolpho *and declares, "I really thought before, young men despised novels amazingly."*

Sometimes Austen's characters realize they need to read more if they are to improve. Toward the end of Mansfield Park, *Fanny Price becomes "a chuser of books!" and introduces her sister to an upward path toward gentility by encouraging her to read.*

The intimacy thus begun between them was a material advantage to each. By sitting together upstairs, they avoided a great deal of the disturbance of the house; Fanny had peace, and Susan learnt to think it no misfortune to be quietly employed. They sat without a fire; but *that* was a privation familiar even to Fanny, and she suffered the less because reminded by it of the east-room. It was the only point of resemblance. In space, light, furniture, and prospect, there was nothing alike in the two apartments; and she often heaved a sigh at the remembrance of all her books and boxes, and various comforts there. By degrees the girls came to spend the chief of the morning upstairs, at first only in working and talking; but after a few days, the remembrance of the said books grew so potent and stimulative, that Fanny found it impossible not to try for books again. There were none in her father's house; but wealth is luxurious and daring—and some of hers found its way to a circulating library. She became a subscriber—amazed at being any thing in *propria persona,* amazed at her own doings in every way; to be a renter, a chuser of books! And to be having anyone's improvement in view in her choice! But so it was. Susan had read nothing, and Fanny longed to give her a share in her own first pleasures, and inspire a taste for the biography and poetry which she delighted in herself.

In this occupation she hoped, moreover, to bury some of the recollections of Mansfield which were too apt to seize her mind if her fingers only were busy; and especially at this time, hoped it might be useful in diverting her thoughts from pursuing Edmund to London, whither, on the authority of her aunt's last letter, she knew he was gone. She had no doubt of what would ensue. The promised notification was hanging over her head. The postman's knock within the neighbourhood was beginning to bring its daily terrors—and if reading could banish the idea for even half an hour, it was something gained.

In Chapter 10 of Sense and Sensibility, *Marianne has realized her lack of sense and resolves on a course of self-improvement:*

"When the weather is settled, and I have recovered my strength," said she, "we will take long walks together every day. We will walk to the farm at the edge of the down and see how the children go on; we will walk to Sir John's new plantations at Barton Cross, and the Abbeyland; and we will often go to the old ruins of the Priory and try to trace its foundations as far as we are told they once reached. I know we shall be happy. I know the summer will pass happily away. I mean never to be later in rising than six, and from that time till dinner I shall divide every moment between music and reading. I have formed my plan and am determined to enter on a course of serious study. Our own library is too well known to me to be resorted to for anything beyond mere amusement. But there are many works well worth reading at the park; and there are others of more modern production which I know I can borrow of Colonel Brandon. By reading only six hours a day, I shall gain in the course of a twelve-month a great deal of instruction which I now feel myself to want."

In Chapter 5 of Emma, *we hear Mr. Knightley's (and Jane Austen's) attitudes toward the importance of reading and the necessity of steady application and discipline in becoming well informed. Mrs. Weston (as the former Miss Taylor, former governess of Emma Woodhouse) is speaking to Mr. Knightley:*

"I can imagine your objection to Harriet Smith. She is not the superior young woman which Emma's friend ought to be. But on the other hand, as Emma wants to see her better informed, it will always be an inducement to her to read more herself. They will read together. She means it, I know."

"Emma has been meaning to read more ever since she was twelve years old. I have seen a great many lists of the drawing-up, at various times, of books that she meant to read regularly though—and very good lists they were, very well chosen, and very neatly arranged—sometimes alphabetically, and sometimes by some other rule. The list she drew up when only fourteen—I remember thinking it did her judgment so much credit, that I preserved it some time, and I dare say she may have made out a very good list now. But I have done with expecting any course of steady reading from Emma. She will never submit to anything requiring industry and patience, and a subjection of the fancy to the understanding. Where Miss Taylor failed to stimulate, I may safely affirm that Harriet Smith will do nothing. You never could persuade her to read half so much as you wished. You know you could not."

Rachel Hadas

(b. 1947)

Rachel Hadas lives in Manhattan and is the author of several books of poems, including Other Worlds Than This.

"Books," wrote Milton, "are not absolutely dead things, but do contain a potency of life in them as active as that soul whose progeny they are." At the Turin Book Fair in May 1988, Joseph Brodsky had this to say about reading:

> Since we are all moribund and since reading books is time-consuming, we must devise a system that allows us a semblance of economy. Of course there is no denying the possible pleasure of holing up with a fat, slow-moving, mediocre novel; still, we all know that we can indulge ourselves in that fashion only so much. In the end, we read not for reading's sake but our own.

What's odd about this is Brodsky's relegation of pleasure and indulgence to the realm of sin. No doubt we do read for our own sake, and no doubt we acquire (for example) knowledge from what we read. But if reading failed to provide a whole bouquet of delights, among them the apparently incompatible joys of solitude and community, it wouldn't be so addictive.

One of the first books I was able to read to myself all the way through, and so read over and over again, was *The Princess and the Goblin.* The magical grandmother in that tale, whose name is Irene, tells her great-great-great (etc.) granddaughter, whose name is also Irene, that a name is one of those things one can give away and keep at the same time. Books are like that too. Both Brodsky and Milton stress the relative durability of books,

the way, like names, they outlast their creators while simultaneously expressing those creators' activity of soul. (One can't, perhaps, say a name has a creator—"bearer" might be better, and if
books can have begetters, why not bearers too?) Brodsky: "Even
the worst of them [books] outlast their authors—maybe because
they occupy a smaller amount of physical space than those who
penned them." This physical compactness seems to be highly
compatible with, perhaps even necessary for, not only the actual
survival of the books but also the incredibly potent, durable,
condensed, and varied kinds of pleasure books bestow on readers.

For pleasure—*pace* Brodsky—is what makes us read, certainly what keeps us reading. The pleasures of reading for reading's sake or for the sake of learning could be articulated as
follows: pleasure is what keeps us reading until we've finished
the book, learning is what remains after we've closed the book.
But why separate what belongs together? Rapt readers do not
consider why they're rapt. In my family, at least, we would all
read even if condemned to instant amnesia (and Plato long ago
warned that reading and writing induce forgetfulness), because
reading feels good now. What is that if not reading for reading's sake? Yet the matter can never rest there, because no
matter how woolly-headedly forgetful we become, a good deal
of what we've read does somehow, in bits and pieces and unpre-
dictable ways, stay with us.

Once the artificially severed aspects of pleasure and memory
are reunited, it's obvious that each enhances the other. Reading
is one of the handful of human experiences that can be felt as
joyful at the moment it's taking place; even so, the pleasure is
greater in retrospect. And unlike a memorable meal, or a hike
up a mountain, or an ecstatic hour with a lover, reading effort-
lessly and innocently offers itself to us again, permits us to
compare, to deepen our understanding in an uninvidious way
that lays the blame on nobody should the repeated experience
disappoint us.

Reading is a physical act that can be performed under tre-

mendously varied circumstances and in a bewildering variety of
modes. A snapshot of me aged nine or so shows a pigtailed girl
huddled on the hood of a bulbous 1950s Buick, taking a huge
bite of a cookie (I think it was a Hermit), her eyes glued to her
book. A few years earlier, the family pediatrician had berated
me for reading on my stomach—bad for the eyes? the posture?

Like solitary sex, solitary eating has its own pleasures; but the
pleasures of eating in company, of making love with somebody
(and not just anybody) else, are part of what we often consider
the essence of these activities. With reading, such sharing is
often the exception rather than the rule. Yet many readers, too,
like to have partners: listeners, perhaps, to whom at any moment they can read a tidbit aloud; companions who will ask
them what they're laughing or grimacing at. The joy of diving
into a book and surfacing to share a morsel has been insufficiently praised. Another form of social pleasure in reading (this
is based on my experience of library books) consists of marking
up the margins of books with corrections or comments—a
pleasantly anonymous way of communicating with future readers of the book and mystically perhaps with the author as well.

In my family, and especially since my son has become a
greedy readee, the pleasure of sharing books is also the pleasure
of leaping the generation gap. It occurred to me the other night
that Jonathan (aged four and a half) was ready to be read
"Rikki-Tikki-Tavi." My husband and my mother would both
have loved to have read him the story; since I was the lucky
reader, they listened with, inevitably, more pleasure than the
child hearing it for the first time. A good deal of Jonathan's
pleasure was a reflection of our excitement at the prospect of his
discovering Kipling's story. As he helped me look for *The Jungle Book* in the attic, we discovered we had two copies of it: one
belonging originally to my sister, one with my father-in-law's
name on its flyleaf. I told Jonathan of these two prior owners.
"Were they friends?" he asked.

All this is not to say that children automatically devour what
their elders assure them is delicious. (Note the food metaphor,

which proves pervasive. Orwell tells us in his essay on Dickens that "forced feeding" of Dickens to him as a child initially caused "rebellion and vomiting"; he ponders the irony of having "*David Copperfield* ladled down my throat by masters in whom even then [I] could see a resemblance to Mr. Creakle.") The mysterious process of forming—consciously or not—a child's taste is probably often slow and indirect, indeed painful, just as our own tastes are gradually and often painfully acquired. Love and discomfort are inseparable in the penetrating passage in *Jean Santeuil* where Proust begins by considering books but quickly moves on to murkier waters:

> We often think what a pleasure it would be to talk about books, and other matters, to a very young and intelligent person. Actually, what we might read to him, what we might say, he would think extremely mediocre and, similarly, we should find nothing to interest us in his tastes. We often think that the object of our love flaunts its beauty, which to us is so adorable, on the surface for all to see. In reality, it is deep in ourselves that its beauty is displayed and if to gaze upon it ends by becoming a passion which we find it an agony not to be able to indulge more often, it frequently begins as a yoke the weight of which we find it hard to bear.

Or perhaps all this is about reading after all. The image of a buried and private beauty, a hidden object of desire, is very apt for the intense and solitary satisfaction of reading—a pleasure illegible and incomprehensible, if not wholly unknown, to others. Furthermore, this pleasure is one that often begins by not being especially pleasurable even to the reader. Proust's last sentence could easily refer to the familiar phenomenon of a book's not being enjoyable until we have read and reread it many times. How then do we ever get through that first reading? Yet we do.

The epitome of shared pleasure in reading is the slippery business of reading aloud, and it is here, of course, that the analogy with food and feeding comes into its own. To spoon-feed an adult is an act of tenderness and patience (or so one hopes; condescension and power-mongering are also strong possibilities), but it is also a sad necessity for both the feeder and, above all, the one being fed. Nursing a baby or feeding a small child, on the contrary, is a quintessential icon of the sustaining reciprocal love that nurtures both the one who feeds and the one who is fed. The issue of power, and later of individual taste, comes up here too, the moment we move away from the haloed image of a nursing mother, for the further the child moves from babyhood, the greater the range of choices, possibilities, and attendant problems. Still, it's considered natural for a mother to choose, provide, and prepare the food she then helps the baby to eat. If one of the joys of maturity—as great a triumph, for me, as never having to take a math course again—is reading what one chooses when one wants, then one of the joys of childhood, long past the age of weaning, is being lovingly provided with another kind of fare: books. There will be a time for the inevitable rebellion or disaffection later; but in my experience as child and now as mother, to reject books is to reject love.

Jonathan prefers to snuggle cozily against whoever is reading to him—in a recliner, or lying down before the lights are turned off at bedtime, or (this summer's hit) swinging lazily with the reader in a big hammock. Horizontally suspended, the reader and the one being read to share the illusion of having escaped gravity, and perhaps along with gravity that moribund condition Brodsky darkly refers to. The gentle pendulum of the hammock's swing marks the time—a comparison I owe to James Merrill's poem "A Timepiece," which, not coincidentally, is about not only time but motherhood.

In the absence or abeyance of vertical busyness, of scurrying hither and thither, the time which the hammock's marks is all the freer to cluster, almost like drops of moisture, around the dream of the book. Of the essence here is *otium*, the empty time needed to read, to snuggle, to dream. *Otium* is also an important ingredient of the kind of patience needed to create any book worth spending time over. Here's a chance comparison thrown up by my summer's reading. The late Georges Perec's remarkable novel *Life: A User's Manual* lovingly describes the minutiae of each apartment in a Paris building, devoting a mesmerized and mesmerizing attention to the design on an ashtray, the double renovation of a kitchen, the postcard on a mantelpiece. In Nicholas Von Hoffman's slapdash *Citizen Cohn*, Roy Cohn's 68th Street townhouse is allotted two adjectives—"moldering and crowded." That townhouse would have provided Perec with chapters full of detail—not merely as an extended decorative squiggle or an end in itself but as a crucial piece of a larger pattern, a pattern which would have told us something about Cohn but would also have been beautiful in its own right. Being a journalist, Von Hoffman is too rushed to pause over the townhouse. Is the handling of time what separates the genres of journalism and fiction, or even hackwork and art? Certainly Brodsky's mild sneer at the "fat, slow-moving, mediocre novel" drastically oversimplifies the kinds of pleasure leisureliness affords. Lying in the hammock reading to Jonathan, or reading to myself, I have the time for slow-paced books; I also, I find, have even less patience than usual for bad books.

Still in the hammock, I consider how reading takes over with exquisite tact from the other kinds of nurturance—being fed, changed, carried—that a four-year-old has outgrown. Think of Wilbur in *Charlotte's Web*. Miserably lonely in the strange barn and then at the fairgrounds, the pig begs Charlotte to tell him a story before he goes to sleep. Wilbur is, to say the least, well fed by the Zuckermans, but only Charlotte's attention can feed his hungry heart—and her attention, since it cannot be directly physical, consists of the tales (as well as epithets) she spins for him.

I thought of Charlotte one hot afternoon recently. Reading in the hammock, Jonathan and I noticed a couple of small spiders delicately lowering themselves from the larch boughs over our heads, swaying on their almost invisible strings a few inches above the pages of our book, which happened to be Howard Pyle's *The Wonder Clock*. Apparently it was Charlotte's turn to be read to.

I wonder whether Jonathan will remember those spiders and fairy tales, that hazy July afternoon. Probably not. Yet many of the memories of reading I still retain have the glamour of a slight strangeness—an unusual location (the hammock? the hood of the Buick?), a shared response. Memories float up from childhood but also from different layers of my adult life. Just as for a young child, being read to supplants being nursed, so for an adult reading in the company of a beloved person surely satisfies some of the need for the childish things we are supposed to have put away. How Edenic to have all of another person's attention, to be sharing in the giving and taking of pleasure, to be entertained and (yes, Mr. Brodsky) instructed too! An erotics of reading—is reading all a sexual sublimation? Maybe the other way around.

One summer in Vermont when my half-brother and his family shared the house with us, my sister and I were lucky enough to be read *David Copperfield* by our half-brother David, twenty years our senior. We were old enough to have read it ourselves, but there was no comparison between the book we would have evoked and the ferocious Mr. Murdstone David enacted for us. A couple of summers later, my sister and I, now at the advanced ages of thirteen and ten, were read *Pride and Prejudice* by our mother.

There are winter memories too: notably reading Cicero's *De Senectute* with my father—both of us home from school, tired, lying down, enjoying puzzling out the syntax. I recall something about metaphorical manure-spreading, no doubt to signify the enrichment of old age: *stercorandi*. In another year or so, I would be off to college. My father had only two more years to live.

I don't think it's claiming too much to say that every one of these memories, each of which casts a halo over both the reader and the text, signifies love. And not a vague floundering love, but affection in a highly concentrated, focused shape. It sounds paradoxical, but I'm thinking of *otium* again, of that sense of literate leisure favorable not only to visitations from the Muses but also to their worship, in the form of reading.

It's no coincidence that most of these episodes come from periods of my life (childhood; summertime) when I was not particularly studious, but when time was abundant. Reading to a child, or reading any text with attention, creates its own island where time, however scarce it may really be, feels luxuriant. I guess such islands, and the illusion of endlessness they bestow, are my version of that cant phrase "quality time." The best evocation I've ever seen of literature's power to help us escape from necessity is Primo Levi's "Ulysses Canto" chapter in *Survival in Auschwitz*, where—in the absence of a text—merely remembering, reciting, and trying to translate to a fellow prisoner some of Dante's account of Ulysses in hell is an act of attention wholly sublime and separate in nature from the condition the concentration camp seeks to impose.

Thinking of Levi's experience is humbling; compared to Auschwitz, we all live in enchanted islands. Nevertheless, time is notoriously hard to come by when one is adult, and it isn't summertime. Under these conditions, one way to attain *otium* is by malingering. After all, the absorption and abstraction, and often the reclining posture attendant on reading, give it the character of a mild indisposition anyway. One can be indisposed and keep working, especially if one's work is reading or writing—think of Marat! think of Proust! But the work takes on phenomenological contours reminiscent of the comforts of snuggling in that hammock, reading the afternoon away.

I've always imagined that before Charlotte Corday came along, Marat had a pretty nice time of it soaking in his bath. However itchy he may have been, it was more comfortable to be in the tub than out of it, and he was all set up to do paperwork. I felt like Marat last year when, for a urinary infection, I was advised to soak in a warm bath for quite a long time each day. Naturally, I read. The amniotic immersion, the semirecumbent position, the shut door, the sense of unaccountability to the world: all these sensations engulfed me before I even opened my rather damp book. But aren't these precisely the sensations that accompany any really concentrated reading? Mentally or physically, we shut the door and somehow or other (boldly diving, gingerly tiptoeing) immerse ourselves in the text. And the same goes for writing. Marat's bath was Proust's bed. How apposite that some critic has a memorable image of Proust seated in the lukewarm bath of his novel/life (*roman-fleuve* would seem to be the phrase) soaking a sponge in the murky water and continually squeezing it out over himself.

What I happened to be reading, during the days in my own lukewarm water, were bound volumes of the 1950s radio program "An Invitation to Learning." A kind of Columbia Lit. Hum. over the airwaves, the show featured panel discussions of writers from Seneca and Boethius to Dostoevsky and Hugo. Oddly enough, these "Invitation" volumes, which had presumably been on our Vermont bookshelves for decades, had first attracted my attention the previous summer, when, discreetly waiting outside the bathroom door for my son's imperious summons "Wipe me!" I found myself looking freshly at bookcases whose contents I thought I knew by heart. Why had I never happened to notice those severe yellow and salmon paperbacks before? Here were Alfred Kazin on *The House of the Dead,* and my father defending Seneca from the charge of rhetorical insincerity, and Jacques Barzun—

"Mommy, wipe me!" came the call. Was this juxtaposition what Baudelaire had in mind when he began his wonderful poem "La Voix" with the line *"Mon berceau s'adossait à la bibliothèque"*? (My cradle stood against the bookcase.) . . .

According to Thoreau, another passionate reader (and Baudelaire's almost exact contemporary), "A written word is the choicest of relics. It is something at once more intimate with us and more universal than any other work of art." Intimate and universal: two of the criteria by which poetry is often judged; two of the qualities that come to mind when we observe a mother and child. Literature's ability to be as personal (hence we speak of "character") to many people—to be private in a public way—is part of what makes a book such an ideal gift, since, as Queen Irene says of names, we can keep it and give it away at the same time. In Louis Malle's film *Au Revoir les Enfants*, Jean, the Jewish boy who has been attending the convent school under an assumed name is finally betrayed to the Gestapo. Packing his things before he boards the portentous offscreen train, he gives his beloved books, *The Arabian Nights* and *Sherlock Holmes*, to his gentile friend Julien. "You take them; I've read them all anyway." This friendship, which began with mutual suspicion, began to flourish when the two boys discovered a shared taste for reading with flashlights under the covers.

Kathleen Cambor
(b. 1948)

When I was a child, no one read to me. So I missed the pleasure of the shared chair, the sweetness of the loved voice, the purr of murmured sentences. Now strangers read to me through books on tape, and in some small way become the lost and loving parents. A catalogue is my library, the books are unabridged. The readers' voices are known to me after my years of listening. I trust them. With them as guides I take up books I've long neglected—histories, biographies, certain classics that I ought to have read, but didn't because I never made the time. I've discovered time expands when reading with my ears becomes an option. Such reading can be done while my eyes and hands are doing other things. It can be done in darkness. On anxious, sleepless nights, I can let books and those familiar voices soothe me.

"THE READER LISTENS"

Thus the books are an eloquent farewell token. Part of the retrospective anguish that permeates the film is Julien's failure not only to save Jean but even really to say goodbye to him. In a way, Jean, who knows he is doomed, has the best of it: he has found the perfect parting gift, the channel and symbol of reciprocal love, of which both boys understand the value. And Julien—a.k.a. Louis Malle—has kept these "choicest of relics." Books not only, as Brodsky says, outlast their authors; they can even outlast their owners, which is why it's important to pass your love of a book on to someone else.

—from *Living in Time*

Laura Furman

(b. 1945)

Before I became a mother, I was free to judge other mothers—my own and my friends', my friends as mothers, and strangers I saw hitting their kids in the supermarket. I didn't become a mother in order to be a bad mother or a good one, just a mother, but I soon found that I had a secret idea of being a good mother. I would be attentive and willing. I would be patient and efficient. I wouldn't lose my temper, and I would never carry on a conversation with another adult while my child danced around me, chanting, "Mom, Mom, Mom." I would never read the paper while my child asked the same question again and again. I would keep a zone around my child and me of attention and love. Once I was a mother, relativity set in quickly, along with sleep deprivation. The love is there, but I'm pressed, distracted, somewhere else, and usually feeling guilty. I'm told that being a mother *means* being guilty, which is easy to say and hard to live with. When I read to my son at bedtime, I can fancy myself purely good. I try to let nothing interfere. The machine gets the phone, and I resist jumping up and saying, I'll be back in a minute, when I remember things that must be done. For once my child and I are doing the same thing at the same time. I look forward to our reading time as women who pray might look forward to a prayer before sleep, even though in the best children's books there's hardly a good mother to be found.

I once thought Mrs. Darling was the perfect mother—after all, her children came back from Neverland. Mrs. Darling didn't have a job, much less two jobs, the way plenty of us do. Her set-up sounds enviable. She had wonderful help, and Nana was available twenty-four hours a day. But where it counts, Mrs. Darling is a sister of mine, for her "sweet melt-

ing mouth had one kiss on it that Wendy could never get."
In Mrs. Darling's kiss I recognize a mother who is not always present or giving, either literally or figuratively, one
who holds back something private, a mother like me. I remember her from my childhood reading, and she seemed
simply present and warm, but she had more to her. Mrs.
Darling kept secrets so her children never knew everything
about her, and she had the remarkable ability to rearrange
the thoughts in her sleeping children's minds as she might
straighten their dresser drawers.

When Peter Pan appears, Mrs. Darling sits in the nursery
beside her sleeping children, mending their clothes. She sees
him as a motherable child and of course he is in part: the "most
entrancing thing about him was that he had all his first teeth."
Peter Pan is "gay and innocent and heartless," the spirit of
youth. "When he saw that she was a grown-up, he gnashed the
little pearls at her." He has appeared at the window for mother-
ing but not from a grown-up. Mrs. Darling and Peter are natural enemies in a war of possession, control, and protection in
which the outcome is inevitable and equally a defeat and a
triumph for both sides.

Peter Pan is very much like Mrs. Darling's kiss, seductive
and unavailable, begging for love and flying out the window. I
understand them both with my heart. There are times when I'd
like to fly to Neverland, but I can't leave my chosen life and I
don't want to. In the book's last scene Wendy is ashamed that
she's grown up, and I cried bitterly when she told Peter not to
waste his fairy dust on her. Now the gulf between adult and
child is the topography of my day, and my own kiss, the one I
keep back, is my lifeline. Mrs. Darling may not be perfect but
she's wiser than I remembered.

I live in the mother country, and I stay inside its borders,
wanting my freedom while dreading the moment when my son
will be grown. At little moments, like the one before he drifts
into sleep when he looks up and I am there, reading to him and
thinking of nothing but him, I feel sure that I'm a good enough

mother. Then I look beyond, to the moment when he'll be asleep and I'll have time for myself, and in the looking my pride vanishes like the fairy dust it is.

—from "Mrs. Darling's Kiss"

Franz Kafka

(1893–1924)

Franz Kafka's diary offers observations on reading aloud—and being read to. At a recital of Goethe's poems by a famous German actor, Kafka noted that such performances reminded him of ventriloquism, with the invisible artist acting as the dummy. He narrates his own perils when he describes a reading he gave from Kleist's novella in 1913.

In Toynbee Hall read the beginning of *Michael Kohlhaas*. Complete and utter fiasco. Badly chosen, badly presented, finally swam senselessly around in the text. Model audience. Very small boys in the front row. One of them tries to overcome his innocent boredom by carefully throwing his cap on the floor and then carefully picking it up, and then again, over and over. Since he is too small to accomplish this from his seat, he has to keep sliding off the chair a little. Read wildly and badly and carelessly and unintelligibly. And in the afternoon I was already trembling with eagerness to read, could hardly keep my mouth shut.

—from *The Diaries of Franz Kafka 1910–1913*

His friend, editor, and biographer Max Brod (1884–1968), who was also close to another Prague contemporary, Jiri Langer, was present and insists that Kafka read Kleist's words beautifully, though the selection was a little long and Kafka had to cut as he read. "In addition there was the quite incongruous contrast between this great literature and the uninterested and inferior audience, the majority of whom came to benefit affairs of this kind only for the sake of the free

cup of tea they received." As he shows in this excerpt from his 1915
diary, Kafka finds reading aloud complicated even at home:

January 4. It is only because of my vanity that I like so much
to read to my sisters (so that today, for instance, it is already too
late to write). Not that I am convinced that I shall achieve
something significant in the reading, it is only that I am domi-
nated by the passion to get so close to the good works I read that
I merge with them, not through my own merit, indeed, but
only through the attentiveness of my listening sisters, which has
been excited by what is being read and is unresponsive to unes-
sentials; and therefore too, under the concealment my vanity
affords me, I can share as creator in the effect which the work
alone has exercised. That is why I really read admirably to my
sisters and stress the accents with extreme exactness just as I feel
them, because later I am abundantly rewarded not only by
myself but also by my sisters.

But if I read to Brod or Baum or others, just because of my
pretensions my reading must appear horribly bad to everyone,
even if they know nothing of the usual quality of my reading;
for here I know that the listener is fully aware of the separation
between me and what is being read, here I cannot merge completely with what I read without becoming ridiculous in my
own opinion, an opinion which can expect no support from the
listener; with my voice I flutter around what is being read, try
to force my way in here and there because they want me to, but
don't intend this seriously because they don't expect that much
from me at all; but what they really want me to do, to read
without vanity, calmly and distantly, and to become passionate
only when a genuine passion demands it, that I cannot do; but
although I believe that I have resigned myself to reading badly
to everyone except my sisters, my vanity, which this time has no
justification, still shows itself: I feel offended if anyone finds
fault with my reading, I become flushed and want to read on
quickly, just as I usually strive, once I have begun, to read on

endlessly, out of an unconscious yearning that during the course of the long reading there may be produced, at least in me, that vain, false feeling of integration with what I read which makes me forget that I shall never be strong enough at any one moment to impose my feelings on the clear vision of the listener and that at home it is always my sisters who initiate this longed-for substitution.

—from *The Diaries of Franz Kafka 1914–1923*

Giacomo Leopardi

(1798–1837)

Giacomo Leopardi, the nineteenth-century Italian nobleman and poet, despised being read to, and makes no bones about it. Probably neither his religious, sadistic mother, who "considered beauty a true misfortune, and seeing her children ugly or deformed, gave thanks to God," nor his narcissistic, foolish father read aloud to him when he was a child. But neither did they stop him from reading. His graceful biographer, Iris Origo, noted that between the ages of twelve and eighteen, Leopardi did little but read: "Absorbed by an all-devouring passion for knowledge, for years he allowed himself no time for exercise, no recreation, grudging even the few minutes spent upon his meals. Thus, by the time he was eighteen, he had become narrow-chested, fragile-boned, and hunchbacked."

He declared, "I have miserably and irremediably ruined myself for the remainder of my existence by making my appearance odious, and so rendering despicable all that outer aspect of a man, which yet is the only one which most people look at and take into account."

He found his happiness as well as his misery by reading, as he shows in this description of reading Greek poetry: "If I were to try to describe the indefinable effect that Anacreon's odes have upon me, I could find no more suitable image than the passing breath of a summer wind, scented and refreshing . . . that opens your heart to a happiness that is already gone before one has fully felt or savoured it." For a romantic, this is happiness indeed.

His Pensieri [Thoughts] were written at the end of his life when he was consumptive, suffering from eye disease, heartbroken, and impoverished.

His objections—and solutions—to being read to by the vast number of people he met who thought they were writers make us smile in recognition of our own time when it sometimes seems that there are more writers than readers—and all of them want to read aloud to you.

If I had the genius of Cervantes, I would write a book to purge, as he Spain of counterfeit chivalry, so I Italy, and indeed the civilized world, of a vice which, having regard to the mildness of our present manners, and perhaps also in other respects, is not less cruel nor less barbarous than that remnant of the ferocity of the Middle Ages which the author of *Don Quixote* castigated. I speak of the vice of reading or reciting to others one's own compositions; which vice, though very ancient, was yet until recent times a not intolerable one, because not common; but which now, when everyone writes—and it is extremely difficult to find anyone who is not an author—has become a scourge, a public calamity, and a new tribulation for human life. And it is not a joke but the truth to say that through this vice acquaintances are suspect and friendships perilous; and that there is no hour nor place in which an innocent person has not to fear that he will be assaulted and subjected on the spot, or dragged elsewhither, to the torture of hearing prose without end or thousands of verses, no longer under the pretext of a wish to have the listener's judgment on the merits of the composition, a pretext which formerly it was the custom to assign as the motive for such recitations, but solely and expressly to give pleasure to the author by having a listener, besides the necessary praises which the latter must bestow at the end of the reading.

Speaking seriously, I believe that in very few things are the puerility of human nature, and the extremity of blindness and even of stupidity into which men are led by self-love and vanity, and also the extent to which the mind can cheat itself, so manifestly shown as in this business of forcing others to listen to our compositions. For everyone is conscious of the ineffable annoyance it always is to him to be compelled to listen to the compositions of others; and cannot avoid seeing his friends turn pale with alarm whenever *he* proposes to recite to them, and hears them allege every sort of excuse to avoid the infliction, and even sees them run away from him and shun his company as far as possible: yet with a brazen front, and with tireless persistence like that of a famished bear, he seeks and pursues his prey, no matter where it may take refuge; and having overtaken it, drags it to the place of suffering. And though, during the recitation, he perceives by the yawnings, stretchings, contortions, and a hundred other signs, the deadly agonies which the auditor is undergoing, this does not cause him to desist, but rather urges him the more fiercely to continue barking and shouting for hours, and indeed almost for entire days and nights, until he makes himself quite hoarse, and leaves off at last exhausted but not sated. Yet at such times, and while he is inflicting such torture upon his friend, it is evident that he feels an almost superhuman degree of pleasure, worthy of paradise itself: for we see him leave for this all other pleasures, forget his food and sleep, and everything else in the world. And this pleasure must arise from a firm belief in such readers that they arouse admiration in their hearers, and give delight to them: for otherwise it would be the same to them if they recited to a desert. Now, as I have said, the amount of pleasure of him who hears—I designedly say *hears,* not *listens*—everyone knows by experience, and the reciter sees it: and I know well that many would choose acute bodily suffering rather than such a pleasure. Even writings really beautiful and sublime are apt to become tedious when read by their authors: and it was remarked by a philologist, a friend of mine, that if it is true that the Empress Octavia, hearing Virgil read the sixth book of the *Aeneid,* was overcome with a fainting fit, it is probable that this was caused, not so much by the remembrance (as it is said) of her son Marcellus, as by the weariness induced by the reading.

Such is the nature of mankind. And this vice I speak of, so barbarous and so ridiculous, and so contrary to the sense of a rational creature, is really an ailment implanted in the constitution of man; for there is no nation, however civilized, no condition, nor any age, which is exempt from this infliction. Italians,

French, English, Germans; venerable old men; persons wise in all other respects; men of worth and talent; men quite at home in society, quick to discern follies, and to laugh at them; all become cruel, inconsiderate children when an opportunity occurs of reciting their own compositions. And as it is now, so was it in the time of Horace, who declared it to be quite insupportable; and in that of Martial, who being asked by someone, "Why don't you read your verses to me?" replied, "In order that I may not have to listen to yours": and so, likewise, it was in the last ages of Greece, when, as is narrated, Diogenes the cynic, being, in company with others, all overcome with tedium at such a recitation, and at last seeing the blank page at the end of the book which was being read, said: "Courage, friends; I see land."

In our time, however, the business has become so serious that the supply of hearers, however obtained, no longer suffices to supply the demands of authors. Whence certain ingenious acquaintances of mine, having meditated upon this point, and being convinced that it is imperatively necessary that authors should have proper opportunities of reciting their compositions, have invented a scheme for satisfying this necessity of human nature, and of turning it also, as all such needs should be turned, to private profit. To which end they will shortly open a School, or Academy, or Athenaeum of audition, where, at all hours of the day and night, they or persons employed by them will listen to whoever wishes to read at fixed prices: which will be, for prose, one *scudo* the first hour, two the second, four the third, eight the fourth, and so on, increasing in geometrical progression. For poetry these prices will be doubled. If the reader wishes to read any passage over again, as sometimes happens, an extra *lira* per line will be charged. If any of the listeners fall asleep in the course of the reading, they shall forfeit one-third of the fees due to them. To provide against the occurrence of swoons, convulsions, and other accidents, slight or serious, which may chance, the institution will be supplied with essences and medicines which shall be furnished gratis. Thus will the ears, hitherto unprofitable, be rendered a source of remuneration, and a new pathway for industry, to the increase of the general wealth, be opened.

—from *Pensieri*

Mark Leyner

(b. 1956)

A gifted comic writer gives advice to fathers on reading aloud, having practiced on his infant daughter.

Put simply: It's exceedingly unattractive to sire a child who grows up to be an illiterate simp. Ergo, you must read to the kid regularly and instill a deep and abiding logophilia——any parenting how-to book will tell you as much. Where the guides go astray, particularly in light of your compensatory needs as a swaggering male, is in the recommended syllabus. Notwithstanding conventional wisdom to the contrary, you needn't read children's books to children, especially to very young children.

To illustrate my point, here's a partial list of what I've been reading to Gaby over the past month: military historian John Keegan's The *Mask of Command,* Racine's *Phèdre,* Hans Zinsser's classic *Rats, Lice and History,* and an architectural survey of Kuala Lumpur entitled *The Golden Goiter.* The secret is in the tone. Racine seems to be particularly compelling when read in a high-pitched, squeaky animated-mouse voice.

You'll feel so much better—so much more the alluring outlaw—-reading the delirious confessions of a *poète maudit* to your kid than some allegory about altruistic woodchucks or punctual possums or bears who say good night to their socks. Rimbaud's *A Season in Hell* goes over like gangbusters, especially if each end-stopped line is punctuated by a loud moo or a flatulent spluttering sound. I've found that the lines "I shall detach for you these sparse hideous pages from my notebook of the damned" are most successful when recited in an ascending pitch that accelerates to a crescendo as two fingers scamper from the child's tippy-toes to her chin. This, of course, can be repeated ad infinitum with no discernible diminution of effect.

It's almost impossible to predict which selections will prove most entertaining to your little one. A passage from Edmund White's new biography of Jean Genet describing how one night Genet took too many Nembutals and danced in a pink negligée for a roomful of Black Panthers induces, in Gaby, uncontrollable hysterics that invariably culminate in hiccups. (Please note that reactions to this passage may vary from child to child.)

—from *Tooth Imprints on a Corn Dog*

Mary Leonhardt

I'm not saying you have to let your children plant grass on their wall-to-wall carpeting, but I do think that if you want your children to have a joyous, easy relationship with books—and with learning in general—you have to tolerate a certain amount of disorder. You have to let your kids have some control over their environment—and that will probably mean piles of magazines here, lots of sporting equipment over there. . . . Just keep saying to yourself, in eighteen years they'll go away to college.

PARENTS WHO LOVE READING, KIDS WHO DON'T

Lynn Freed

(b. 1945)

Readings nowadays are a feature of literary life: Graduate students in creative writing programs have practice readings and critiques so that when their time in the sun arrives, they will be ready to perform. It is hard to find a poet or writer who refuses to read, though plenty of them complain about the number of readings they must attend.

Still, large audiences are happy to be read to, by the author or a skilled professional performer. Such popular radio programs as "Selected Shorts," "The Sound of Writing," to name two, bring literature into kitchens and automobiles, to millions of grateful ears, as do the many recorded books available now. (There is a bumper sticker that warns that reading and driving don't mix.) Some works can be better grasped when they are read aloud, at least initially. For many it continues to be a great gift—to be read to—to be given a story or a poem in that direct way. Novelist Lynn Freed was particularly fortunate in her reader.

Only long after I was old enough to read for myself, did I really make the connection between literature and the printed word. My mother, whose first and abiding love was for the theater, preferred to tell her own versions of the stories other parents read to their children from books. This way she could add characters at will, eliminate others, change the plot around and thus string out the story into a series of episodic cliffhangers that would last over a period of weeks or even months. The books themselves remained on our shelves, moldy and full of bookworm in the hot, damp region of South Africa in which we lived.

The first story I remember her delivering was Charles Kingsley's *Water Babies*, one of those strange, English tales for children, in which bad people with money and foul tempers bully small, poor, helpless, good people, often children. Good does triumph in the end, of course, but not before lessons have been learned and the wicked punished. In this particular story, Tom is a very young chimney-sweep, who is employed by the evil Mr. Grimes. Tom runs away, falls into a river, and meets there the water babies of the title, with whom he takes up residence.

My mother, falling into an old literary trap, managed to make the evil characters, both above and below the water, far more appealing than Tom. As she came forth with yet another demon lying in wait for him, and he—a bit stupid, and too good to be true—accomplished another narrow escape, I lay shivering with delight. When I finally came to read the book itself, with its angelic illustrations of the water babies, and even the rather predictably grumpy Mr. Grimes, I felt terribly let down. Not only was my mother's version better, but it seemed truer as well.

What I did take on faith in this story, however—and in so many other stories fed to South African children when I was growing up—was that, contrary to what was true in my world, small white boys could be made to work for a living (girls, too—to wit the many tales of English waifs dressed in rags, who skivvied all day and were then consigned to freezing London attics to pray and shiver through the night). Also that snow fell at Christmas time, that there were fires rather than flower arrangements in fireplaces, and that hedgehogs, toads, foxes, and moles—not monkeys, snakes, and iguanas, the urban animals of my childhood—were the sorts of creatures which, in fiction, would stand up on their hind legs, don clothing, and sally forth into a story.

More than this, I believed that these strange customs and creatures were more real than those of the world I lived in, and far more worthy of fiction. The real world of my childhood— a large, subtropical port on the Indian Ocean with beaches and bush and sugar cane and steaming heat, a strict Anglican girls' school, massive family gatherings on Friday nights and Jewish

holidays, and then my parents' theater world—the plays my
mother directed, my father learning his lines every evening in
the bath, both of them off to rehearsal night after night, leaving
the next episode of her story for me to listen to on a huge reel-
to-reel tape recorder—this world did not exist, not even periph-
erally, in the literature available to me. Nor did I think that it
should.

What I did encounter of indigenous South African literature
came later, much later, at school. There, the odd poem or book
(Roy Campbell, Laurens van der Post) would be included in an
otherwise watertight English syllabus: Shakespeare, Jane Austen, Thackeray, Dickens, Hardy, and, of course, the King James
Bible. There wasn't even any venturing into Bloomsbury or,
across the Atlantic, to America, absolutely not. Our history
teacher, who, like most of the teachers in the school was English, stopped short of teaching the First World War, which,
said she in 1960, was still controversial.

The Africa of popular imagination came to us via the radio.
Until the mid-1970s, there was no television in South Africa,
and so it was radio that offered programs like "Tarzan, King of
the Apes," to which I listened every evening in the kitchen with
the servants. There we stood in rapt silence next to the fridge,
on top of which the wireless sat in a place of honor.

Meanwhile, the fact that I was learning to read did not bring
my mother's nightly episodes to an end, far from it. She moved
on to the Brothers Grimm, to Rudyard Kipling's *Just So Stories*
(a world much more familiar to me than Tarzan's jungle), to
The Wind In The Willows, which never engaged me, not even
her version of it, and then to the plays of J.M. Barrie—*Quality
Street, Peter Pan,* and my favorite, *The Admirable Crichton.*
These she told from the point of view of whichever character
she herself had played on the stage.

The books I was beginning to read for myself—by English
children's author Enid Blyton—were considered lower than
comics by the local cognoscenti, chief among whom was one of
my father's sisters, a psychologist. My mother, a natural foe to

my father's family, to the whole idea of psychology, and, indeed,
to censorship itself (except for Disney, which she would not
countenance), lifted her ample nose in scorn. Blyton's books,
now widely unavailable, might trespass upon the rudimentary
borders of correctitude being laid down, even then, by the likes
of my aunt, but they had me reading for once, lying quietly on
the veranda swingseat or down in the the summerhouse, and
then rushing back into the house to ask my mother to take a
few more out of the library for me the next day.

What Blyton understood very well, even in her Noddie books
for the very young, was the universal desire of children to escape from the sovereignty of adults. And so, the fact that Noddie had his own car, which, like him, was an animated toy, and
that he made off in it with Big Ears, his friend, or that later, in
Blyton's pre-adolescent novels—*Five Go Off in a Caravan, Hollow Tree House, The Naughtiest Girl in the School*—there were
rebels and runaways and naughty children finding adventure
beyond the pale—this was a wonderful thing for a girl living at
the bottom of Africa and dreaming of leaving one day, somehow, for the real world.

Unlike my mother, I was not a natural reader. I read slowly,
and quite haphazardly. As the youngest child in a large household of family and servants, I spent most of my time un-
supervised, much of it outdoors. It was here that I was most
alive to adventure and fantasy, creating grandiose scenarios
from the top of the mango tree, or off on my bicycle to explore.
With books it was different. I read when it was dark, when it
rained, when I was sick, or when I felt like company.

Most of the books in the house were kept in my parents'
study, a cozy room with leather chairs and leaded windows and
piles of scripts stacked around on the floor. It was there that my
mother was to be found during the day, either timing scripts or
drilling a new actor. She allowed me in as long as I didn't
interrupt. And so I read what was available—mostly plays, but
also opera libretti, the odd history, a few biographies, a selection
of popular novels. I'd choose a book, drape myself across a

chair, and then laugh silently, once again, at *Lady Windemere's Fan*.

One day I came upon a collection of books I'd never noticed—right in the back corner, behind the piles of scripts. They were books on the Holocaust. As soon as I discovered their existence, I returned to them obsessively, reading book after book and then rereading them, looking up words I did not understand, scrutinizing the horrifying photographs so that, even to this day, they are burned into memory.

Unlike the comfortable remove at which I felt myself from the horrors of received children's fiction, nothing separated me from the Holocaust. It seemed quite able to reach off the shelf, out of a book, and swallow me into it. Other children I knew dreaded bogeymen under the bed— emblems, no doubt, of the revolution their parents expected to happen one day. My demons, however, were Nazis with guns and gas ovens. Having one's throat slit by the next door neighbor's servant some day in the distant future seemed mild by comparison.

As I grew older, my mother did not stop playing Mother Goose; she simply changed the old bedtime format. Driving along, she would tell me the story of a play she had just read, or a novel she was adapting for Lux Radio Theatre, or about an aunt, whose suitor had demanded a dowry that her mother had refused to pay, and everyone had landed up marrying the wrong person, and now look how unhappy they all were. I knew, of course, not to trust her version of things, but at the same time, over the years, I found myself reading a book or seeing a play or an opera in a kind of stereoscope: what was written, and then what could have happened, what should have happened.

My mother is very old now, almost blind, and often confused. She cannot read the old books, neatly stacked on the shelves of her apartment, nor can she bear to be read to. But almost every day she sees goblins with pointed hats lurking on the veranda, men riding up the driveway on horseback, elegant ladies coming in for tea in the guise of her nurse. Together with so much else from her life—her husband, her home, and us, her audience—her text has vanished. And so she is doing the best she can with what's left to her: the imagination.

—from "A Child's Reading in South Africa"

Linda Pastan

(b. 1932)

Poet Linda Pastan lives in Maryland. Her books include Imperfect
Paradise *and* PM/AM: New and Selected Poems.

McGuffey's First Eclectic Reader

The sun is up
The sun is always up.
The silent "e"
keeps watch;
and 26 strong stones
can build a wall of syllables
for Nell and Ned
and Ann:

Rab was such a good dog,
Mother. We left him
under the big tree
by the brook
to take care of the dolls
and the basket.

But Rab has run away.
The basket's gone back to reeds
through which the night wind
blows; and mother was erased;
the dolls are painted harlots
in the Doll's Museum.

Where did it go, Rose?
I don't know;
away off, somewhere.
The fat hen
has left the nest.

I hand my daughter
this dusty book.
Framed in her window
the sky darkens to slate:
a lexicon of wandering stars.
Listen, child—the barking
in the distance
is Rab the dog star
trotting home
for dinner.

—from *PM/AM: New and Selected Poems*

Eudora Welty

(b. 1909)

*Both a writer's writer and a reader's writer, Eudora Welty is proba-
bly the only (certainly the senior) American writer to have an
Internet E-mail application named after her.*

I learned from the age of two or three that any room in our
house, at any time of day, was there to read in, or to be read to.
My mother read to me. She'd read to me in the big bedroom in
the mornings, when we were in her rocker together, which
ticked in rhythm as we rocked, as though we had a cricket
accompanying the story. She'd read to me in the dining room
on winter afternoons in front of the coal fire, with our cuckoo
clock ending the story with "Cuckoo," and at night when I'd
got in my own bed. I must have given her no peace. Sometimes
she read to me in the kitchen while she sat churning, and the
churning sobbed along with *any* story. It was my ambition to
have her read to me while *I* churned; once she granted my wish,
but she read off my story before I brought her butter. She was
an expressive reader. When she was reading "Puss in Boots,"
for instance, it was impossible not to know that she distrusted
all cats.

It had been startling and disappointing to me to find out
that storybooks had been written by people, that books were
not natural wonders, coming up of themselves like grass. Yet
regardless of where they came from, I cannot remember a
time when I was not in love with them—with the books
themselves, cover and binding and the paper they were
printed on, with their smell and their weight and with their
possession in my arms, captured and carried off to myself.
Still illiterate, I was ready for them, committed to all the
reading I could give them.

Neither of my parents had come from homes that could afford to buy many books, but though it must have been something of a strain on his salary, as the youngest officer in a young insurance company, my father was all the while carefully selecting and ordering away for what he and Mother thought we children should grow up with. They bought first for the future.

Besides the bookcase in the livingroom, which was always called "the library," there were the encyclopedia tables and dictionary stand under windows in our dining room. Here to help us grow up arguing around the dining-room table were the *Unabridged Webster,* the *Columbia Encyclopedia, Compton's Pictured Encyclopedia,* the *Lincoln Library of Information,* and later the *Book of Knowledge.* And the year we moved into our new house, there was room to celebrate it with the new 1925 edition of the *Brittannica,* which my father, his face always deliberately turned toward the future, was of course disposed to think better than any previous edition.

In the "library," inside the Mission-style bookcase with its three diamond-latticed glass doors, with my father's Morris chair and the glass-shaded lamp on its table beside it, were books I could soon begin on—and I did, reading them all alike and as they came, straight down their rows, top shelf to bottom. There was the set of Stoddard's *Lectures,* in all its late nineteenth-century vocabulary and vignettes of peasant life and quaint beliefs and customs, with matching halftone illustrations: Vesuvius erupting, Venice by moonlight, gypsies glimpsed by their campfires. I didn't know then the clue they were to my father's longing to see the rest of the world. I read straight through his other love-from-afar: the *Victrola Book of the Opera,* with opera after opera in synopsis, with portraits in costume of Melba, Caruso, Galli-Curci, and Geraldine Farrar, some of whose voices we could listen to on our Red Seal records.

My mother read secondarily for information; she sank as a hedonist into novels. She read Dickens in the spirit in which she would have eloped with him. The novels of her girlhood that had stayed on in her imagination, besides those of Dickens and Scott and Robert Louis Stevenson, *Jane Eyre, Trilby, The Woman in White, Green Mansions, King Solomon's Mines.* Marie Corelli's name would crop up but I understood she had gone out of favor with my mother, who had only kept *Ardath* out of loyalty. In time she absorbed herself in Galsworthy, Edith Wharton, above all in Thomas Mann of the *Joseph* volumes.

St. Elmo was not in our house; I saw it often in other houses. This wildly popular Southern novel is where all the Edna Earles in our population started coming from. They're all named for the heroine, who succeeded in bringing a dissolute, sinning roué and atheist of a lover (St. Elmo) to his knees. My mother was able to forgo it. But she remembered the classic advice given to rose growers on how to water their bushes long enough: "Take a chair and *St. Elmo.*"

To both my parents I owe my early acquaintance with a beloved Mark Twain. There was a full set of Mark Twain and a short set of Ring Lardner in our bookcase, and those were the volumes that in time united us all, parents and children.

Reading everything that stood before me was how I came upon a worn old book without a back that had belonged to my father as a child. It was called *Sanford and Merton.* Is there anyone left who recognizes it, I wonder? It is the famous moral tale written by Thomas Day in the 1780s, but of him no mention is made on the title page of this book; here it is *Sanford and Merton in Words of One Syllable* by Mary Godolphin. Here are the rich boy and the poor boy and Mr. Barlow, their teacher and interlocutor, in long discourses alternating with dramatic scenes—danger and rescue allotted to the rich and the poor respectively. It may have only words of one syllable, but one of them is "quoth." It ends with not one but two morals, both engraved on rings: "Do what you ought, come what may," and "If we would be great, we must first learn to be good."

This book was lacking its front cover, the back held on by strips of pasted paper, now turned golden, in several layers, and the pages stained, flecked, and tattered around the edges; its garish illustrations had come unattached but were preserved, laid in. I had the feeling even in my heedless childhood that this was the only book my father as a little boy had of his own. He had held onto it, and might have gone to sleep on its coverless face: he had lost his mother when he was seven. My father had never made any mention to his own children of the book, but he had brought it along with him from Ohio to our house and shelved it in our bookcase.

My mother had brought from West Virginia that set of Dickens; those books looked sad, too—they had been through fire and water before I was born, she told me, and there they were, lined up—waiting for *me*.

I was presented, from as early as I can remember, with books of my own, which appeared on my birthday and Christmas morning. Indeed, my parents could not give me books enough. They must have sacrificed to give me on my sixth or seventh birthday—it was after I became a reader for myself—the ten-volume set of *Our Wonder World*. These were beautifully made, heavy books I would lie down with on the floor in front of the dining-room hearth, and more often than the rest volume 5, *Every Child's Story Book,* was under my eyes. There were the fairy tales—Grimm, Andersen, the English, the French, "Ali Baba and the Forty Thieves"; and there was Aesop and Reynard the Fox; there were the myths and legends, Robin Hood, King Arthur, and Saint George and the Dragon, even the history of Joan of Arc; a whack of *Pilgrim's Progress* and a long piece of *Gulliver*. They all carried their classic illustrations. I located myself in these pages and could go straight to the stories and pictures I loved; very often "The Yellow Dwarf" was first choice, with Walter Crane's Yellow Dwarf in full color making his terrifying appearance flanked by turkeys. Now that volume is as worn and backless and hanging apart as my father's poor *Sanford and Merton*. The precious page with Edward Lear's

"Jumblies" on it has been in danger of slipping out for all these years. One measure of my love for *Our Wonder World* was that for a long time I wondered if I would go through fire and water for it as my mother had done for Charles Dickens; and the only comfort was to think I could ask my mother to do it for me.

Katherine Mansfield
(1888–1923)

J. read the Tchechov aloud. I had read one of the stories myself and it seemed to me nothing. But read aloud, it was a masterpeice. How was that?

JOURNAL (1922)

I believe I'm the only child I know of who grew up with this treasure in the house. I used to ask others, "Did you have *Our Wonder World?*" I'd have to tell them *The Book of Knowledge* could not hold a candle to it.

—from *One Writer's Beginnings*

IV
Reading Ahead

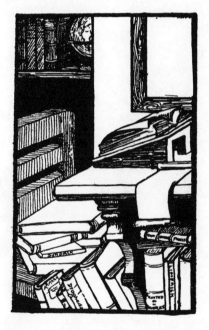

"For every reader who dies today, a viewer is born, and we seem to be witnessing, here in the anxious mid-nineties, a final tipping of the balance." So writes Jonathan Franzen in a recent consideration of American culture, especially as it relates to the written (and the read) word. Sven Birkerts is even more pessimistic about the future of reading and writing: ". . . The elusive angel of history has detached itself from the printed word and taken up residence in the circuitry of electronic systems."

There are others, just as intelligent and articulate, who salute those very electronic circuits as liberators of a literate citizenry from the traditional cultural gatekeepers: the editors, writers, and publishers who dominate the media.

Media critic Jon Katz, writing in Wired, *reminds us that "Newspapers, news magazines, and the network news have all lost consumers. Their audiences are aging, the advertising revenue on which they depend is increasingly fragmented. . . . Computers and modems have enabled millions of people to communicate directly with one another, thus making them less dependent on a handful of papers, magazines, and newscasts for all of their information on public policy." He suggests that the self-named neo-Luddites who are objecting vociferously to the New Media are doing so to protect their cultural dominance.*

Indeed, writer Kirkpatrick Sale, who claims to be protecting the natural world from this electronic assault, himself assaulted a computer onstage at Town Hall in New York, to the cheers and applause of an audience that would have wept had any book been burned.

What has this debate to do with reading, with our sense of ourselves as bookworms who started as young readers, have used books to understand our world and ourselves, and turn to books for pleasure, solitude, and knowledge?

There is no doubt that the new inventions have had an effect on us all, and Jonathan Franzen's statement is hard to argue with; there are those who might say that someday no readers will be born, only viewers! Those of us who teach writing would be the last ones to deny the effect of television and the movies on the reading habits of our young.

Many TV and binary babies don't know or care about fairy tales and nursery rhymes. Language seems slow to them. "Screenagers" they've been called. They respond to the intense visual image that is blown up, then dissolves, then reappears. They are most comfortable writing with passive voice in the present tense. They have trouble writing descriptions of places or people except in the most general terms, and their characters have no past to resonate in the eternal present. They can write slick action scenes. They are great at laconic dialogue. Mostly, they haven't read much that they remember. Their meaningful cultural references are to movies and TV. The few who do read on their own read for the story, for what happens next. "Their inner world," Birkerts says, "is constituted from images, sounds, and spoken words. . . . Bring them face-to-face with the demands of cultivated literacy, and they gasp like stranded fish."

An American historian reminds us that our people have always foreseen the self-immolation or salvation of civilization due to technology. In 1982, Daniel Boorstin (b. 1914) addressed the Library of Congress. In his seminal speech titled "A Nation of Readers," he asked us to remember the disasters predicted at the coming, five centuries ago, of the printed book and to consider the potential displacements brought about by the radio, the telephone, the automobile, Rural Free Delivery!

Boorstin said RFD, skeptically viewed by the postal service when it began in the 1890s, was christened (in 1911) "the great university in which 36 million of our people receive their daily lessons from the newspapers and magazines of the country."

In 1964, Marshall McLuhan stressed that repeated contact with new media restructures the consciousness of its users. He said individuals "interiorize" new communication technologies by making them a "part of themselves." Indeed, there are those marketing lots in the Global Village on the Internet, a place that is not a place.

An American lust for information (and lots of it) produced a struggle among books and newspapers and periodicals, and now among the printed word and television and the Internet. Boorstin said that American institutions have always "been biased toward the recent and the up-to-date, toward information rather than knowledge," but he also reminds us that "every book reader can find momentary refuge from the present," from the artificially energized. The book reader is not at the mercy of a flood of flickering images, the fiendish VCR, the urgent commercial "messages," the Mad Clicker, the power outage, the Internet connection that is temporarily unavailable. The person who works hard at the computer company all day is not going to come home and boot up; settling down with a good book is a far more likely choice.

We cannot decide here whether or not this altered literacy, from books to film to TV and now perhaps to the Internet, is simply change or a sign of impending doom. More and more people are writing letters, articles, and having electronic conversations on-line. Our librarians don't yet know how to capture and preserve our electronic communication as they have in the past our words on paper. Meanwhile we've learned to use computers and to enjoy the access they give us to great libraries.

Our selections in "Reading Ahead" remind us that, finally, books are to hold and to accompany. Books have a valuable physical presence that electronic information does not have. A computer-company employee in Austin, Texas, and an Oxford Fellow in Classics agree—books have always been more than vehicles for facts.

Those who have placed such a premium on reading and its civilizing properties worry that reading is literally disappearing down the tube. Perhaps the recent spate of books about reading and book-collecting represents ardent readers drawing their wagons into a circle. Reading is in the air, these days, at least among the self-selected elite who care deeply about it. We have seen the proliferation of book discussion groups and reading lists, and of bookstores where you can sit down in an easy chair or sip a latte *while you browse.*

"As readers," Boorstin said, "we are refugees from the flood of contemporaneous mathematicized homogeneity. There we are at home with ourselves."

Arnold Bennett

(1867–1931)

Like some present-day seeers into the future of media, Bennett understood the potential of a vast new reading public and believed in getting this public to read by whatever means. The writer and critic John McCarey called Arnold Bennett the "hero" of his book The Intellectuals and the Masses *(1992): Bennett's writings "represent a systematic dismemberment of the intellectuals' case against the masses." Bennett was often scorned by the literary establishment as a result of his advocacy, and his writing, according to McCarey, is still undervalued.*

Literary Taste *is an exhortation, a sermon, a plea for self-improvement through reading. Bennett shows how a library of English works indispensable to a comprehensive collection may be compiled, and he provides a list of 337 titles from the beginning of English literature to the end of the nineteenth century for what Bennett describes as the surprisingly small outlay of about £27.*

Bennett is best known for his novels, set in the Staffordshire "Five Towns" of Stoke-on-Trent, Tunstall, Burslem, Hanley, and Longton, about the drab lives in ugly surroundings of his working-class characters.

He was a great believer in the power of literature to change people's lives and was a champion of education for the masses. The Education Act of 1870 produced what Bennett called "a new, eager reading public with no tradition of self-culture by means of books." He set out to show people how they could develop literary taste by scrimping to buy books, by diligent and regular reading of certain works, and by thinking about this reading. In his 1909 Literary Taste and How to Form It *he says, ". . . the spirit of literature is unifying; it joins the candle and the star. . . ." According to Bennett, responsible readers must spend at least as much time thinking about what they read as they spend reading.*

You, O serious student of many volumes, believe that you have a sincere passion for reading. You hold literature in honor, and your last wish would be to debase it to a paltry end. You are not of those who read because the clock has just struck nine and one can't go to bed till eleven. You are animated by a real desire to get out of literature all that literature will give. And in that aim you keep on reading, year after year, and the gray hairs come. But amid all this steady tapping of the reservoir, do you ever take stock of what you have acquired? Do you ever pause to make a valuation, in terms of your own life, of that which you are daily absorbing? Do you ever satisfy yourself by proof that you are absorbing anything at all, that the living waters, instead of vitalizing you, are not running off you as though you were a duck in a storm?

—from *Literary Taste and How to Form It*

Vartan Gregorian

(b. 1934)

Professor of history and president of Brown University, and former president of the New York Public Library, Vartan Gregorian, in an address to the 174th Stated Meeting of the American Academy of Arts and Sciences, "A Place Elsewhere: Reading in the Age of the Computer," tries to mediate between the rock of old-time reading and the hard place of electronic access.

President Gregorian begins by describing important shifts in mass-communication technology, from the building of the cathedral in the fifteenth century ("an awesome engine of communication") to the printed book, then on to our recent "new life as a computer-using population." The information explosion in the last decade has resulted in what he calls the fragmentation of knowledge—that is, we have organized ourselves into "ever more-specialized communities." He feels the prediction of an electronic global village has been proved wrong; instead we are retreating into insulated citified communities of the "like-minded".

At the same time, President Gregorian reminds us the new technology presents "new resources for the establishment of coherence, connection, and meaning" and that there are many things the computer can do a lot better than we can. Every year, computers and software become cheaper and easier to use and the real revolution will manifest itself, he says, in how we organize our social structures to adapt to these technological changes.

This brings him to the anxiety among pessimists like Sven Birkerts, who sees a shift from the book to electronic circuits, and Mario Vargas Llosa, who fears the effects of an audio-visual culture more easily manipulated by power and money. President Gregorian, more optimistic, says, "High technology . . . will not be able to eliminate the culture of the written word."

Going from books to computers is no mere change of medium. Indeed, I am concerned about the second part of the computer-book dilemma: In the age of the computer, where, precisely, is the book? And what of the library? Libraries (and museums) are the DNA of our civilization. The library is the center for the book and of the book. The library embodies and symbolizes the book, one of mankind's most imaginative and extraordinary inventions.

When the late Jorge Luis Borges, one of the greatest contemporary writers and a former librarian, became blind, he imagined paradise in the form of a library.

Reading provides renewal. What is renewed is the imagination. Through books, the independent imagination is able to take the measure of everyday events from a point just beyond their reach. Reading constitutes a self-renewal in the imaginative and the human act. We are obliged to wonder how we would be poorer, what kind of experience we would be missing, and what strengths we would lack if we did not read.

The qualities we would miss by not reading are active, imaginative collaboration and critical distance. These qualities have implications for what a library is and ought to be and ought to do. The library is not only a place, an information center. It is a center for knowledge *and* a center for learning. The library always has provided and always will provide *a place elsewhere*—an imaginative retreat, an imaginative recreation, an imaginative rebirth.

The rapidly changing fashions in technology must not obscure the enduring substance we take for granted, traditionally signified by the ancient Greek term *logos* (word). If language, as many anthropologists believe, defines men and women and organizes their activities, reading is inarguably a necessity. Literacy presupposes the ability to negotiate linguistic forms. Reading enhances this ability. To read is to be fully human.

Today, the desirability and prevalence of books seem to guarantee, to some degree, the persistence of reading. Throughout history, the relationship between the book as a container of information and knowledge and insight, and the reader as receiver, has been a dialectical and collaborative one. This relationship has always assumed a process: understanding and digestion. The process has never been a passive one. This is why Rabelais advised his sixteenth-century reader to eat his copy of Pantagruel. Books cannot nourish, or even be said to exist, until they are digested. This is true even at a time when consumption has replaced digestion. There are modern authors who require that we recall our original responsibilities as readers. We make the book as the book makes us.

The collaboration between the book and the reader is intimate, private. We must not forget that pleasure, discretion, silence, and creative solitude are the primary characteristics of a life of reading, its most tangible justification and most immediate reward. Solitude may appear now to be an unaffordable luxury, yet any book creates for the reader a place elsewhere. A person reading is a person suspended between the immediate and the timeless. This suspension serves a purpose that has little to do with escaping from the real world, the sin avid readers are most commonly accused of. Transcending the limitations of time and space is one of the primary pleasures of the act of reading, for it allows not only the renewal of one's imagination but also the development of one's mind.

Whether a work of fiction or a work of science, a book primarily appeals, first of all, to the mind. Reading makes what we read our own. In truth, one cannot ever merely read; one rereads. Rereading makes a reader an active reader, a creative reader, an understanding reader. Furthermore, in a fragmented culture in which we seem to rely more and more on the specialist, the reader remains the only autonomous unit and the only possible synthesizer. Rereading is an expression of personal desire, will, and freedom. In the age of the computer, such reading is a risky activity: it both isolates and liberates through new connections. The stakes are enormous. Like any art, craft, or sport, reading becomes more rewarding as we master its intricacies to higher and higher degrees. Our skill, our learning, and our commitment to the book or the text has determined and always will determine, for each of us, the kind of experience the book or the text provides. So I am not pessimistic about the future of the book.

The risks and rewards of reading are becoming more widely understood. The pleasures of reading remain. To paraphrase [Virginia] Woolf, I would add the following lines about all readers in libraries everywhere: "Look! They need no rewards. We have nothing to give them here. As bibliophiles, as lovers of libraries and builders of libraries, they are the people of the book, and therefore they are readers, and therefore they are blessed."

—from "A Place Elsewhere: Reading in the Age of the Computer"

Sven Birkerts

(b. 1957)

Essayist, reviewer, critic, and teacher, Sven Birkerts is passionate about the experience of reading that he fears soon will be lost. His urgent voice alarms us, persuades us to beware the epochal shift taking place between print and electronic media. "Paging the Self: Privacies of Reading" is an observation that traces his own self-formation through the kind of reading unattainable from the post-print world.

I'm going to take it as an axiom that the act of reading plays a vital role in the forming and conditioning of sensibility in the life of the committed reader. What interests me is to try to puzzle out the nature of that role. But before I do, I feel that I should pause over the word *sensibility*. It is, I realize, a "humanist" term that is slipping from usage; in our age of hard-edged critical terminology it suggests a fin-de-siècle preciosity. What is sensibility, besides being the counterpart to *sense*? It is neither self nor ego; neither identity nor personality. While these are designations for something one either *has* or *is*, sensibility is more of a construct. The old sense of the word is a refinement or cultivation of presence; it refers to the part of the inner life that is not given but fashioned: a defining, if cloudy, complex of attitudes, predilections, and honed responses. And for this very reason I want to have the term available. For while it can be many things, serious reading is above all an agency of self-making. When undertaken freely, the effort of engaging a book shows a desire to actualize and augment certain inner powers. The reader assumes the possibility of deepened self-understanding, and therefore recognizes the self as malleable. Reading is the intimate, perhaps secret, part of a larger project, one that

finally has little to do with the more societally oriented concep-
tions of the individual.

To talk about reading and the part it plays in developing the
sensibility I will need to distinguish not only among different
kinds of reading, but also to point out some of the ways in
which reading changes across the trajectory of the reader's career. The process that begins, in most cases, with being read to,
and which activates the most intense sorts of identifications in
the independent reading of childhood, is something else again
in adolescence, and again in full-fledged maturity and yet again,
I would guess, in later years. But because from adulthood on we
are talking about sensibilities that have more or less crystallized,
we may gain more by looking at the reading years of childhood
and adolescence.

Being read to, while not strictly reading, is nonetheless not an
entirely passive absorption either, as any parent can tell you.
The child fleshes out the narrative through imaginative projection, and questions the text constantly. "Why is he crying?" "Is
she going to get hurt?" She also engages the book itself, looking
at the illustrations, monitoring the momentum of the turning
pages, and, with the increase of aptitude, noting the correlation
between what is being read out and the placement of words on
the page. I see my daughter, now five, hovering on the brink of
literary independence. She still loves being read to, but she
breaks the flow of the story constantly by fastening on some
word and working to sound it out. I can almost see the cognitive machinery at work. My hope is that as my daughter ac-
quires mastery over words and meanings she will also discover
that specialized and self-directed inwardness that makes private
reading so rewarding.

Independent childhood reading seems to continue and elaborate upon the process of imaginative projection initiated
through listening. It is, beautifully and openly, a voluntary participation in an ulterior scheme of reality. We might almost call
it pure escape, except that getting *away* is probably less important than getting *to*. Early childhood reading is free indulgence

of fantasy and desire, done because it feels good. I remember the sensation of reading (Freudians can note this) as one of returning to a warm and sage environment, one that I had complete control over. When I picked up a book it was as much to get back to something as it was to set off to the new. The last thing the child thinks about is self-improvement; nor is he, in any obvious sense, trying to figure out the terms of existence (though such figuring probably goes on unconsciously).

The main difference between childhood reading and reading undertaken later is that in the former, futurity—the idea of one's life as a project, or adventure, or set of possibilities—has not yet entered the calculation. The child reads within a bubble. He is like Narcissus staring at his lovely image in the water's mirror. He is still sealed off from any notion of the long-term unfolding of the life, except in the perfected terms of fantasy: *I, too, will be a pirate* . . .

The change comes with adolescence, that biological and psychological free-fire zone during which the profoundest existential questions are not only posed, but lived. Who am I? Why am I doing what I'm doing? What *should* I do? What will happen to me? It is in adolescence that most of us grasp that life—our own life—is a problem to be solved, that a set of personal unknowns must now be factored together with the frightening variables of experience. The future suddenly appears—it is the space upon which the answers will be inscribed. The very idea of futurity now becomes charged with electricity.

This self-intensity, which pushes toward the future as toward some kind of release, is highly conducive to reading. The book—the novel, that is—becomes the site for testing transformations. Indeed, whatever else it may be, diversion or escape, the novel at this stage of life is primarily a screen that will accept various versions and projections of the self.

These projections are different from those of the child reader. The child manipulates fantasy stuff that is still undiluted by the reality principle. The boy dreaming of river rafts or space travel is not yet constrained by the impediments that will eventually curb and instruct his desires. Not so for the adolescent. A different reality has announced itself. Socially, sexually, and even within the bosom of the family, that thing grownups call "life" has begun to bare its face.

Adolescence is the ideal laboratory for the study of reading and self-formation. Or maybe I should say, a laboratory for studying the *ideal* impact of reading on that formation. For of course it is no secret that fewer and fewer adolescents now turn to reading on their own. Private reading still exists, but more exclusively—organized sports and "lessons" as well as seductive electronic games have made deep inroads upon the expanses of dreamy solitude that were once the given of preadult years. And it is precisely this reading, not that done for school assignments, that concerns me here.

How does reading work on the psyche during what is surely its most volatile period of change? There is no pinning it down, naturally, but we might begin with the most obvious sort of answer: the role of specific books and characters. We get reports of this influence all the time in interviews and memoirs. The subject (usually someone who has achieved something noteworthy) tells of *living* with Tom Sawyer or David Copperfield or Elizabeth Bennett. There follows the desire to do what Tom did, to be like young Elizabeth. These recognitions are eventually externalized as ideals and in that form guide the behavior along after the spell of the reading passes. I vividly remember situations in which I acted in a certain way—more bravely, more recklessly—because I believed that was what Jack London would have done (I had all but memorized Irving Stone's romantic biography *Jack London: Sailor on Horseback*). To be sure, books are not the only places where adolescents can look for role models. Ever vigilant, they pick up moves and attitude display from rock stars, athletes, and sulky actors.

But the identifications we take from books go deeper. They form the very basis of childhood play, and run like a stream alongside the less-rooted transactions of adolescence. They often function as a kind of (pardon the jargon) "meta-narrative." If one is *not* Tom Sawyer or Elizabeth Bennett or whoever (and identifications usually are not absolute) one nevertheless performs in a magnetic field that somehow contains them. The admiring reader acts in a world that is half that of the book and half that of the real life circumstance. Every action is ennobled and exaggerated in significance because the reader imagines it brightly transposed onto the field of the book—the field of a higher and more lasting reality.

Later, as adult claims displace childish needs and as the adolescent matures, reading takes on a slightly different function. Now the reader begins to borrow from the book a sense of consequential destiny that is so absent from the daily routine. For what the novel transmits, over and above its plot and character, is the bewitching assumption of connectedness. Purpose. Meaning. The characters and situations, products of the author's creative intention, are knit together into a larger wholeness. The least movement or action *tends toward;* every action is held within the larger context which is, implicitly, artistically purposeful. Our own lives may drift every which way toward the future, but the lives of the characters are aimed toward determined ends. As readers we take this in, unconsciously, and we may begin to conceive of our own actions under this same aspect of fatedness. Certainly we do so while we are reading or otherwise still in thrall to the book. And we thereby become important—just when we need to most. Our lives feel pointed toward significance and resolution; we feel ourselves living toward meaning, or at least living in the light of its possibility. I don't know that this more sustained self-charge is available anywhere else but in books. Movies are too compacted and visually determinate to encourage such operations. They don't last long enough, nor do cinematic images impinge on the memory in the same way that do the images we coproduce. And certainly little in the day-to-day world conveys to the adolescent some larger momentum toward meaning. He needs something with which to fend off the most obvious version of futurity, that incarnated in his parents, whose lives must appear tyrannized by empty ritual and pettiness.

My own shields, I remember, were other alienated solitaries.

I searched high and low for novels with troubled protagonists. I soothed myself and fortified myself with novels by Thomas Wolfe, William Goldman, J.D. Salinger, and others. Their situations became the stuff of my own cocoon; they were with me as I sharpened my grievances against the world. When I went against my parents and teachers I was drawing strength from their example. I took onto myself some of what I saw as their specialness. They *had* to be special, for they were the subjects of their own books. I was special, too—subject at least of my life.

Again, I am talking about the reading of fiction—novels and stories that are, to a greater or lesser degree, simulations of reality. This does not mean that I am privileging the genre above all others, but there is a very special transformation that takes place when we read fiction that is not experienced in nonfiction. This transformation, or catalyzing action, can be seen to play a vital part in what we might call, grandly, existential self-formation.

When we read a sentence from a work of nonfiction—a history or a study of some topic, say—the words intersect with the psychic continuum, but they do not significantly modify it. We do what we need to in order to pay attention, to receive the information, but we do not reposition the self. Consider, for example, this straightforward sentence from the *Columbia History of the World:* "When we talk about human evolution, we are dealing with two different kinds of processes: the evolution of the human body and the evolution of human behavior." As we read the words, we decode the syntactical logic of the statement and extract the idea content, the sense. If there is an authorial "voice," we don't focus upon it. The prose is a conveyor for the concept, a means to an end. We make a place for it in that interior zone where we process verbal information, but we don't ourselves change. Unless, of course, we encounter an idea that can be translated into relevant personal terms and thus affect our understanding of ourselves. But even then we react less to the words than to the implications we dig out for ourselves.

Now open a novel:

> If you really want to hear about it, the first thing
> you'll probably want to know is where I was born,
> and what my lousy childhood was like, and all that
> David Copperfield kind of crap, but I don't feel like
> going into it, if you want to know the truth.

This, too, is information, but it is obviously information of a
very different kind. Reading the earlier sentence about evolution, we make no significant internal adjustment because it is
not ourselves—as selves—that we hear addressed. In the second
sentence, the opening of J. D. Salinger's *Catcher in the Rye,* the
voice is primary. The voice proposes a self and we must greet it
accordingly. We therefore heed the casual, alienated, deter-
minedly forthright tone and filter the sense of the statement
through that. But we cannot heed and filter so long as our own
self is in dormancy—either we decide to engage Holden Caulfield's voice or we close the covers on the book.

Salinger, via Holden, posits a world. Holden's world. And
the reader who would hear more about it is forced to open up a
subjective space large enough to contain it. The opening of that
space is the crucial move, for it requires the provisional loosen-
ing of whatever fixed attitudes and preconceptions we may
have. In that space, two versions of reality will be stirred together—the reader's and the author's. A hybrid life will start
up. Not the author's life, not fully the character's, and not quite
our own though all these must be present for the mysterious
catalysis of reading.

To read the book we must, in effect, bracket off our own
reality and replace it with Holden's. Better, we must use what
we know of our world to create his. His can only exist at the
expense of ours, though—this is the law of fiction. We agree to
suspend our self-grounded posture, or place in the "real" world,
in order to make room for Holden's alternative sense of things.
We create the textures of his reality with what we have learned
from our own. But we don't disappear, either. Our awareness,
our sense of life, gets filtered into the character, where it becomes strangely detached from us. The novel, in a manner of

speaking, smelts its reader, extracting responsive emotions and apprehensions and then showing them forth in an aesthetic frame. Distanced from these parts of ourselves, then, we (especially as adolescents) possess them in a semiobjectified form. We begin to understand how they matter in the larger human ecology.

We don't entirely become Holden, but we abide by the terms of the world he narrates to us, agreeing to its provisions at least for the duration of our reading. We slip free from our most burdensome halter of contingent identity in order to experience the consciousness of another. This consciousness and its world are, in turn, the product of the author's consciousness. And as we read, we find that Holden's (or any character's) world manifests a kind of wholeness. This fictional world has meaning, even if Holden's own life does not appear to. Unconsciously we attune ourselves to the unitary scheme that underlies the disorder he pitches around in. This scheme, like the white page that underlies the printed words, is the surface that holds our projections. And when we close the book, we return to ourselves. Those projections stream back, only now they have been tested and modified into new shapes and they become elements in our understanding of life. We do not learn so much from the novel itself, the lessons of its situations, as we do from having strayed free of our customary boundaries. On return, those boundaries seem more articulated, more our own; we understand their degree of permeability, and this is a vital kind of knowing.

I recall from adolescent reading the powerful sensation of double consciousness, how I went about as if in the active possession of a secret. The secret had less to do with whatever specific narrative I was caught up in, and much more with the knowledge that I had a gateway out of the narrow, baffling, and often threatening world of high school.

What does all this have to do with self-formation? How does it differ from simple escape? I have to answer with my own reader's conviction, my sense that sufficient exposure to the coherent and meaningful realities represented in the pages of novels began to lay down the traces of an expectation in me. They awoke a whole set of private determinations about my life in the future—the life I *had* to have. Even when the awareness of meaning or the sense of fatedness were not to be gathered from my surroundings, novels gave me the grounds, the incentive, to live *as if.* Indeed, more than anything else, reading created in me the awareness that life could be lived and known as a unified whole; that the patterns which make meaning are disclosed gradually. That awareness, I admit, gets harder to sustain with the passing of time—life feels much less concentrated as one grows away from the urgencies of adolescence—but I would not dream of surrendering it. Without that faith, that sense of imminent resolution, the events of the day-to-day would be like some vast assortment of colored beads without a string to hold them together.

—from *The Gutenberg Elegies*

Rob Turk

(dates unknown)

Here is a letter to the Austin Chronicle, *dated February 1995 that kindly reassures Luddites everywhere that the new machines are not out to ruin their reading lives. KUT refers to the local National Public Radio station, and Celis White is a local beer.*

Dear *Chronicle* Staff:

I just finished reading this week's edition and I wanted to write in to express my appreciation for the fine Internet-related articles. While enthusiastic about this new media and its potential to reshape the way people communicate, I want to encourage you all to keep faith in the printed word. Books, magazines, newspapers as we now experience them are already a wonderfully interactive and affordable media. As public Internet access increases, and as subscriber entertainment services such as "interactive" television and video-on-demand access increases, new avenues will be explored by many people. However, the intellectual stimulus of novels, essays, reviews, and editorials will continue to thrill us for some time, and access to them won't be meted out by hardware and software savvy and resources, but by the tried-and-true method of visits to the local library, bookstore, or magazine stand. Now don't get me wrong. I happen to be working for a computer company that is interested in having an informed work force, and the information (documents and data) those people require will be distributed (by me) with this technology. Frequently revised documents can and should be distributed electronically, and tools evolving because of the Internet are making that solution more and more accessible. Also, sharing ideas and information is more efficient along these (T1:) lines. But after a 15-hour workday with my computer, I for one enjoy stretching out on the sofa, listening to KUT, with a magazine or novel in hand, and a Celis White nearby. Books are easier on the eyes than terminal screens; they are portable, entertaining, and thought-provoking (as is beer). If there is a day when a monitor is as easy on the eyes as a collection of Donald Barthelme stories and I don't have to wait until two in the morning to log in to my access provider (who will remain nameless here!), then I too will embrace the electronic frontier as more than a tool, but as sustenance. Hey, I'm lucky to have access at all, right?

There is tremendous potential for people to communicate freely and effectively with one another with the Internet. Telecommunicating promises to relieve cities of traffic congestion and improve workers' morale, if only more employers would encourage it. Artists, writers, philosophers, and mystics will find a larger audience, and democratic principles will flourish because of decreased dependency on huge amounts of capital to get a point across or to rally support. The Internet as tool can only increase efficiency and information by making knowledge more accessible.

The *Chronicle* informs, entertains, and enlightens many people, and it is encouraging that its staff has embraced this media (r)evolution. Keep up the good work. By the way, the ad campaign referred to in the page two editorial is not an IBM campaign (they've got the hip nuns and the French gentleman with the data-storage dilemma) but an AT&T campaign that, while hokey, at least helps prepare the television viewer for a potentially exciting future. We just have to make sure everyone is fed, clothed, housed, informed, and happy, and that environmental degradation, cultural intolerance, and the devestations of warfare don't eliminate all these sparkling, telecommunicating-from-the-beach-for-some-reason (who wants to think about their work while sunbathing in Cozumel!?!!!) possibilities.

—Letter to the *Austin Chronicle*

Don Fowler

(b. 1953)

In a review of Geoffrey Nunberg's The Future of the Book, *Don Fowler, Fellow and Tutor in Classics at Jesus College, Oxford, settles what's left for the poor old book.*

There is no doubt that major changes are occurring in the world of the book; the problem is that the changes are so rapid that even those who celebrate the changes cannot keep up with them. Geoffrey Nunberg is extremely cautious and sceptical about the grand claims of the cybernauts, but still declares quite categorically that "if we take the book in its broad sense to refer simply to bound, printed volumes, then most books will likely disappear soon". As he goes on to say, however, these books are not the stuff of futurologist *Angst* or excitement; not many are celebrating the passing of the parts catalogue, the technical manual, and the phone book. More significant may be the disappearance of academic print journals and monographs, as self-publication on the World Wide Web becomes a respectable branch of this vanity industry. The situation in which academic authors obtain subsidies from their institutions to pay publishers to publish monographs to sell to the same set of institutions has ripe potential for cutting out the middle men, which is already being exploited. Perhaps here too, however, the cries of anguish on the streets will be muted. The concern of many of the more pessimistic prophets is in fact less the disappearance of the "real" book than its fetishization, its removal from its utilitarian roots: the worry that books will be like horses or canal boats, no longer used because they are the best way to deliver information but because they bear cultural value. This opposition between function/meaning and use just looks like a tedious hangover from modernism, however, and one which neglects the varying uses to which books have always been put. There is nothing more natural about reading a book to find out the population of Zambia than using it to impress a friend, seduce a lover, or prop up a table. Books have always been more than glorified information delivery boys.

—from "Beyond the Book?"

Kevin Kelly and Kirkpatrick Sale

(b. 1934, 1937 resp.)

Kirkpatrick Sale, the author of Rebels Against the Future: The Luddites and Their War on the Industrial Revolution, *calls himself a "modern-day Luddite." In this excerpt from an interview with Kevin Kelly, author of a book on neo-biological technology and editor of* Wired *magazine, they are talking about forms of resistance to new technology. Sale observed that so far resistance has been mainly intellectual and political.*

KELLY: Yet you did smash a computer recently, right?

SALE: I did.

KELLY: I hope it made you feel better.

SALE: It was astonishing how good it made me feel! I cannot explain it to you. I was on the stage of New York City's Town Hall with an audience of 1,500 people. I was behind a lectern, and in front of the lectern was this computer. And I gave a very short, minute-and-a-half description of what was wrong with the technosphere, how it was destroying the biosphere. And then I walked over and I got this very powerful sledgehammer and smashed the screen with one blow and smashed the keyboard with another blow. It felt wonderful. The sound it made, the spewing of the undoubtedly poisonous insides into the spotlight, the dust that hung in the air . . . some in the audience applauded. I bowed and returned to my chair.

Toward the end of the same interview Kelly suggests that computers can be made so that they have less impact on nature.

SALE: But then how are we going to use the computer?! What do you use that technology for?! Here's how: it's going to be used for the dominance and exploitation of nature for our benefit.

KELLY: We dominate nature at first so that we can survive, but beyond survival I believe the focus of technology, culture, and civilization is on human creativity, to allow humans to be creative, to allow every human born to have a chance to create, to write a book, to make a film, to make music, to love, to understand the universe. I think that's what technology is for. I think that's why we're here. It's not to worship nature.

—from "Interview with the Luddite"

Robert Graves
(1895–1985)

How much of the averagely interesting book is actually read nowadays by the averagely interested person? It can only be a small part, and of that small part a good deal is lost because, though the eye goes through the motions of reading, the mind does not necessarily register the sense.

THE READER OVER YOUR SHOULDER

V
QUEEN LEAR

In times of difficulty, readers often turn to literature to under-stand the wordless world about them. It is also the case that some-times reading leads to more, and worse, trouble.

David Denby

(b. 1943)

Film critic and journalist David Denby returned to his alma mater,
Columbia College, to retake the basic Humanities course in the new
light of multiculturalism and his own intellectual development.
During that time, his mother became increasingly ill. He narrates
his experience in his book Great Books: My Adventures with
Homer, Rousseau, Woolf, and Other Indestructible Writers of
the Western World.

My mother died the way she did everything, decisively and in
great haste. I had been away with my wife and two sons in
California, and the night we returned to New York I called her,
as I always did when I got back from a trip. It was February,
1991, and she was seventy-five. When no one answered, I knew
she was in trouble, and part of me thought, *She's gone.* I was
sure of it, even though I'd talked to her a few days earlier and
she had been fine. It was impossible—it was inconceivable—
that she wouldn't be home when her family came back from a
trip. At times, she seemed to live for moments of reunion; they
occurred every day, or almost every day, when I made my
regular call. Sometimes she seemed amazed when I called, as if
I had been shunning her. If I did neglect to call for a few days,
amazement was replaced by grief: it was her lot to have a son
who had forgotten his mother; a rift had opened up between us
that she would now, with great relief, close.

I entered her apartment, two gently murmuring New York
policemen at my heels, with the disbelief one experiences when
a catastrophe actually happens: unaccountably not a movie or a
dream or a premonition but the thing itself unfolding—an acci-
dent, a fight, a body on the ground. My mother was lying in her
bathtub, naked; the shower was on. Her face was black, and her

lips were pressed together in a frown. I searched for her pulse and turned off the shower, which was cold. There was a small amount of dark blood on the back of the tub—from her mouth, probably. Why was the shower cold? Perhaps she had been stricken while taking a shower and had fallen. Was it a stroke? I was sure that it wasn't a heart attack: she had a heart like Tolstoy's. Had she collapsed before she could adjust the shower? The hot water could not have run out in a large modern apartment building in New York—or could it? I left the bathroom and went out into the living room and sat down on the sofa.

A doctor arrived; he was a small, fussy man, a Haitian in a New York public job. The cops were like angels, silent now, consoling me with lengthy, moist-eyed glances in my direction—they had mothers, too—but the doctor talked a great deal, and actually rubbed his hands together and bowed. Dimly, I noticed that the moment had changed: it no longer had the congealed, this-can't-be-happening-but-it-is quality. Reality was taking over; farce was taking over. The doctor and one of the policemen struggled to get the body out of the tub and onto the floor of the bathroom. Then the doctor rubbed his hands and chattered some more. There had been no foul play; he would order an autopsy. She had died the previous day, perhaps as much as twenty-four hours ago. I closed my eyes and leaned back into the sofa.

I had a peculiar, unsought intimacy with *King Lear*—the great, baleful monument of dramatic poetry—and not just because I had seen movie versions of it and read it a few times since college. In the years before my mother died, when she was in trouble in ways that I couldn't understand or grapple with, I had thought about *King Lear* more than anyone would want to. She *is* King Lear, I would say angrily to my wife after an impossible phone call or visit, the joke seeming staler and less illuminating each time. She was also my mother, Ida Denby, unhappy as hell and eager to let me know it.

Surely, I'm not alone in my uneasy relation to this play. *Lear* may exert its effects on us differently from other literary monuments. It's a great work that comes and finds us. If it *doesn't* suggest something intimate to us, it risks seeming outrageous and improbable, a preposterous fable with overwrought emotions and extravagantly embittered poetry, a wave of misery and negation. As I read the play in 1992, much of it—details of the action, bits of poetry—came back readily enough, and with the force of accusation. I was unsettled right at the opening by its hardness and harshness, the sense of catastrophe unfolding as a kind of joke. Lear, a tough old bastard, intelligent but without insight, gives up the power of the kingship yet refuses to give up the precedence and trappings of his royal position. We don't know why he does this. Apart from the folly of unkinging himself, he is not in any sense failing. He describes himself later as "every inch a king," and he is. His abdication is a mystery, a mystery compounded by vanity and wrath.

But this doesn't quite capture the strangeness of it. The play is set in motion by an excessive parental demand for love. The demand for love: could anything be more homely and banal? Before the first scene, Lear has decided to award the largest portion of his kingdom to Cordelia, his youngest daughter and his favorite. But then, seeking confirmation, and promising to reward in kind, Lear asks each of his three daughters how much she loves him. It is a dreary, embarrassing command performance of affection. Disgusted, Cordelia proudly eschews the effusive protestations of her sisters ("I cannot heave my heart into my mouth"), and Lear, in a rage, immediately dispossesses her.

The play starts with folly and error, and goes downhill from there. The two flattering daughters, Goneril and Regan, divide the land and almost immediately betray their father, progressively stripping him of honor, privilege, comfort, and shelter. Little can be said in extenuation of the way Goneril and Regan behave: they want their father dead. But their depredations and Cordelia's prideful silence can both be seen, at least in part, as a revolt against the humiliating demand for love.

Shakespeare was nothing if not apocalyptic at this stage of his career (*Macbeth* was his next tragedy), and, once the bonds of family love are broken, everything goes. The frame of the state, the physical universe itself crack and split, and the elements whirl into contention. Civilization gives way to barbarism, shelter to brutal exposure, fellow-feeling to feral and carnivorous appetite. Lear himself casts off his old manner, his sanity, his clothes: it is a process, violent beyond belief, of unraveling, unhousing, and undressing, until the King is out in a storm with his few remaining loyal subjects and, for the first time in his life, senses what poor and miserable people must suffer.

Man without protection from the elements—without civilization, laws, forms of respect—is nothing, and Lear, now remorseful and anguished, needs to feel the nothingness in his own skin.

Lear harrows himself, attains something like a new consciousness; the forces of good rally and join him, and he is reconciled with Cordelia and with his old friend Gloucester, who has undergone a similarly lacerating ordeal of misjudgment, betrayal, and renewal. Redemption of a sort is possible, almost achieved, but help arrives too late. The bodies pile up, including Lear's and Cordelia's.

Beginning in banality and dismay, *Lear* goes right to the edge of annihilation, with a richness of bleak imagery, a sense of the entire natural world in revolt against normal usage, and, at times, an almost manic high foolishness that is no less amazing on the third or fourth reading.

A few years ago, when I worried about my mother, I would think constantly of *Lear;* now, reading *Lear* again, I thought constantly of *her.* The play is about fierce pre-Christian aristocrats, not Jewish-American middle-class mothers; but Ida Denby was the Lear of my life.

She was born during the First World War, and in the Depression she became one of those women who just went out and launched a career, without benefit of education or professional training, and certainly without a theory of women's rights and capabilities. She became a businesswoman by necessity and instinct, and much later, in the sixties and seventies, she was puzzled by the emergence of a modern feminist consciousness. She couldn't see the need for it; talk of "patriarchy" and "the oppression of women" only amused her. In truth, I don't think she could imagine anyone holding her back. She had wanted to make money—no, she had *had* to make money—and so she had dropped out of school at fourteen and begun working (her four brothers stayed in school and eventually went to college). By the time she reached her early twenties, she was sailing to Europe on the *Mauritania* and buying ladies' sportswear in Paris for American department stores. She was a short Jewish girl (about five feet one) from Washington Heights, and was not especially articulate. Untutored, she put herself together (a favorite phrase of hers) and somehow acquired a stone-crushing self-confidence combined with an unshakable system of concealing her ignorance of everything that wasn't necessary to her work, her family, her travel, her clothes, and her table. Until her final decade, I never knew her to be anything other than a tremendous success in life.

And I never knew her to be conscious of her effect on people, or to be aware of when she had faked her way through something or had lied. My mother was possibly the most *innocently* egotistical human being who has ever lived. In other words, she was a happy woman. She was also a heroine. I knew that when I was a very small boy.

When I was thirteen or fourteen—dressed in my gray flannel slacks and blue blazer, the perfect gentleman—I would accompany her on visits to a manufacturer's plant in Pennsylvania or on Long Island. She would barge in, head for the boss's office, sit on the edge of his desk, her legs crossed and exposed (she had good legs), and say something like "When are you going to get that fucking shipment of blouses to me?" This was around 1956, when not many women executives talked that way. Of course, she was showing off for her little boy. Trembling a bit, I thought, My own movie star! Barbara Stanwyck! She was fast, spontaneous, devastating. She teased the men she worked with, and got away with things that men wouldn't have tried. As far as I could tell, they were fond of her, a prefeminist "working girl" of the thirties and forties who could join them in the shouted give-and-take of a Seventh Avenue showroom as machinery clattered in the background.

Unfortunately, she told off salesgirls, too. She was hell to go shopping with, and I was occasionally humiliated by her dominating ways. Having worked in the forties at McCreery's, the long-gone department store at Fifth and Thirty-fourth—according to family legend, she was the first Jew at McCreery's—she knew all about salesgirls. If a clerk refused to go look for something or take back a purchase she would browbeat the girl until she broke, and I would suffer along with the clerk. "I saw you on Saturday at Doubleday's," a girl in my eighth-grade class said to me once. "You were with your mother. You were crying."

Yet I counted myself lucky. And my father, who was awed by her and crazy about her, was lucky too, because she was loving and easy at home. With us, she would try to run everything, and then, suddenly, she would pull back. Home was not business—she knew that, and she relented. In any case, she was happy with my father, a costume jewelry manufacturer and an adroit, low-pressure salesman. He was a quiet and refined sort of guy, not a fighter, but a gentleman who dressed like Fred Astaire. She loved him and doted on me, her only child, her prince. I have a picture of her now in my living room. She is lying on a hospital bed, her head propped up on her arm, and she is fully made up: lipstick, eyebrows, Rita Hayworth hair— the works. She is almost beautiful. And all this while lying on a hospital bed! A photographer had apparently been called to her bedside to provide evidence that Ida Denby had put herself together. I was, I believe, born just a few days before this picture was taken. The look on her face is a cross between triumph and impatience.

The prince had no complaints. When I heard Jewish-mother

jokes, when I read *Portnoy's Complaint,* I would think that I should be the victim of the joke—but I knew that it wasn't so. My mother's spiritedness released people from embarrassment and anger.

And then my father died. He had been ill for some years, weak from angina, and my mother, by sheer will power, had kept him alive, buoying his mood and nursing him when necessary, even retiring for a while and living with him in the country. He died very abruptly, in 1980. We were in a bank on Thirty-fourth Street, he and I, looking at papers in the vault, and he had a moment's warning, a surge of pain. "Not good," he said. "Let's continue our business." And he went on looking at the papers. But a minute or so later, he leaned forward and, without a word, lost consciousness. It was over before I realized what was happening. I called for an ambulance and after that took in nothing until a paramedic, not realizing who I was, felt my father's pulse and said, "This one's a stiff." I immediately forgave him—he had seen, no doubt, several other corpses that day. I also never forgave him.

Both my parents died suddenly in New York City, and, if I can speak with the selfishness of a survivor, and of an only child, each death was, for me, both easy and hard, since there was no time to say anything. I had, through much of my life, taken my gentle father for granted; we both lived in the shadow of a powerful woman, and at some level I had wanted him to be as strong as my mother. I thought of him as someone who was appended to her, someone to whom she had shown mercy; I hadn't realized how much work went into being her constant companion. But after he died I saw it clearly enough. He had absorbed much of her energy, taken her aggressiveness into himself and neutralized it. "You can wear her down," he had once confided to me, with a sigh. "But you can never make her stop." I don't think he wanted her to stop.

When my father died, my mother, then in her mid-sixties, most astonishingly fell apart. And she got worse and worse. After a few years, muttering something about taxes, she abruptly and mysteriously quit working, and became, still arrayed in battle dress, a warrior without a campaign. All at once, she was that diminished person, a widow; she had no arena in which to expend her energy, her desire for command, her anger. She furiously managed her apartment in New York and a house on Long Island and refused to do much else. Nothing was good enough for her. She would go out with no man—not even for dinner—and refused any chance to make new friends, even as she scared off many of the old ones. In a state of constant irritation, she would denounce companions of thirty years' standing. Only a few young women, loyal acolytes from her business days, retained her interest.

I suppose there was no mystery in this. She had lost her husband, her son (to marriage), and her business—a three-way reduction of power. A freewheeling big spender, generous to a fault, my mother no longer commanded expense accounts and travel budgets; she could not invite people to her house or apartment, because she didn't have the spirit to entertain them, and as a guest at someone else's house she was restless, and accusatory. If the whole day wasn't planned around her, she was miserable. "This doesn't work for *me*," she would wail.

I listened and suffered with her, and I grew embarrassed. She had been masterful for half a century, and now she couldn't seem to find herself. I made suggestions, offering to introduce her to this or that experience, but she would do nothing that I proposed, and at times my sympathy would drain away. Would she go to lectures or join in activities with other retired people at the Ninety-second Street Y, one of the best-run cultural institutions in the city? She was furious. Sit with housewives? She who had been everywhere, done everything? It was out of the question.

"You're killing me with this stuff!"

"With the suggestion that you go to the Y?"

"You're killing me."

All right. Would she visit her brothers and sisters in Florida, then? No, there was nothing to do there, no one to talk to but old people. She would not go down there. She would *die* in Florida.

"What am I supposed to do?" I asked my wife.

"Ask your mother."

Very funny, but my mother was telling me in her way exactly what I was supposed to do. I was supposed to know her and to love her, and that love must be unabashed, unreserved, and unseeing. She wanted to be taken care of, and yet she wouldn't accept care.

Now, for the first time, my mother's dropping out of school at fourteen hurt her badly. She had few interests to draw on or cultivate, and she was too proud, after years of achievement, to accept instruction. She lacked the patience to read fiction and the information and curiosity to read, say, history, so she read biographies of actresses, duchesses, and gigolos and went to the movies a great deal. For once, I could help, but there were never enough movies or the right ones, and the complaints arrived like a pelting rainstorm on my head. Tradesmen and dentists cheated her; everyone lied. She was suddenly helpless, she who had been a master of trade. For years, I had been wary of her— I had loved her, but I had been wary—and now she wanted everything done for her. She would never consider visiting a shrink; the sole meeting I was able to arrange with a psychiatric social worker turned into a comic disaster. And so, unseen and unseeing, she was relentless in her woe, and there were days when I shut my heart against her.

With my mother in mind, I thought that *King Lear* was about the anguish that ensues when the ravages of time invert the accustomed relation between parent and child. As my mother's situation grew worse, her short-term memory began to go (this happened when she was about seventy), and she forgot appointments and addresses and even ran out into the city in her robe and slippers a few times.

A woman who had bullied many people (though not me) had become almost abject, and once or twice I noticed in myself the same thing I had been noticing in others—a secret fascination with the scandal of her weakness. People's eyes would come alive with horrified excitement when she was late for a dinner party. She would eventually show up, blaming someone else for her lateness, and everyone would be relieved, yet still eager to hear the *details* of it. (Her pride helped her there; she never admitted a thing.)

The layers of upper-middle-class armature, the clothes and jewels and furs and furniture that she had so happily earned and enjoyed; the New York restaurant-going and theater-going that she had so lovingly mastered—none of this could protect her. Her condition was becoming dangerous, and I was paralyzed. Suddenly, she seemed naked, and I had no idea how to clothe her. She unhoused herself one day, showing up at our apartment haggard and drawn, and lived with us for a while, sleeping in the living room and wandering the apartment gray-faced, her gloom relieved only by my oldest son, then six, whom she adored.

She wanted to live in her own apartment, and when she went home we hired companions to live with her and look after her, all of them trained to deal with "difficult" older people. But she couldn't bear to have anyone monitoring her, and fired them all, accusing each one, after a few weeks, of incompetence or stealing. She seemed as mad as a hatter. Did she have Alzheimer's? The question became unavoidable. My wife and I took her to a well-known neurologist, who asked her such questions as "Who is the President of the United States?" Like so many doctors, he had a profound detestation of what he took to be senility. There was nothing he could do about it, and he was openly contemptuous during the examination. She had become that infinitesimal thing, a patient no longer competent.

I was almost ready to put my mother in a "home"—which would have been a defeat for all of us, almost the modern equivalent of Regan and Goneril's driving Lear out into the storm—but my wife was not. The neurologist's haughty manner so enraged her that she insisted that my mother see another doctor—a young man, but one who knew something about geriatrics—and from the moment my mother entered the new doctor's office the clouds began to lift for us. He quickly established that she had an excess of calcium in her blood—a condition that her old doctor had wrongly attributed to Padget's disease, and one that can, in some cases, cause dementia. Within weeks, a benign tumor was discovered in one of her parathyroid glands, and the gland was removed. In the hospital the day after the operation, when my mother was still in pain, I noticed that she was speaking more logically than she had spoken in years. The nurses were slow, but they were not trying to destroy her, she said. No, they simply had problems taking care of everybody. My wife had saved my mother's life.

Ida Denby quickly regained her sense, her apartment, and some of her peace of mind, and almost enjoyed her last few years. She was better, significantly better, but she still raged against her situation and demanded more love than I could give her. The illness had exacerbated her troubles, but even when she got better her fundamental nature and situation remained unchanged. She was a powerful person who had let go of the reins yet still wanted to control a team of horses.

All the people she had made feel lazy or unsuccessful in the past fastened on her troubles and then, after her operation, refused to hear that she had got better. Even after she was much improved, I couldn't persuade any of them to call her up. "Being weak, seem so," Regan says to Lear when the old King, no longer in office, complains about his emissary being put in the stocks. It is a vile remark. But it's almost understandable, too, because powerful people, as they age, often become obsessed with loyalty and the signs and flourishes of respect while failing to notice how much their children and friends need to maintain their own *self*-respect.

Unlike Regan and Goneril, I did my parent no great harm—I took care of her in the slightly distant but steady way that wary only sons take care of mothers—but I was often in a rage. No matter, I told myself at the time. It was duty that was required in grown-up sons. What you felt was beside the point.

You had obligations, and you had to fulfill them. She had never failed me, and I could not fail her. But when she died my tears were produced as much by relief as by sorrow.

Whatever else *King Lear* does, it brings you back to the inescapable struggle for power between parents and children. It suggests that the basic human relations in begetting and dying can be intolerable. Lear is hardly the only parent to demand too much love from his children. Did I not want my sons to accept my reading, my culture, my tastes—a demand for love in its way as relentless as any other? And who hasn't had moments in which he wished his parents gone, as Goneril, Regan, and Edmund did? I know there were days when I wanted my mother off my back, out of my life. Shakespeare begins with such awkward stuff and splits the earth wide open with it.

At my mother's funeral, a young cantor sang so beautifully that he almost purged the regrets and ambivalence that were choking me. After her young friends made eulogies, I was ready to say something. "From the beginning to last week, she was my strength, my authority, my sword and shield." That was certainly true. And then I told her story as I've told it here, but without the dismaying coda of her final years.

When Lear loses everything and fears he will go insane, his loving Fool, who continues to attend him, speaks to him in penetrable riddles: a seeming madness to mirror Lear's madness, a manic yet utterly faithful critique of Lear's actions and state. And, similarly, Edgar, Gloucester's good son, speaks to his deluded father and to Lear in the character of Poor Tom, a noisy addlepate who thinks that the universe has conspired against him. Shakespeare's poetry of pretended madness is made almost unbearably moving by the deeply loving intention behind it: the Fool and Edgar hope to nurse the two tormented old men back to mental health with their provocations, while hateful Goneril and Regan speak to Lear in the tones of the coldest rationality, trying to check his anguished demands with

reason. How many knights shall Lear retain when he stays with
either of his daughters?

> LEAR: *[To Goneril]* I'll go with thee.
> Thy fifty yet doth double five-and-twenty,
> And thou art twice her love.
> GONERIL: Hear me, my lord.
> What need you five-and-twenty? ten? or five?
> To follow in a house where twice so many
> Have a command to tend you?
> REGAN: What need one?
> LEAR: O reason not the need! Our basest beggars
> Are in the poorest things superfluous.
> Allow not nature more than nature needs,
> Man's life is cheap as beast's. Thou art a lady:
> If only to go warm were gorgeous,
> Why, nature needs not what thou gorgeous
> wear'st,
> Which scarcely keeps thee warm.
>
> (2.4. 253–265)

The famous lines mortified me as I read the play again,
because I had been forever trying to reason with my mother,
trying to separate her real difficulties from her imagining of
difficulty. When she went alone to her country house for the
weekend, disaster attended her hours: power lines fell down on
the house; the lawn developed gaping holes; pipes burst; ants
ravaged the kitchen. Catastrophe followed catastrophe—the ob-
jective world a mockery of her fallen state. Her return to the
city, on Sunday night, would be capped with a damage report
on the telephone. But how much of it was true? None of this
happened when my wife and I were with her. So I would try to
sort it out, try to get *her* to sort it out, and she would grow
angrier and angrier, as if I were the one pulling down power
lines on her head.

Was I really helping her with my logical, patient questions, my attempts to bring her around? If only I could have loosened up, let fly my fancy, any fancy that worked, and tried a loving cure—like the Fool or Edgar! Reading *King Lear* again, I saw a bit of Goneril and Regan's stony rigor breaking through my exasperated relation to my mother in her later years. I revenged myself on her long-held strength by refusing to enter her madness. How could I not have realized that, emotionally, she needed reassurance, not reality.

My mother did not understand much of what was going on with her when she was ill, and afterward she did not admit she *had* been ill. She wouldn't even credit the young doctor with saving her sanity. After a few hapless attempts, I never spoke of the matter again. My mother did not know that she possessed an unconscious. She had the noble, infuriating density of a fully achieved ego, a pre-Freudian personality. You could not hold a mirror up to her nature. That was partly the source of her strength—and of her capacity for happiness. Throughout our lives together, I was always struggling to get her to see herself, but she would not be my student.

—from *Queen Lear*

Katherine Mansfield

(1888–1923)

Katherine Mansfield, celebrated for her resonant and beautifully written stories, led a short and restless life, traveling from her native New Zealand to settle in England, and from there to Germany, Switzerland, and France. She complained often in her letters and journal of the discomforts of her temporary housing, and she, like many other travelers, found a particular solace in reading.

If there is a book to be read, no matter how bad that book is, I read it. I will read it. Was it always so with me? (*Journal*, 1922)

She had always read a great deal, as most writers do, although some of her reading was for the purpose of writing book reviews for the Athenaeum *and other journals edited by her husband, John Middleton Murry, and therefore in the category of literary duty rather than private pleasure.*

Putting my weakest books to the wall last night I came across a copy of *Howard's End* and had a look into it. But it's not good enough. E. M. Forster never gets any further than warming the teapot. He's a rare fine hand at that. Feel this teapot. Is it not beautifully warm? Yes, but there ain't going to be no tea. (*Journal*, 1917)

When I read Dr. Johnson, I feel like a little girl sitting at the same table. My eyes grow round. I don't only listen; I take him in *immensely*. (*Journal*, 1919)

Especially after her tuberculosis took hold and made it impossible for her to spend winters in England, she became fierce for reading material.

Can I have the *Times Lit. Sup.?* I freeze, I burn for the printed word. (Letter to John Middleton Murry [18 September 1920], France)

. . . During the past two nights I have read *The Dynasts.* Isn't it queer how a book eludes one. And then suddenly it opens for you? I have looked into this book before now. But the night before last when I opened it I suddenly understood what the poet meant, and how he meant it should be read! *The point of view* which is like a light streaming from the imagination and over the imagination—over one's head as it were—the chorus and the aerial music. (Letter to John Middleton Murry [24 May 1921], Switzerland)

I read less and less, or fewer and fewer books. Not because I don't want to read them, I do—but they seem so high up on the tree. It's so hard to get at them and there is nobody near to help . . . On my bed at night there is a copy of Shakespeare, a copy of Chaucer, an automatic pistol, and a black muslin fan. This is my whole little world. (Letter to Lady Ottoline Morrell [June 1921], Switzerland)

But the more poetry one reads the more one longs to read! (Letter to the Countess Russell [October 1921], Switzerland)

In fact, isn't it a joy—there is hardly a greater one—to find a new book, a living book, and to know that it will remain with you while life lasts? . . . (Letter to John Middleton Murry [7 February 1922], Paris)

Katherine Mansfield felt a special attachment to the work of Anton Chekhov (1860–1904). Working with her friend S. S. Koteliansky, she was one of the earliest translators of Chekhov into English, and she wrote to Koteliansky in August 1919:

I have re-read *The Steppe*. What can one say? It is simply one of *the* great stories of the world—a kind of Iliad or Odyssey. I think I will learn this journey by heart. One says of things: they are immortal. One feels about this story not that it *becomes* immortal—it always was. It has no beginning or end. [Chekhov] just touched one point with his pen (.———.) and then another point: *enclosed* something which had, as it were, been there forever.

In 1921, she copied out sentences from Chekhov's "Misery" in her Scrapbook and wrote:

I would see every single French short story up the chimney for this. It's one of the masterpieces of the world.

Chekhov had tuberculosis much of his adult life, but only after 1884 was his illness made public. He, too, lived from hotel to hotel, seeking respite from winter, dampness, and his disease. Mansfield wrote on December 14, 1919, to Koteliansky from Menton:

I shall try and get well here. If I *do* die perhaps there will be a small private heaven for consumptives only. In that case I shall see Chekhov. He will be walking down his garden paths with fruit trees on either side and tulips in flower in the garden beds. His dog will be sitting on the path, panting and slightly smiling as dogs do who have been running about a great deal.

In her Scrapbook, *she copied out snatches from Chekhov's letters from 1900 and 1904, then underlined certain phrases and words, to echo and to second Chekhov.*

"I am torn up by the roots, I am not living a full life, I don't drink, though I'm fond of drinking; I love noise and don't hear it—in fact, I am in the condition of a transplanted tree which is hesitating whether to take root or to begin to wither." (February 10, 1900)

So am I exactly.

"I live on the ground floor." (June 12, 1904)

"My health has improved. I don't notice now as I go about that I am ill; my asthma is better, nothing is aching." (June 16, 1904)

"I confess I dread the railway journey. It's stifling in the train now, particularly with my asthma, which is made worse by the slightest thing." "I like the food here very much, but it does not seem to suit me; my stomach is constantly being upset. Evidently my digestion is hopelessly ruined. It is scarcely possible to cure it by anything except fasting—that is, eating nothing, and that's the end of it. And the only remedy for asthma is not moving." (June 28, 1904)

Who reads between the lines here? I at least. K.M.

She was reading Chekhov as one dying person reads another.

How much do we know of Chekhov from his letters? Was that all? Of course not. Don't you suppose he had a whole longing life of which there is hardly a word? Then read the final letters. He has given up hope. If you de-sentimentalize those final letters they are terrible. There is no more Chekhov. Illness has swallowed him. (*Journal,* 1922)

. . . About being like Chekhov and his letters. Don't forget

he died at 43. That he spent—how much? of his life chasing
about in a desperate search after health. And if one reads "intu-
itively" the last letters, they are terrible. What is left of him?
"The braid on German women's dresses . . . bad taste"—and
all the rest is misery. Read the last! All hope is over for him.
Letters are deceptive, at any rate. It's true he had occasional
happy moments. But for the last 8 years he knew no *security* at
all. We know he felt his stories were not half what they might
be. It doesn't take much imagination to picture him on his
deathbed thinking "I have never had a real chance. Something
has been all wrong." (Letter to John Middleton Murry, 15 October 1922)

*In her last months, Katherine Mansfield sought solace in a bookless
world, at a mystical commune in Fontainebleau, and from there she
wrote her faithful friend on October 24, 1922:*

Don't send the book. Why should you? I don't want any
books at present.

Katherine Mansfield died on January 9, 1923.

Gustave Flaubert

(1821–1880)

Flaubert advised his friend, Louise Collet (1810–1876), poet, novelist, "intrigante," and one of his models for Emma Bovary, "Read if you want to live!"

Emma Bovary, Flaubert's celebrated escapist, fills her boredom with dreamy sentimental thrills that she gets from reading novels. The pursuit of emotions, the monotony of daily existence, and the fact that dreams never equal reality, lead Emma Bovary to disaster.

Emma enters a convent when she is about thirteen and there commences a life based on fantasy.

She becomes rapt over The Lives of the Saints, *secretly reads novels concerned with affairs of the heart, grows enamored of Sir Walter Scott, cultivates a passion for Jeanne d'Arc, Mary Stuart, and other ill-starred ladies. Emma trembles over book engravings of young girls kissing doves and daydreaming on sofas. Carried away by these and other visions, she balks at taking final vows and finally leaves the convent.*

Later, after she has married and has grown quickly bored with Charles Bovary, her dull doctor husband, and with living in provincial Yonville, there is a seduction scene at a dinner table in which Emma is talking to the young law clerk, Monsieur Léon, about reading. Her husband is present along with several others, but the lovers-to-be talk right over their heads.

"My wife doesn't care about gardening," said Charles; "although she has been advised to take exercise, she prefers always sitting in her room reading."

"Like me," replied Léon. "And indeed, what is better than to sit by one's fireside in the evening with a book, while the wind beats against the window and the lamp is burning?"

"What, indeed?" she said, fixing her large black eyes wide open upon him.

"One thinks of nothing," he continued; "the hours slip by. Motionless we traverse countries we fancy we see, and your thought, blending with the fiction, playing with the details, follows the outline of the adventures. It mingles with the characters, and it seems as if it were yourself palpitating beneath their costumes."

"That is true! that is true!" she said.

"Has it ever happened to you," Léon went on, "to come across some vague idea of one's own in a book, some dim image that comes back to you from afar, and as the completest expression of your own slightest sentiment?"

"I have experienced it," she replied.

"That is why," he said, "I especially love the poets. I think verse more tender than prose, and that it moves far more easily to tears."

"Still in the long-run it is tiring," continued Emma. "Now I, on the contrary, adore stories that rush breathlessly along, that frighten one. I detest commonplace heroes and moderate sentiments, such as there are in nature."

"In fact," observed the clerk, "these works, not touching the heart, miss, it seems to me, the true end of art. It is so sweet, amid all the disenchantments of life, to be able to swell in thought upon noble characters, pure affections, and pictures of happiness. For myself, living here far from the world, this is my one distraction; but Yonville affords so few resources."

"Like Tostes, no doubt," replied Emma; "and so I always subscribed to a lending library."

—from *Madame Bovary*

The French have a term for "escapism"—bovarysme! *Emma Bovary was a woman who read too much.*

Jonathan Greene

(b. 1943)

Poet, book designer, and proprietor for thirty years of Gnomon Press, a publisher of literary and photographic works, Jonathan Greene is the author of fifteen books. He and his wife raise Lincoln Longwool sheep on the banks of the Kentucky River.

The Ideal Reader

Some use for old poems—

the mice in the basement
found them, chewed over
what the critics ignored,
a letter-by-letter
close reading!

An audience the mailing lists
overlooked, my work judged good
enough to live in, Grade A
nesting matter!

—from *Idylls*

Ursula K. Le Guin

(b. 1929)

A widely published writer of fantasy and science fiction, Ursula K. Le Guin writes engaged and imaginative work that transcends genre, including The Left Hand of Darkness *and* The Dispossessed. *Le Guin lives in the Pacific Northwest.*

Messages came, Johanna thought, usually years too late, or years before one could crack their code or had even learned the language they were in. Yet they came increasingly often and were so urgent, so compelling in their demand that she read them, that she do something, as to force her at last to take refuge from them. She rented, for the month of January, a little house with no telephone in a seaside town that had no mail delivery. She had stayed there several times in summer; winter, as she had hoped, was even quieter than summer. A whole day would go by without her hearing or speaking a word. She did not buy the paper or turn on the television, and the one morning she thought she ought to find some news on the radio she got a program in Finnish from Astoria. But the messages still came. Words were everywhere.

Literate clothing was no real problem. She remembered the first print dress she had ever seen, years ago, a genuine *print* dress with typography involved in the design—green on white, suitcases and hibiscus and the names *Riviera* and *Capri* and *Paris* occurring rather blobbily from shoulder-seam to hem, sometimes right side up, sometimes upside down. Then it had been, as the saleswoman said, very unusual. Now it was hard to find a T-shirt that did not urge political action, or quote lengthily from a dead physicist, or at least mention the town it was for sale in. All this she had coped with, she had even worn. But too many things were becoming legible.

She had noticed in earlier years that the lines of foam left by waves on the sand after stormy weather lay sometimes in curves that looked like handwriting, cursive lines broken by spaces, as if in words; but it was not until she had been alone for over a fortnight and had walked many times down to Wreck Point and back that she found she could read the writing. It was a mild day, nearly windless, so that she did not have to march briskly but could mosey along between the foam-lines and the water's edge where the sand reflected the sky. Every now and then a quiet winter breaker driving up and up the beach would drive her and a few gulls ahead of it onto the drier sand; then as the wave receded she and the gulls would follow it back. There was not another soul on the long beach. The sand lay as firm and even as a pad of pale brown paper, and on it a recent wave at its high mark left a complicated series of curves and bits of foam. The ribbons and loops and lengths of white looked so much like handwriting and chalk that she stopped, the way she would stop, half willingly, to read what people scratched in the sand in summer. Usually it was "Jason + Karen" or paired initials in a heart; once, mysteriously and memorably, three initials and the dates 1973–1984, the only such inscription that spoke of a promise not made but broken. Whatever those eleven years had been, the length of a marriage? a child's life? they were gone, and the letters and numbers were also gone when she came back by where they had been, with the tide rising. She had wondered then if the person who wrote them had written them to be erased. But these foam words lying on the brown sand now had been written by the erasing sea itself. If she could read them they might tell her a wisdom a good deal deeper and bitterer than she could possibly swallow. Do I want to know what the sea writes? she thought, but at the same time she was already reading the foam, which though in vaguely cuneiform blobs rather than letters of any alphabet was perfectly legible as she walked along beside it. "Yes," it read, " 'esse hes hetu tokye to' ossusess ekyes. Seham hute' u." (When she wrote it down later she used the apostrophe to represent a kind of stop of click

like the last sound in "Yep!") As she read it over, backing up
some yards to do so, it continued to say the same thing, so she
walked up and down it several times and memorized it. Pres-
ently, as bubbles burst and the blobs began to shrink, it changed
here and there to read,"Yes, e hes etu kye to' ossusess kye. ham
te u." She felt that this was not significant change but mere loss,
and kept the original text in mind. The water of the foam sank
into the sand and the bubbles dried away till the marks and
lines lessened into a faint lacework of dots and scraps, half
legible. It looked enough like delicate bits of fancywork that she
wondered if one could also read lace or crochet.

When she got home she wrote down the foam words so that
she would not have to keep repeating them to remember them,
and then she looked at the machine-made Quaker lace tablecloth on the round dining table. It was not hard to read but was,
as one might expect, rather dull. She made out the first line
inside the border as "pith wot pith wot pith wot" interminably,
with a "dub" every thirty stitches where the border pattern
interrupted.

But the lace collar she had picked up at a second-hand
clothes store in Portland was a different matter entirely. It was
handmade, hand written. The script was small and very even.
Like the Spencerian hand she had been taught fifty years ago in
the first grade, it was ornate but surprisingly easy to read. "My
soul must go," was the border, repeated many times, "my soul
must go, my soul must go," and the fragile webs leading inward
read, "sister, sister, sister, light the light." And she did not know
what she was to do, or how she was to do it.

—from "Texts"

Leslie Marmon Silko

(b. 1948)

Novelist and poet Leslie Marmon Silko was born in Albuquerque, New Mexico, and grew up on the Laguna Pueblo reservation. Of mixed Caucasian, Mexican, and Laguna Indian heritage in a family with a tradition of communal storytelling and reading, her work is concerned with the struggles of native peoples to hold on to their culture. In her essay "Books: Notes on Mixtec and Maya Screenfolds, Picture Books of Pre-Conquest Mexico" Silko describes how, in 1540, magnificent Maya and Aztec folding books were destroyed when European invaders burned the great libraries of the Americas. After they destroyed the books, they destroyed the people and took their land.

My great-grandmother's house had a tall bookcase full of my great-grandfather's books. My grandparents' house also had rooms with shelves of books. We had books. My parents kept books at their bedsides. My father used to read at the table at lunchtime, and we did too. It was years before I realized it is considered impolite to read at the table. I remember waiting until I was alone in the house, and then I'd go find *Lolita* or *Lady Chatterley's Lover* half hidden under my dad's side of the bed.

I have a friend who grew up in a house without books. There was a Bible and there were cattle growers' magazines, but he was in the sixth or seventh grade before a cousin going off to war gave him the first books he ever owned. My friend still suffers with insatiable lust for books. While his father and uncles counted cattle, my friend counted his books. My friend couldn't tell one cow from another, but he knew how to spot the books he wanted whenever the high school basketball team took a trip to the big city.

The heyday of the cattle drives and open range didn't last long. Stampedes, storms, angry Indians, and bandits never did get to that great old cowboy Charles Goodnight, but lawyers and their books laid old Goodnight low. No wonder the cowboys distrusted books. They must have distrusted my friend too, when they sensed his passion for books. They clung to their old life, the old cowboy culture, with its devotion to livestock and to the land long after the heyday of the cowboys had passed. These cowboys believed in action, not words, certainly not the printed word.

Hundreds of years before, proclamations, letters, and edicts came to the Americas from monarchs and popes admonishing the settlers to obey the laws. In the Americas, the printed word, like the spoken word, had to be ignored if the settlers were to reap the riches they all desired. If you could not read the king's or the pope's edict, then you could not be held accountable. If you were ignorant of the pope's edict then you were blameless before God. So illiteracy and the aversion to books that is found through the Americas descends from colonial times. Ignorance was blissful and profitable.

My great-grandmother and Aunt Susie had been sent away to Carlisle Indian School in Pennsylvania, and both women had returned with a profound sense of the power of books. The laws were in books. The King of Spain had granted the Laguna Pueblo people their land. The Laguna Pueblo people knew their land was protected by a land grant document from the King of Spain. The Anglo-Americans who swarmed into the New Mexico Territory after 1848 carried with them no such documents. The Pueblo people fared better than other tribes simply because of these documents. The land grant documents alerted the Pueblo people to the value of the written word; the old books of international law favored the holders of royal land grants. So, very early, the Pueblo people realized the power of written words and books to secure legitimate title to tribal land. No wonder the older folks used to tell us kids to study: learn to read and to write for your own protection.

Grandma A'mooh used to read to me and my sisters over and over from a tattered little book called *Brownie the Bear.* My father and my uncles also remember *Brownie the Bear.* People told stories constantly, but Grandma A'mooh made a point of reading to us from a book too, perhaps because she feared we'd prefer listening to reading (who wouldn't?). But when I got to school and there were no beloved grandmas or aunts to tell me stories, I remembered that books tell stories too, and whenever I felt alienated and lonely in school, I would begin to read a story, and immediately I felt that happy secure feeling come over me as it did whenever Grandma A'mooh began telling me a story. I used to make up stories for my sisters and cousins because I learned very early that I got the same pleasure from telling stories as I felt when I was a listener.

Later, in fifth grade, I learned that when it was not possible to be soothed by hearing a story or by telling a story aloud, I could evoke that same feeling of well-being by writing down a story I made up myself. Fifth grade was when my sisters and I had to commute to Albuquerque to school, and I was very unhappy. Mrs. Cooper, the fifth-grade teacher, asked us to make up a story that used the words in our spelling list at least once. The spelling list had the word *poplar,* and I remember I had a character sliding down the smooth bark of the poplar tree. Of course I had no idea what a poplar tree looked like.

A book was the cause of the only big quarrel my great-grandmother ever had with her daughter-in-law Aunt Susie. The old-time Pueblo people abhorred confrontations, especially with family members. So I was almost grown and Grandma A'mooh had passed on before my mother ever discussed the incident. The quarrel had occurred years before, and few people knew about it; but Grandma A'mooh was very fond of my mother and told her the story.

It seems that when the War Department surveyed graduates of the Carlisle Indian School, they noted shocking recidivism; the graduates who had once looked so well scrubbed and earnest in their dark suits and long dresses "went back to the blanket" as soon as they returned home. They abandoned civilized clothing; they grew their hair long again, and they refused to speak English.

The U.S. government had taken every precaution to sever the Indian students' ties with their families and tribes. Children were taken by force, if necessary, put on the train, and sent thousands of miles to the boarding school in Carlisle, Pennsylvania. The government did not allow the children to return home for visits in the summer. Instead the Indian students were hired out to Carlisle families for domestic and farm work. The government policymakers believed that if the Indian children were kept far enough away from their families and homeland long enough, the Indian School graduates might never return to the reservations but instead melt into the cities in the east to work as maids and farmhands.

What was needed was an extension program that would reach Carlisle graduates after they returned home, to reinforce all of the civilizing and instruction given at the boarding school. Thus it was that the book *Stiya: The Story of an Indian Girl* came to be. Marion Bergess, a white woman who worked as a teacher and dormitory matron at Carlisle, wrote the novel under the fake Indian name Tonka. The U.S. War Department published the book in 1881; as far as I know, distribution was limited to Indian boarding school graduates.

The book was written from the point of view of a young Pueblo girl named Stiya after she has returned home from Carlisle and struggles to retain her new identity and "civilized" ways despite growing hostility and pressure from her family and from the Pueblo community where she grew up. Marion Bergess revealed the whites' perspective of Pueblo people as she described the sights and smells of the village, which repel Stiya and even nauseate her. Bergess projected all of her own fears and prejudices toward Pueblo life into her Stiya character. Stiya refuses to wear traditional Pueblo clothing and she speaks only English although her family absurdly insists she speak their "gibberish." She refuses to go to the plaza for the sacred *ka'tsina* dances because they are "lewd." Just when she seems most alone, when the pressure of the tribal elders seems almost to break her, the government arrests and imprisons those same elders for performing "obscene" pagan dances. Stiya is right and good; all the others are wrong, bad and dirty—very, very dirty. Bergess could not emphasize too much the filth and the odors she imagined in Stiya's village.

There are a number of authentic memoirs and autobiographies of Indian women who went away to Indian Boarding School around 1900. Helen Sekaquaptewa describes the experience in her book *Me and Mine: The Life Story of Helen Sekaquaptewa,* and Polingasi Qoyawayma (Elizabeth Q. White) also describes her experiences after returning from a government boarding school in her book *No Turning Back.* Although the readjustment to village life was not easy for these young Indian women, still the reader is struck by the overwhelming love and respect that the women have for their families and communities despite the numerous conflicts that did arise between the boarding school graduates and village traditionalists.

By contrast, the Stiya character Bergess created is detached from land and from village life. The Stiya character has no affection for any family member; every aspect of Pueblo life is repugnant; vile odors and flies abound. Stiya is filled with self-loathing when she remembers that she grew up in this place. She has only loathing for the traditional Pueblo ways. Stiya wonders how she can possibly endure the squalor, and these questions were exactly the sort that the U.S. Department of War wanted Indian School graduates to ask themselves. It was never too late for a Carlisle graduate to move to the city.

All Carlisle Indian School graduates who returned to their home reservations received a copy of *Stiya* in an attempt to inoculate them against their "uncivilized" families and communities. I don't know what year this was, but since Aunt Susie was already married to Uncle Walter, it must have been around 1900.

As soon as the parcels from Carlisle began to arrive at the post office, there must have been a stir of excitement among the Carlisle graduates. Those who had graduated some years before would have been one of the first to finish reading *Stiya* because she loved to read. Grandma A'mooh began reading the book but, as she read, she became increasingly incensed at the libelous portrayal of Pueblo life and people. There was a particularly mendacious passage concerning the Pueblo practice of drying meat in the sun. The meat was described as bloody and covered with flies. Grandma A'mooh was outraged.

About this time, Aunt Susie came over. Aunt Susie loved discussions and she was anxious to find out what Grandma thought about the book. But Grandma A'mooh was in no mood for discussion; she told Aunt Susie the only place for this book was in the fire, and she lifted the lid on her cookstove to drop in the book.

Aunt Susie was a scholar and a storyteller; she believed the *Stiya* book was important evidence of the lies and the racism and bad faith of the U.S. government with the Pueblo people. Grandma A'mooh didn't care about preserving historical evidence of racist, anti-Indian propaganda; a book's lies should be burned just as witchcraft paraphernalia is destroyed. Arguments and face-to-face confrontations between mother-in-law and daughter-in-law were avoided if possible, but that day they argued over a book.

Aunt Susie could not persuade my great-grandmother that the book should be spared for future Pueblo historians. So finally Aunt Susie said, "Well, if you are going to burn the book, then give it to me." According to Pueblo etiquette, it would have been unthinkable for my great-grandmother to refuse her daughter-in-law's request for the book, especially since my great-grandmother was about to destroy it. So Grandma A'mooh gave Aunt Susie her copy of the *Stiya* book, and our side of the family didn't have a copy of the notorious book. Years passed before I ever saw a copy of the book, in the rare book room of the University of New Mexico Library in Albuquerque.

Jamaica Kincaid
(b. 1949)

When I was a child I loved to read. I loved *Jane Eyre* especially and read it over and over. I didn't know anyone else who liked to read except my mother, and it got me in a lot of trouble because it made me into a thief and a liar. I stole books, and I stole money to buy them. . . . Books brought me the greatest satisfaction. Just to be alone, reading, under the house, with lizards and spiders running around . . .

"THROUGH WEST INDIAN EYES"

Books like *Stiya,* purportedly written by Indians about Indian life, still outnumber books actually written by Indians. It is because of books like *Stiya* that Native American communities concern themselves with the origins and authorship of so-called Indian novels and Indian poetry. Books have been the focus of the struggle for the control of the Americas from the start. The great libraries of the Americas were destroyed in 1540 because the Spaniards feared the political and spiritual power of books authored by the indigenous people. As Vine Deloria has pointed out, non-Indians are still more comfortable with Indian books written by non-Indians than they are with books by Indian authors.

Now, fewer than five hundred years after the great libraries of the Americas were burned, a great blossoming of Native American writers is under way.

—from *Yellow Woman and a Beauty of the Spirit*

Jiri Langer

(1894–1943)

Poet, folklorist, and mystic, Jiri Langer grew up in Prague in a comfortable and not particularly observant middle-class Jewish home, and sought a mystical rebirth in the tiny isolated Chassidic villages of eastern Galicia. Chassidism has ancient roots but has evolved since the mid-eighteenth century into the forms he found. It was a world that ended in the Holocaust.

Langer gathered stories and customs of rabbi-saints and their followers into Nine Gates to the Chassidic Mysteries *(1937), a work of folklore, anthropology, and devotion. Entertaining to read, as Langer intended. "It is not the purpose of this book to present a philosophical analysis of Chassidic learning. Certainly it is easy enough to bore one's readers and misuse their patience, but it is not godly." Chassidic society had a great reverence for books and a passion for reading, as Langer describes here.*

Books are greatly respected here, worshipped, in fact. Nobody, for instance, sits on a bench if there is a book anywhere on it. That would be an affront to the book. We never leave a book face downwards or upside down, but always face upwards. If a book falls to the ground we pick it up and kiss it. When we have finished reading we kiss the book before we put it away. To throw it aside, or put other things on top of it is a sin. Yet the books are nearly all woefully dilapidated by constant use. When a book is so badly torn that it cannot be used, the caretaker takes it to the cemetery and buries it. Even the smallest scrap of paper with Hebrew characters printed on it must not be left lying about on the floor, or trodden on; it must be buried. For every Hebrew letter is a name of God. We never leave books open except when we are actually learning from them. If we are obliged to slip away for a moment, and do not wish to close the book, we may leave it open so as not to lose the place, but we must cover it with a cloth. If anyone notices another person going away from a book without closing or covering it, he goes over and shuts it himself; but first he will look at the open page and read a few lines of it. If he were to shut the book without reading it at all, his act of closing it would weaken *the power of memorizing* in the other person who left the book open. The parchment scroll of the Law, which is hand-written, is held in even greater respect than printed books.

The Nazi occupation of Czechoslovakia in 1939 presented drastic choices to Jews: one of Langer's brothers committed suicide rather than go to his death in a concentration camp, the other escaped to France and then to England. The Gestapo was open to bribes, and the Danube route was open to Istanbul and then to Palestine, where Langer had long wished to go. For the October journey he packed his suitcases with two hundred books, which helped him very little to eat or stay warm when the slow, open barge on the Danube foundered because of Nazi harassment and freezing weather. He arrived in Palestine in mid-February, already ill with the nephritis that eventually killed him. He bequeathed his books to the Tel Aviv library, and on his deathbed this great reader was able to see the proofs of his small book of poetry that he called Me'at Tsori (A Little Balsam).

The Torah is the holiest of all things for us—the Five Books of Moses in Hebrew, exquisitely and faultlessly written, in black china-ink, on white parchment calf leather, by the hands of a highly skilled scribe. It is a scroll several yards long whose two ends are wound on two wooden sticks. We call it the Tree of Life.

The parchment scroll of the Torah is most precious. So also is the velvet mantle in which we clothe it; beautifully embroidered, it is adorned with the ancient symbol of the six-pointed shield of David. On the tips of the Tree of Life we place silver crowns with little bells; on the neck of the scroll, wrapped in its mantle, we hang a little silver hand with the index finger extended, and on the scroll itself a silver shield. The Torah is kept in the House of Prayer, in a sacred ark behind a magnificent curtain.

On the holy Sabbath and festivals, when the Torah is carried through the synagogue during the services, we rise from our seats before it with greater respect than other peoples before their kings. We touch and kiss its mantle. If—God forbid—by an unhappy chance the Torah should fall to the ground, we should fast seven times to cleanse away the disgrace. When for any reason the scroll can no longer be used for reading aloud, we bury it in the cemetery with due honour.

God has entered into the Torah and its holy letters, and in this way has given Himself to us. Before the world was, the Torah was, the mysterious Law of God. It was written *in white fire on black fire,* says the Talmud. And in the holy Zohar it is written: "God and the Torah and Israel are one and the same."

The Torah is read out to the people every Sabbath and festival. In the course of the year we read it right through and begin again at the beginning. This has been going on for thousands of years. It is not easy to read from the Torah, for it has no vowels and no diacritical marks to distinguish the letters. You cannot recognize the Hebrew *ch* from *k, v* from *b, s* from *t,* and so on. Every word has its own melody and has to be intoned when read out. The next word has an entirely different melody. A skilled reader must know all this by heart if he is not to cut a sorry figure. A devout audience is very critical and excitable.

Each little letter of the Torah hides a profound mystery. The more sublime mysteries are contained in the vowels while those that are still more sublime are to be found in the annotations. But the most sublime mysteries of all lie submerged in the undefined sea of whiteness which surrounds the letters on all sides. No one is able to unravel this mystery, none there are that can fathom it. So infinite is the mystery of the whiteness of the

parchment that the entire world we live in is incapable of com-
prehending it. No vessel is fit to receive it. Only in the world to
come will it be understood. Then shall be read not what is
written in the Torah, but what is not written: the white parchment.

There are thousands upon thousands of readers who are adept at reading swiftly and impeccably from the Torah. But none
indeed can be compared with the holy Reb Urele of Strelisk!

The holy Reb Sholem of Belz once came to Strelisk for the
festival of Pentecost. It was on this festival that God gave us the
ten commandments. Every year at Pentecost we read the appropriate chapter in the Torah. Reb Sholem had been invited to
come and see how his teacher read.

All at once the parchment disappeared before Sholem's sight
and he beheld the Torah as it had been before the creation of
the world: *a white flame on a black flame.*

Naturally only a disciple like the holy Reb Sholem can behold the sacred Torah, and even then only when it is read by a
saint like the holy Urele. . . .

Langer wrote this passage from Reb Urele's point of view:

When I was a little boy and the teacher had just taught me to
read, he once showed me two little letters, like square dots in
the prayer book, and said: "Urele, you see these two letters side
by side? That's the monogram of God's name, and wherever
you see these two quadrangular dots side by side, you must
pronounce the name of God at that spot, even if it is not written
in full." I continued reading with my teacher until we came to a
colon. It also consisted of two square dots, only instead of being
side by side they were one above the other. I imagined that this
must also be the monogram of God's name and so I pronounced
the name of God at this spot. But my teacher told me:

"No, no, Urele, that does not mean the name of God. Only

where there are two sitting nicely side by side, where the one looks on the other as an equal—only there is the name of God; where one is under the other and the other is raised above his fellow—there the word of God is not. . . ."

—from *Nine Gates to the Chassidic Mysteries*

Laura Jensen

(b. 1948)

For her quiet, harrowing poetry, Laura Jensen has received grants from the National Endowment for the Arts, the Ingram Merrill Foundation, the Washington State Arts Commission, and, in 1993, the Lila Acheson Wallace-Readers Digest Writers' Award. She lives in Tacoma, Washington.

Destinations

The smell of cooked ground turkey is as heavy
as the sandalwood incense I burn by the sink
where the dishes dry in the rack. A wealthy time
superimposes indecision on an unclear, fattened
image, hazy in light from the white evening
window. The plants may blossom before summer ends.

I walk in the evening, leave the harsh
shouts of the crowd of children or the stereo
blaring downstairs or the sounds passing cars
make at the corner stop sign. The dark eases
some of this, when wind rises and the ash leaves
sigh, but in the heat of the early evening
I walk past the houses where their sprinklers
wash the lawns in that slow repetition.

I cannot bring myself to go nowhere. I cannot
visit the crowded park where the sounds of people
multiply. I need a destination. The last time
I walked I left twenty-four exposures, over a year
in pictures, at the Safeway. There is a book at
the library. And I need to borrow a saw from home.

My father insists on wrapping it in newspaper
like a fish for me while I look at my pictures
with my mother. Sometimes I forget
my friend who stands pale on my porch
visiting from California, or the poets at the
wintry marina, or one who looks up laughing,
sun brightening her deck and the freeway below it
and the friend who came back from Montana
and her daughter petting the cat. (The cat had
watched mole holes in the garden, then vanished
the next day and was never heard from again.)

My father wraps the saw and says he bought that
before I was born, when they lived at the old place.
When he was in England, some sergeants got him
to make a scabbard for their axes, and a scabbard
for another axe at the hospital. Pharmacists
were jacks of all trades then, I suppose.

The book from the library keeps me up all weekend.
It is about Christina, in England after World War One,
where her husband died in a PBS serial I saw
three times and kept the music on my tape recorder.

At the end all her plans have turned out badly. She
rushes a fence in the sunset. The whole story suddenly ends.
I cry for an hour. I have not cried like that,
over anything, for a long, long time.

　　　—from *Shelter*

Frederick Douglass

(1817?–1895)

Frederick Douglass was born into slavery on the Eastern Shore of Maryland around 1817. His owners, named Auld, having made the mistake of teaching young Douglass the alphabet and how to spell simple words, came to see the danger of allowing him access to newspapers and books. In his presence, Hugh Auld shouted that "learning would spoil *the best nigger [sic] in the world." Douglass converted into teachers "all the little white boys" he met on the streets of Baltimore, and got them to teach him how to read from bits of print he found in the gutter. He says he learned to write on boards and on the tops of flour barrels.*

A change of owners brought Douglass extremely cruel treatment until one day he turned on his tormentor. From that moment, Douglass was determined to become his own master. He bided his time and at the age of twenty-one, hopped a train out of Baltimore and went on to New York, where he discovered how few opportunities there were for a free Negro to earn a living. He had a letter of introduction to Nathan Johnson, a prosperous Negro in New Bedford, and it was Johnson who suggested he take the name "Douglass" from Sir Walter Scott's Lady of the Lake, *which Johnson had been reading at the time.*

Every week, Douglass read William Lloyd Garrison's Liberator *and was so deeply moved he became a regular subscriber. He says, "The paper became my meat and my drink, my soul was set all on fire. . . ." He began to attend abolitionist meetings and took a job as a lecturer for the Massachusetts Anti-Slavery Society.*

Douglass continued his self-education and went on to become an orator, a writer, an editor, and a leader in the national abolition movement. After Reconstruction, he became consul general to the Republic of Haiti, and an international spokesman for his people.

The following anecdote, "Learning to Read and Write," is from My Bondage and My Freedom, *originally a small volume of 125 pages, which sold for fifty cents in 1845. By 1848, 11,000 copies had been published in this country and it had gone through nine editions in England.*

Douglass points up the power of knowledge as he narrates the course of his literacy, and connects it directly to his next enormous life-change—freedom.

The frequent hearing of my mistress reading the Bible—for she often read aloud when her husband was absent—soon awakened my curiosity in respect to this *mystery* of reading, and roused in me the desire to learn. Having no fear of my kind mistress, . . . I frankly asked her to teach me to read; and, without hesitation, the dear woman began the task, and very soon, by her assistance, I was master of the alphabet, and could spell words of three or four letters. My mistress seemed almost as proud of my progress, as if I had been her own child; and, supposing that her husband would be as well pleased, she made no secret of what she was doing for me. Indeed, she exultingly told him of the aptness of her pupil, of her intention to per-servere in teaching me, and of the duty which she felt it teach me, at least to read *the Bible*. . . .

Master Hugh was amazed at the simplicity of his spouse, and, probably for the first time, he unfolded to her the true philoso-phy of slavery, and the peculiar rules necessary to be observed by masters and mistresses, in the management of their human chattels. Mr. Auld promptly forbade the continuance of her instruction; telling her, in the first place, that the thing itself was unlawful; that it was also unsafe, and could only lead to mis-chief. To use his own words, further, he said, "if you give a nigger an inch, he will take an ell"; . . . "it would forever unfit him for the duties of a slave"; and "as to himself, learning would do him of harm—making him disconsolate and un-happy"; . . . "If you learn him now to read, he'll want to know how to write; and, this accomplished, he'll be running away with himself." . . .

His discourse was the first decidedly anti-slavery lecture to which it had been my lot to listen. Mrs. Auld evidently felt the force of his remarks, and, like an obedient wife, began to shape her course in the direction indicated by her husband. The effect of his words, *on me,* was neither slight nor transitory. . . . "Very well," thought I; "knowledge unfits a child to be a slave." I instinctively assented to the proposition; and from that moment I understood the direct pathway from slavery to freedom. . . .

I lived in the family of Master Hugh, at Baltimore, seven years, during which time—as the almanac makers say of the weather—my condition was variable. . . . My mistress . . . not only ceased to instruct me, herself, but set her face as flint against my learning to read by any means. . . . I was most narrowly watched in all my movements. If I remained in a separate room from the family for any considerable length of time, I was sure to be suspected of having a book, and was at once called upon to give an account of myself. All this, however, was entirely *too late.* The first, and never to be retraced, step had been taken. In teaching me the alphabet, in the days of her simplicity and kindness, my mistress had given me the *"inch,"* and now, no ordinary precaution could prevent me from taking the *"ell."*

Seized with a determination to learn to read, at any cost, I hit upon many expedients to accomplish this desired end. The plea which I mainly adopted, and the one by which I was most successful, was that of using my young white playmates, with whom I met in the street, as teachers. I used to carry; almost constantly, a copy of Webster's spelling book in my pocket; and, when sent on errands, or when play time was allowed me, I would step, with my young friends, aside, and take a lesson in spelling. I generally paid my *tuition fee* to the boys, with bread, which I also carried in my pocket. For a single bisquit, any of my hungry little comrades would give me a lesson more valuable to me than bread. Not every one, however, demanded this consideration, for there were those who took pleasure in teaching me, whenever I had a chance to be taught by them. I am strongly tempted to give the names of two or three of those little boys, as a slight testimonial of the gratitude and affection I bear them, but prudence forbids; not that it would injure me, but it might, possibly, embarrass them; for it is almost an unpardonable offense to do anything, directly or indirectly, to promote a slave's freedom, in a slave state. . . .

When I was about thirteen years old, and had succeeded in learning to read, every increase of knowledge, especially respecting the Free States, added something to the almost intolerable burden of the thought—"I AM A SLAVE FOR LIFE." . . . Fortunately, or unfortunately, about this time in my life, I had made enough money to buy what was then a very popular school book, viz: the "Columbian Orator." I bought this addition to my library, of Mr. Knight, on Thames street, Fell's Point, Baltimore, and paid him fifty cents for it. . . . I met there one of Sheridan's mighty speeches, on the subject of the Catholic Emancipation, Lord Chatham's speech on the American war, and speeches by the great William Pitt and by Fox. These were all choice documents to me, and I read them, over and over again, with an interest that was ever increasing, because it was ever gaining in intelligence; for the more I read them, the better I understood them. The reading of these speeches added much to my limited stock of language, and enabled me to give tongue to many interesting thoughts, which had frequently flashed through my soul, and died away for want of utterance. . . . The dialogue and the speeches were all redolent of the principles of liberty, and poured floods of light on the nature and character of slavery. With a book of this kind in my hand, my own human nature, and the facts of my experience, to help me, I was equal to a contest with the religious advocates of slavery. . . . The more I read, the more I was led to abhor and detest slavery, and my enslavers. . . . As I read, behold! the very discontent so graphically predicted by Master

Hugh, had already come upon me. I was no longer the light-hearted, gleesome boy, full of mirth and play, as when I landed first at Baltimore. Knowledge had come; light had penetrated the moral dungeon where I dwelt; and, behold! there lay the bloody whip, for my back, and here was the iron chain; and my good, *kind master,* he was the author of my situation.

—from *My Bondage and My Freedom*

Mike Rose

Mike Rose began teaching children in the Teacher Corps in El Monte, a traditionally Mexican-American community in East Los Angeles. Since then he has often worked with students labeled "slow" or remedial as he was at one time in his own life. "I was lucky," he says, "I got redefined."

After serving in the Vietnam War, he tutored English and reading in the Veteran's Program housed in an old UCLA Extension Program building in depressed downtown LA. His students had sustained injuries of the body and mind, and were people with what Rose calls "dreary school memories," whose response to any institution was an "existential gag reflex." They were also people who desperately wanted to change their lives.

As their teacher, Rose wanted them to think about thinking and to read with a critical eye. He wanted to give them "a little insight into how to pick the academic lock." They had to "be let into the academic club."

What emerged for Rose, after teaching adults and becoming increasingly involved in counseling and crisis intervention, was the "majesty of small progress." It was a powerful revelation, he says, that "even at the extreme, there is possibility."

The Veteran's Program, like many language and literacy programs, paid teachers by the course. Wages were fairly low, so I had to teach a lot and over the years ended up working in a variety of settings. I tutored in a community college writing center and counseled CETA workers in a summer job-training program. For a brief while, the administrators of the Veteran's Program tried offering some English, humanities, and mathematics courses right on a military facility. So every Tuesday and Thursday evening I drove the freeway out to an Air Force base on the southwestern edge of Los Angeles County, engaging a roomful of uniformed men and women in discussion about *The Old Man and the Sea* or a Grace Paley story or "Blackie, the Electric Rembrandt." Extension also ran a college preparation program for people in low-level law-enforcement jobs—parole aides and the like—people who came from poor backgrounds and had only high school diplomas, if that. The program was housed in the downtown center, so I would walk from the third floor to the first to teach a survey of world literature: Introductory Humanities. Each class had an intimidating range of ability. There was Domingo, a parole aide whose gang tattoos had faded along his weathered skin, whose writing was a halting scribble. But there was also Reba, who carried two notebooks and was very quiet and who, it turned out, was a more fluent and assured writer than speaker—for in writing her self-consciousness could not muffle her words.

My own higher education did not include serious study of the classics or of European literature before the twentieth century, so I didn't know much about some of the books I had to teach. I had read *Don Quixote* and Voltaire and Dostoyevski, but I knew little about Greek or Roman drama, or the epics and tales of the Middle Ages, or Dante. So I was explaining things like the origins of Greek tragedy, the evolution of its structure, and the way it was performed that I had learned in a flurry the week before: sketching out the stage on butcher paper, acting out alone in my apartment the placement of characters and the turns of the chorus, doing the things I would do later with the class to help them visualize the action. I drew maps and flowcharts of the events and stood people up and marched them through key scenes. Because the language of so much of what we were reading was difficult, I prepared lists of questions to guide the students' study, showed them how to read play dialogue, asked them to talk to me about the basic themes of the books—honor, vaulting ambition, betrayal—and relate those themes to their own lives and to the events currently in the news. I tried to humanize the distant eras we were studying—

telling the class, for example, about the German burgomaster who wrote to Voltaire asking, "In confidence, is there a God or not?" (asking, too, that the philosopher answer by return mail). But still, for some, it was the wrong time and place—the reading was laborious and remote. They would need courses preliminary to this one, and they would need a dramatic change in the demands and derailing seductions and random catastrophes that their neighborhoods threw their way. Domingo, the tattooed parole aide, dropped the class after three weeks.

For others, it worked. The readings started to take hold—in a variety of ways. Blanche, who was about fifty, sat there laughing out loud as she read a prose rendering of Chaucer: "It was the best bout she'd had in years—he thrust away like a madman, hard and deep." "Hard and deep," sighed Blanche, shaking her head. She started tapping the desk: "Mmm hmm. Hard and deep. My, my." Reba, the quiet one, began spending her break asking me questions, wanting to know, in her soft voice, what her library might have that would help her. She asked me about college. Did I think she'd have a chance? I got her a catalogue from the local community college, and we started talking about courses.

And there was Olga. Olga reminded me of the tough girls I had seen in El Monte. Hair teased, heavy mascara. She was older—the lines of a hard life across her forehead, along her cheeks—but she was still rebellious. She fought me all the way on *Macbeth*. She complained about the language—"How do you expect us to *read* this stuff?"—and about the length, and about its sheer distance from us. I'd sit with her and drag her through a scene, paraphrasing a speech, summarizing a conflict. Sometimes I'd force her to direct her anger at the play, to talk at it, make her articulate exactly why she hated it, be as precise as she could about how it made her feel to sit here with this book. Finally, we finished *Macbeth*. One night in that eggshell basement lunchroom, she wrapped her hands around her cola and

began to tap it on the table: "You know, Mike, people always
hold this shit over you, make you . . . make you feel stupid
with their fancy talk. But now *I've* read it, I've read Shakespeare, I can say I, *Olga*, have read it. I won't tell you I like it,
'cause I don't know if I do or I don't. But I like knowing what
it's about."

I have a vivid memory of sitting on the edge of my bed—I
was twelve or thirteen maybe—and listening with unease to a
minute or so of classical music. I don't know if I found it as I
was turning the dial, searching for the Johnny Otis Show or the
live broadcast from Scribner's Drive-In, or if the tuner had
simply drifted into another station's signal. Whatever happened,
the music caught me in a disturbing way, and I sat there, letting
it play. It sounded like the music I heard in church, weighted,
funereal. Eerie chords echoing from another world, I leaned
over, my fingers on the tuner, and, in what I remember as
almost a twitch, I turned the knob away from the melody of
these strange instruments. My reaction to the other high culture
I encountered—*The Iliad* and Shakespeare and some school-
book poems by Longfellow and Lowell—was similar, though
less a visceral rejection and more a rejecting disinterest, a sense
of irrelevance. The few Shakespearean scenes I did know—saw
on television, or read or heard in grammar school—seemed
snooty and put-on, kind of dumb. Not the way I wanted to talk.
Not interesting to me.

There were few books in our house: a couple of thin stories
read to me as a child in Pennsylvania *(The Little Boy Who Ran
Away,* an *Uncle Remus* sampler), the M volume of the *World
Book Encyclopedia* (which I found one day in the trash behind
the secondhand store), and the Hollywood tabloids my mother
would bring home from work. I started buying lots of Superman and Batman comic books because I loved the heroes' virtu-
ous omnipotence—comic books, our teachers said, were bad for
us—and, once I discovered them, I began checking out science

fiction novels from my grammar school library. Other reading material appeared—the instructions to my chemistry set, which I half understood and only half followed, and, eventually, my astronomy books, which seemed to me to be magical rather than discursive texts. So it was that my early intrigue with literacy—my lifts and escapes with language and rhythm—came from comic books and science fiction, from the personal, nonscientific worlds I created with bits and pieces of laboratory and telescopic technology, came, as well, from the Italian stories I heard my uncles and parents tell. It came, too, from the music my radio brought me: music that wove in and out of my days, lyrics I'd repeat and repeat—"gone, gone, gone, jumpin' like a catfish on a pole"—wanting to catch that sound, seeking other emotional frontiers, other places to go. Like rocker Joe Ely, I picked up Chicago on my transistor radio.

Except for school exercises and occasional cards my mother made me write to my uncles and aunts, I wrote very little during my childhood; it wasn't until my last year in high school that Jack MacFarland sparked an interest in writing. And though I developed into a good reader, I performed from moderately well to terribly on other sorts of school literacy tasks. From my reading I knew vocabulary words, and I did okay on spelling tests—though I never lasted all that long in spelling bees—but I got C's and D's on the ever-present requests to diagram sentences and label parts of speech. The more an assignment was related to real reading, the better I did; the more analytic, self-contained, and divorced from context, the lousier I performed. Today some teachers would say I was a concrete thinker. To be sure, the development of my ability to decode words and read sentences took place in school, but my orientation to reading—the way I conceived of it, my purpose for doing it—occurred within the tight and untraditional confines of my home. The quirks and textures of my immediate environment combined with my escapist fantasies to draw me to books. "It is what we are excited about that educates us," writes social historian Elizabeth Ewen. It is what taps our curiosity

and dreams. Eventually, the books that seemed so distant, those
Great Books, would work their way into my curiosity, would
influence the way I framed problems and the way I wrote. But
that would come much later—first with Jack MacFarland
(mixed with his avant-garde countertradition), then with my
teachers at Loyola and UCLA—an excitement and curiosity
shaped by others and connected to others, a cultural and linguistic heritage received not from some pristine conduit, but
exchanged through the heat of human relation.

Virginia Woolf
(1882–1941)

One summer day at Monk's House, Virginia Woolf
"went in and found the table laden with [unread]
books": "I looked in and sniffed them all. I could not
resist carrying . . . one off and broaching it."

READING NOTEBOOKS

A friend of mine recently suggested that education is one
culture embracing another. It's interesting to think of the very
different ways that metaphor plays out. Education can be a
desperate, smothering embrace, an embrace that denies the
needs of the other. But education can also be an encouraging,
communal embrace—at its best an invitation, an opening. Several years ago, I was sitting in on a workshop conducted by the
Brazilian educator Paulo Freire. It was the first hour or so and
Freire, in his sophisticated, accented English, was establishing
the theoretical base of his literacy pedagogy—heady stuff, a
blend of Marxism, phenomenology, and European existential-
ism. I was two seats away from Freire; in front of me and next
to him was a younger man, who, puzzled, finally interrupted
the speaker to ask a question. Freire acknowledged the question

and, as he began answering, he turned and quickly touched the man's forearm. Not patronizing, not mushy, a look and a tap as if to say: "You and me right now, let's go through this together." Embrace. With Jack MacFarland it was an embrace: no-nonsense and cerebral, but a relationship in which the terms of endearment were the image in a poem, a play's dialogue, the winding narrative journey of a novel.

More often than we admit, a failed education is social more than intellectual in origin. And the challenge that has always faced American education, that it has sometimes denied and sometimes doggedly pursued, is how to create both the social and cognitive means to enable a diverse citizenry to develop their ability. It is an astounding challenge: the complex and wrenching struggle to actualize the potential not only of the privileged but, too, of those who have lived here for a long time generating a culture outside the mainstream and those who, like my mother's parents and my father, immigrated with cultural traditions of their own. This painful but generative mix of language and story can result in clash and dislocation in our communities, but it also gives rise to new speech, new stories, and once we appreciate the richness of it, new invitations to literacy.

—from *Lives on the Boundary*

Richard Wright

(1908–1960)

Richard Wright was born on a plantation near Natchez, Mississippi. Later in his life, he went to Chicago and got a job in the Federal Writers' Project (the WPA). Native Son *(1940) brought him recognition and financial independence, and after World War II he moved to Paris, where he lived until his death.*

Wright was always a reader and describes reading second-hand copies of Flynn's Detective Weekly, Argosy, *and* All-Story Magazine. *When he was fifteen, with fewer than three years of formal schooling, he went to work and began living on his own. The following passage is from* Black Boy *(1945), his autobiographical novel.*

One morning I arrived early at work and went into the bank lobby where the Negro porter was mopping. I stood at a counter and picked up the Memphis *Commercial Appeal* and began my free reading of the press. I came finally to the editorial page and saw an article dealing with one H. L. Mencken. I knew by hearsay that he was the editor of the *American Mercury,* but aside from that I knew nothing about him. The article was a furious denunciation of Mencken, concluding with one, hot, short sentence: "Mencken is a fool."

I wondered what on earth this Mencken had done to call down upon him the scorn of the South. The only people I had ever heard denounced in the South were Negroes, and this man was not a Negro. Then what ideas did Mencken hold that made a newspaper like the *Commercial Appeal* castigate him publicly? Undoubtedly he must be advocating ideas that the South did not like. Were there, then, people other than Negroes who criticized the South? I knew that during the Civil War the

South had hated northern whites, but I had not encountered such hate during my life. Knowing no more of Mencken than I did at that moment, I felt a vague sympathy for him. Had not the South, which had assigned me the role of a non-man, cast at him its hardest words?

Now, how could I find out about this Mencken? There was a huge library near the riverfront, but I knew that Negroes were not allowed to patronize its shelves any more than they were the parks and playgrounds of the city. I had gone into the library several times to get books for the white men on the job. Which of them would now help me to get books? And how could I read them without causing concern to the white men with whom I worked? I had so far been successful in hiding my thoughts and feelings from them, but I knew that I would create hostility if I went about this business of reading in a clumsy way.

I weighed the personalities of the men on the job. There was Don, a Jew; but I distrusted him. His position was not much better than mine and I knew that he was uneasy and insecure; he had always treated me in an an offhand, bantering way that barely concealed his contempt. I was afraid to ask him to help me to get books; his frantic desire to demonstrate a racial solidarity with the whites against Negroes might make him betray me.

Then how about the boss? No, he was a Baptist and I had the suspicion that he would not be quite able to comprehend why a black boy would want to read Mencken. There were other white men on the job whose attitudes showed clearly that they were Kluxers or sympathizers, and they were out of the question.

There remained only one man whose attitude did not fit into an anti-Negro category, for I had heard the white men refer to him as a "Pope lover." He was an Irish Catholic and was hated by the white Southerners. I knew that he read books, because I had got him volumes from the library several times. Since he, too, was an object of hatred, I felt that he might refuse me but would hardly betray me. I hesitated, weighing and balancing the imponderable realities.

One morning I paused before the Catholic fellow's desk.

"I want to ask you a favor," I whispered to him.

"What is it?"

"I want to read. I can't get books from the library. I wonder if you'd let me use your card?"

He looked at me suspiciously.

"My card is full most of the time," he said.

"I see," I said and waited, posing my question silently.

"You're not trying to get me into trouble, are you, boy?" he asked, staring at me.

"Oh, no, sir."

"What book do you want?"

"A book by H. L. Mencken."

"Which one?"

"I don't know. Has he written more than one?"

"He has written several."

"I didn't know that."

"What makes you want to read Mencken?"

"Oh, I just saw his name in the newspaper," I said.

"It's good of you to want to read," he said. "But you ought to read the right things."

I said nothing. Would he want to supervise my reading?

"Let me think," he said. "I'll figure out something."

I turned from him and he called me back. He stared at me quizzically.

"Richard, don't mention this to the other white men," he said.

"I understand," I said. "I won't say a word." A few days later he called me to him.

"I've got a card in my wife's name," he said. "Here's mine."

"Thank you, sir."

"Do you think you can manage it?"

"I'll manage fine," I said.

"If they suspect you, you'll get in trouble," he said.

"I'll write the same kind of notes to the library that you wrote when you sent me for books," I told him. "I'll sign your name."

He laughed.

"Go ahead. Let me see what you get," he said.

That afternoon I addressed myself to forging a note.

Now, what were the names of books written by H. L. Mencken? I did not know any of them. I finally wrote what I thought would be a foolproof note: *Dear Madam: Will you please let this nigger boy*—I used the word "nigger" to make the librarian feel that I could not possibly be the author of the note—*have some books by H. L. Mencken?* I forged the white man's name.

I entered the library as I had always done when on errands for whites, but I felt that I would somehow slip up and betray myself. I doffed my hat, stood a respectful distance from the desk, looked as unbookish as possible, and waited for the white patrons to be taken care of. When the desk was clear of people, I still waited. The white librarian looked at me.

"What do you want, boy?"

As though I did not possess the power of speech, I stepped forward and simply handed her the forged note, not parting my lips.

"What books by Mencken does he want?" she asked. "I don't know, ma'am," I said, avoiding her eyes.

"Who gave you this card?"

"Mr. Falk," I said.

"Where is he?"

"He's at work, at the M— Optical Company," I said. "I've been in here for him before."

"I remember," the woman said. "But he never wrote notes like this."

Oh, God, she's suspicious. Perhaps she would not let me have the books? If she had turned her back at that moment, I would have ducked out the door and never gone back. Then I thought of a bold idea.

"You can call him up, ma'am," I said, my heart pounding.

"You're not using these books, are you?" she asked pointedly.

"Oh, no, ma'am. I can't read."

"I don't know what he wants by Mencken," she said under her breath.

I knew now that I had won; she was thinking of other things and the race question had gone out of her mind. She went to the shelves. Once or twice she looked over her shoulder at me, as though she was still doubtful. Finally she came forward with two books in her hand.

"I'm sending him two books," she said. "But tell Mr. Falk to come in next time, or send me the names of the books he wants. I don't know what he wants to read."

I said nothing, She stamped the card and handed me the books. Not daring to glance at them, I went out of the library, fearing that the woman would call me back for further questioning. A block away from the library I opened one of the books and read a title: *A Book ot Prefaces.* I was nearing my nineteenth birthday and I did not know how to pronounce the word "preface." I thumbed the pages and saw strange words and strange names. I shook my head, disappointed. I looked at the other book; it was called *Prejudices.* I knew what that word meant; I had heard it all my life. And right off I was on guard against Mencken's books. Why would a man want to call a book *Prejudices*? The word was so stained with all my memories of racial hate that I could not conceive of anybody using it for a title. Perhaps I had made a mistake about Mencken? A man who had prejudices must be wrong.

When I showed the books to Mr. Falk, he looked at me and frowned.

"That librarian might telephone you," I warned him,

"That's all right," he said. "But when you're through reading those books, I want you to tell me what you get out of them."

That night in my rented room, while letting the hot water run over my can of pork and beans in the sink, I opened *A Book of Prefaces* and began to read. I was jarred and shocked by the style, the clear, clean, sweeping sentences. Why did he write like that? And how did one write like that? I pictured the man as a raging demon, slashing with his pen, consumed with hate, denouncing everything American, extolling everything European or German, laughing at the weaknesses of people, mocking God, authority. What was this? I stood up, trying to read what reality lay behind the meaning of the words. . . . Yes, this man was fighting, fighting with words. He was using words as a weapon, using them as one would use a club. Could words be weapons? Well, yes, for here they were. Then, maybe, perhaps I could use them as a weapon? No. It frightened me. I read on and what amazed me was not what he said, but how on earth anybody had the courage to say it.

Occasionally I glanced up to reassure myself that I was alone in the room. Who were these men about whom Mencken was talking so passionately? Who was Anatole France? Joseph Conrad? Sinclair Lewis, Sherwood Anderson, Dostoevski, George Moore, Gustave Flaubert, Maupassant, Tolstoy, Frank Harris, Mark Twain, Thomas Hardy, Arnold Bennett, Stephen Crane, Zola, Norris, Gorky, Bergson, Ibsen, Balzac, Bernard Shaw, Dumas, Poe, Thomas Mann, O. Henry, Dreiser, H. G. Wells, Gogol, T. S. Eliot, Gide, Baudelaire, Edgar Lee Masters, Stendhal, Turgenev, Huneker, Nietzsche, and scores of others? Were these men *real*? Did they exist or had they existed? And how did one pronounce their names?

I ran across many words whose meanings I did not know, and I either looked them up in a dictionary or, before I had a chance to do that, encountered the word in a context that made its meaning clear. But what strange world was this? I concluded the book with the conviction that I had somehow overlooked something terribly important in life. I had once tried to write, had once reveled in feeling, had let my crude imagination roam, but the impulse to dream had been slowly beaten out of me by experience. Now it surged up again and I hungered for books, new ways of looking and seeing. It was not a matter of believing or disbelieving what I read, but of feeling something new, of being affected by something that made the look of the world different.

As dawn broke I ate my pork and beans, feeling dopey, sleepy. I went to work, but the mood of the book would not die; it lingered, coloring everything I saw, heard, did. I now felt that I knew what the white men were feeling. Merely because I had read a book that had spoken of how they lived and thought, I identified myself with that book. I felt vaguely guilty. Would I, filled with bookish notions, act in a manner that would make the whites dislike me?

I forged more notes and my trips to the library became frequent. Reading grew into a passion. My first serious novel was Sinclair Lewis's *Main Street.* It made me see my boss, Mr. Gerald, and identify him as an American type. I would smile when I saw him lugging his golf bags into the office. I had always felt a vast distance separating me from the boss, and now I felt closer to him, though still distant. I felt now that I knew him, that I could feel the very limits of his narrow life. And this had happened because I had read a novel about a mythical man called George F. Babbitt.

The plots and stories in the novels did not interest me so much as the point of view revealed. I gave myself over to each novel without reserve, without trying to criticize it; it was enough for me to see and feel something different. And for me, everything was something different. Reading was like a drug, a dope. The novels created moods in which I lived for days. But I could not conquer my sense of guilt, my feeling that the white men around me knew that I was changing, that I had begun to regard them differently.

Whenever I brought a book to the job, I wrapped it in newspapers—a habit that was to persist for years in other cities and under other circumstances. But some of the white men pried into my packages when I was absent and they questioned me.

"Boy, what are you reading those books for?"

"Oh, I don't know, sir."

"That's deep stuff you're reading, boy."

"I'm just killing time, sir."

"You'll addle your brains if you don't watch out."

I read Dreiser's *Jennie Gerhardt* and *Sister Carrie* and they revived in me a vivid sense of my mother's suffering; I was overwhelmed. I grew silent, wondering about the life around me. It would have been impossible for me to have told anyone what I derived from these novels, for it was nothing less than a sense of life itself. All my life had shaped me for the realism, the naturalism of the modern novel, and I could not read enough of them.

Steeped in new moods and ideas, I bought a ream of paper and tried to write; but nothing would come, or what did come was flat beyond telling. I discovered that more than desire and feeling were necessary to write and I dropped the idea. Yet I still wondered how it was possible to know people sufficiently to write about them? Could I ever learn about life and people? To me, with my vast ignorance, my Jim Crow station in life, it seemed a task impossible of achievement. I now knew what being a Negro meant. I could endure the hunger. I had learned to live with hate. But to feel that there were feelings denied me, that the very breath of life itself was beyond my reach, that more than anything else hurt, wounded me. I had a new hunger.

In buoying me up, reading also cast me down, made me see what was possible, what I had missed. My tension returned, new, terrible, bitter, surging, almost too great to be contained. I no longer *felt* that the world about me was hostile, killing; I *knew* it. A million times I asked myself what I could do to save myself, and there were no answers. I seemed forever condemned, ringed by walls.

I did not discuss my reading with Mr. Falk, who had lent me his library card; it would have meant talking about myself and that would have been too painful. I smiled each day, fighting desperately to maintain my old behavior, to keep my disposition seemingly sunny. But some of the white men discerned that I had begun to brood.

"Wake up there, boy!" Mr. Olin said one day.

"Sir!" I answered for the lack of a better word.

"You act like you've stolen something," he said.

I laughed in the way I knew he expected me to laugh, but I resolved to be more conscious of myself, to watch my every act, to guard and hide the new knowledge that was dawning within me.

If I went North, would it be possible for me to build a new life then? But how could a man build a life upon vague, unformed yearnings? I wanted to write and I did not even know the English language. I bought English grammars and found them dull. I felt that I was getting a better sense of the language from novels than from grammars. I read hard, discarding a writer as soon as I felt that I had grasped his point of view. At night the printed page stood before my eyes in sleep.

Mrs. Moss, my landlady, asked me one Sunday morning:

"Son, what is this you keep on reading?"

"Oh, nothing. Just novels."

"What you get out of 'em?"

"I'm just killing time," I said.

"I hope you know your own mind," she said in a tone which implied that she doubted if I had a mind.

I knew of no Negroes who read the books I liked and I wondered if any Negroes ever thought of them. I knew that there were Negro doctors, lawyers, newspapermen, but I never saw any of them. When I read a Negro newspaper I never caught the faintest echo of my preoccupation in its pages. I felt trapped and occasionally, for a few days, I would stop reading. But a vague hunger would come over me for books, books that opened up new avenues of feeling and seeing, and again I would forge another note to the white librarian. Again I would read and wonder as only the naïve and unlettered can read and wonder, feeling that I carried a secret, criminal burden about with me each day.

That winter my mother and brother came and we set up housekeeping, buying furniture on the installment plan, being cheated and yet knowing no way to avoid it. I began to eat warm food and to my surprise found that regular meals enabled me to read faster. I may have lived through many illnesses and survived them, never suspecting that I was ill. My brother obtained a job and we began to save toward the trip north, plotting our time, setting tentative dates for departure. I told none of the white men on the job that I was planning to go north; I knew that the moment they felt I was thinking of the North they would change toward me. It would have made them feel that I did not like the life I was living, and because my life was completely conditioned by what they said or did, it would have been tantamount to challenging them.

I could calculate my chances for life in the South as a Negro fairly clearly now.

I could fight the southern whites by organizing with other Negroes, as my grandfather had done. But I knew that I could never win that way; there were many whites and there were but few blacks. They were strong and we were weak. Outright black rebellion could never win. If I fought openly I would die and I did not want to die. News of lynchings were frequent.

I could submit and live the life of a genial slave, but that was impossible. All of my life had shaped me to live by my own feelings and thoughts. I could make up to Bess and marry her and inherit the house. But that, too, would be the life of a slave; if I did that, I would crush to death something within me, and I would hate myself as much as I knew the whites already hated those who had submitted. Neither could I ever willingly present myself to be kicked, as Shorty had done. I would rather have died than do that.

I could drain off my restlessness by fighting with Shorty and Harrison. I had seen many Negroes solve the problem of being black by transferring their hatred of themselves to others with a black skin and fighting them. I would have to be cold to do that, and I was not cold and I could never be.

I could, of course, forget what I had read, thrust the whites out of my mind, forget them; and find release from anxiety and longing in sex and alcohol. But the memory of how my father had conducted himself made that course repugnant. If I did not want others to violate my life, how could I voluntarily violate it myself?

I had no hope whatever of being a professional man. Not only had I been so conditioned that I did not desire it, but the fulfillment of such an ambition was beyond my capabilities. Well-to-do Negroes lived in a world that was almost as alien to me as the world inhabited by whites.

What, then, was there? I held my life in my mind, in my consciousness each day, feeling at times that I would stumble and drop it, spill it forever. My reading had created a vast sense of distance between me and the world in which I lived and tried to make a living, and that sense of distance was increasing each day. My days and nights were one long, quiet, continuously contained dream of terror, tension, and anxiety. I wondered how long I could bear it.

—from *Black Boy*

Antonia White
(1899–1980)

Antonia White is the author of four novels and a book of short stories, all of heartbreakingly fine quality. Elizabeth Bowen wrote that in Frost in May *(1933) "Antonia White's style as a storyteller is as precise, clear and unweighty as Jane Austen's." Although the name of the heroine changed from Nanda Grey to Clara Batchelor in the trilogy (1950–54) that followed* Frost in May, *the novels are roughly autobiographical; but to say this does not take away from their standing as works of art. White's fragile women, who are ill-equipped to be full participants in their society and who break in various ways, are close in intensity to Jean Rhys's powerless women characters. Like Rhys, Antonia White's true subject is madness, when exterior accidents become interior demons. When Nanda reaches for a book, the reader feels danger ahead.*

The naïve quality of Nanda's transgression in the following passage arouses our feelings of protectiveness toward this young reader and of exasperation with her elders. Nanda's trouble with reading begins during a visit from her parents to her convent school. She goes on to worse difficulty after her First Communion when she is sick and reads to pass the time in the school infirmary. We end with part of a meditation on "Dangers of the World" (particularly those presented by reading).

"The nuns have lovely flowers here," said Mrs. Grey romantically. "I suppose they feel they must have *some* light and colour in their lives." She went on poking the bed.

"We've got a Scotch gardener," Nanda told her father. "His name's MacAlister. Mother Frances says he gets up in the middle of the night to curl the petals of the chrysanthemums."

The school bell began to ring.

"I must go," sang out Nanda, with a kind of relief. "That's for Benediction."

"Good gracious, I nearly forgot this," said Mr. Grey, fumbling in the pocket of his overcoat and producing a parcel. "I met Mrs. Appleyard the other day, and she happened to say that it was Marjorie's birthday next week. So I thought perhaps it would be nice for you to give her a present."

"Thank you, Daddy. Yes, I'd like to," said Nanda, though she had certain misgivings.

The present turned out to be a rather nicely illustrated edition of *Dream Days,* a book which Nanda had not read. The pictures of castles and dragons looked exciting; she wondered whether she could somehow manage to skim through it herself before handing it on to Marjorie, who wouldn't, she was pretty sure, think much of it.

"It looks a lovely book," she said rather sadly.

"I'll give you one in your Christmas stocking if you like," Mr. Grey promised.

"You *are* a dear, Daddy," Nanda muttered, fervently kissing him good-bye. "I must simply fly or I'll be late. Good-bye, Mummy."

The others were already lined up by the time she arrived breathlessly in the junior schoolroom; there was only just time to slip *Dream Days* into her desk and snatch up her veil before Mother Frances gave the signal to advance.

After Benediction on Sundays, the Junior School were allowed to read for an hour before supper. Their library consisted of three shelves of *Lives of the Saints* and *Letters from Missionaries* of the early nineteenth century. In a small locked case there were some more frivolous works, including several volumes of Andrew Lang's fairy tales, some Little Folks annuals, *Alice in Wonderland,* and the works of Edward Lear. But these were storybooks, only doled out for an hour or two on the major holidays that occurred two or three times a term. Nanda's own choice for the week, not entirely a free one, since Mildred was the librarian, was a small red *Lives of the English Martyrs.* Being a very quick reader, she came to the end of it while there was still half an hour of "free study" to be filled. She did not want to go over the martyrdoms again, having supped full enough of hangings and drawings and quarterings. In fact, the account of the pressing to death of the Blessed Margaret Clitheroe had nearly turned her sturdy stomach. The exciting green volume of *Dream Days* seemed to burn through her desk; she felt she *must* look at it or go mad. But on the other hand, it was quite obviously a story-book. Probably she had no right to have it in her possession at all; in any case, she ought to ask Mother Frances's permission before actually reading it. She temporised. At any rate, there could be no harm in writing Marjorie's name in it. She took the book out and wrote laboriously on the flyleaf: "Marjorie Appleyard. With best wishes for her birthday. From Fernanda Grey." Her desk was conveniently far from Mother Frances's table, and Mother Frances herself seemed deeply absorbed in correcting exercise books.

Nanda had sternly meant to put *Dream Days* away at once. But somehow page after page slipped over, and before she knew it she was hopelessly enmeshed. She woke with a gasp as a thin, shapely hand blotted out the page in front of her.

"Very interesting, Nanda," said Mother Frances, smoothly. "Is this your library book?"

"No, Mother."

"It's a story-book, isn't it? Did your parents give it you in the parlour?"

"Yes. . . . I mean no, Mother."

"Be truthful, my good child. Which do you mean, yes or no?"

"Well, it was given me to give someone else."

"Oh, indeed," said Mother Frances very softly, opening her harebell eyes surprisingly wide. "Hasn't Mildred told you that we don't take things in the parlour either for ourselves or for other people?"

"Yes, I did, Mother," piped the odious Mildred, who had screwed round on her chair and was fairly goggling with curiosity. "I did, only Nanda was so excited she didn't listen."

"That was a pity, wasn't it, Nanda?" said Mother Frances, sweetly. "I'm afraid perhaps I'll have to take your exemption to remind you about that. And of course, I'll have to take the book as well." As she shut up *Dream Days* she saw the writing on the flyleaf. "Marjorie Appleyard," she mused. "Let's see . . . Marjorie's not *related* to you, is she, Nanda?"

"No, Mother," said Nanda, a little sullenly.

"Just remember, will you, that at Lippington we do not give presents, even birthday presents, except to relatives. We do not encourage particular friendships among little girls."

Nanda was conscious of a hot sense of injustice as Mother Frances moved gracefully away with the offending book under her arm. Her eyes pricked, and she felt horribly homesick. To stop herself from crying, she tried to concentrate once more on the sufferings of Blessed Margaret. "As she lay on the scaffold," she read stubbornly, "with a smile of heavenly patience on her face, the executioners lowered a heavy oaken door on to her prostrate form. On this door they piled a mass of great weights, and, to cause her still more exquisite torment, they" . . . but the rest of the passage was obscured by a fog of tears.

Two days later, Mother Frances called Nanda up to her table. In front of her lay the wretched copy of *Dream Days*.

"Look, Nanda," she said amiably, "I have managed to take Marjorie's name out quite well." The flyleaf, indeed, showed only the faintest ghost of yellow letters. "But I just wanted to say this to you. You are a new child and a convert, and you have not quite got into our ways yet. It is not for me to criticise what your father considers suitable reading matter for you . . . in the holidays, that is. This book will remain in your trunk till you go home for Christmas. But I think that you ought to knew that the tone of this book is not at all the kind of thing we like at Lippington. Apart from its being by a non-Catholic writer, it is morbid, rather unwholesome and just a *little* vulgar." Mother Frances gave her a chilling smile. "That is all, dear child." Nanda turned to fly. Her ears were red-hot.

"Oh, Nanda," said the musical voice.

"Yes, Mother?"

"I think your stocking's coming down. The left one."

Feeling rather defiant, she stuffed the Francis Thompson
that Léonie had given her for her First Communion into the
pocket of her dressing-gown. She was rather surprised that it
had not been confiscated long ago. Wrapped in brown paper, it
passed for an ordinary school poetry book. Her conscience did
not prick her much, for Francis Thompson was, after all, a
Catholic poet, and she boldly scattered her essays with quota-
tions from his works. She quite understood the fuss that had
been made about Léonie's own copy of Shelley, for Shelley was
an atheist and there might be corruption lurking in his most
innocent poems. One day, Léonie had broken away from the
others at recreation and strolled round the lake, reading *The
Revolt of Islam* quite openly and with an air of cynical detachment. There had been a memorable scene in which Mother
Percival, pink with anger, had snatched the book from Léonie,
and Léonie, very politely, had taken back her Shelley and flung
it into the lake, saying: "If the book is so scandalous, that is the
best place for it. It can hardly corrupt the little fishes." Strangely
enough, Léonie had not been punished.

The infirmary rooms at Lippington were bare and dismal.
There was plenty of space in each for two beds at least, but in
no circumstances were children allowed to share a bedroom.
The walls of Nanda's were painted a dirty green, and the only
decorations were a chipped plaster crucifix, a shell, with a
sponge as hard as cork, that had once held holy water, and a
spotty steel engraving of Leo XIII. Round the high, narrow bed
ran a curtain, whose rusty rings jangled at every movement and
effectively disturbed the patient's sleep. But to Nanda the
shabby room, with the grim, old-fashioned dentist's chair in the
corner, the spluttering gas jet and the empty grate, looked like
paradise. . . .

After the first day or two, Nanda began to feel well enough to enjoy life in the infirmary. Her temperature was still a little above normal, so that there was a comfortable justification for remaining in bed, but she was allowed to read and to do some old jig-saw puzzles that were very puzzling indeed, since about a third of the pieces were missing. The infirmary library included a few books that down in the school would have been classed as story-books and the competition for these was keen. Nanda was lucky; instead of back numbers of *Stella Maris* or *The Messenger of The Sacred Heart,* Sister Jones brought her a frivolous, secular work called *St. Winifred's or the World of School.* On the flyleaf of this was written in a nun's beautiful script: "Certain pages of this book have been cut out, as the matter they contain is both vulgar and distasteful to the mind of a modest reader. Their excision does not interfere with the plot of the story." The book had been still further censored. Several paragraphs were inked out, and wherever the word "blackguard" appeared, a careful hand had pasted a strip of thick, but unfortunately, transparent paper over it. Nanda was a voracious reader. She devoured *St. Winifred's* so fast that by tea-time she had finished it. When Sister Jones appeared, bearing a tray with the unaccustomed luxury of hot buttered toast, Nanda begged for a fresh book. But Sister Jones was firm. "You'll not get another book till tomorrow, Miss Nanda," she assured her, "unless it's a lesson-book. There can't be much the matter with you if you can read that fast."

"But, Sister," Nanda implored her, "it's hours before you put the lights out."

"Then, you can say your rosary, miss."

"Will you come back later and talk to me, then? It's so awfully dull here alone."

Sister Jones pursed her lips.

"Good gracious, child, do you think I've nothing else to do? You can say some of the prayers Mother Regan and I haven't time to say for ourselves, what with all this sickness in the house." She shut the door so smartly that Nanda half expected to hear a key turn in the lock. It would probably be two hours before anyone came in again. How was she going to get through such an eternity of time? Sleep was impossible. And three slim bars of toast, even if she counted ten between each nibble, could hardly last more than a few minutes. Then she remembered the Francis Thompson in her dressing-gown pocket. In a few minutes she was stumbling through *The Mistress of Vision* between gulps of sugary tea.

> "Secret was the garden,
>   Set in the pathless awe
> Where no star its breath may draw.
>   Life that is its warden
> Sits behind the fosse of death.
>   Mine eyes saw not and I saw.
> It was a mazeful wonder,
>   Thrice threefold it was enwalled
> With an emerald
>   Sealéd so asunder,
> All its birds in middle air
>   Hung a dream, their music thralled."

She read on and on, enraptured. She could not understand half, but it excited her oddly, like words in a foreign language sung to a beautiful air. She followed the poem vaguely as she followed the Latin in her missal, guessing, inventing meanings for herself, intoxicated by the mere rush of words. And yet she felt she did understand, not with her eyes or her brain, but with some faculty she did not even know she possessed. Something was happening to her, something that had not happened when she made her First Communion. She shut the book and tried to make out what it was. But she could not think at all, she could only go on saying to herself some words that had once caught her fancy and that now seemed to have a real meaning. "Too late have I known thee, too late have I loved thee, O Beauty ever ancient and ever new." But she did not want to go on. She did not want to be led into prayers and aspirations. This new feeling, whatever it was, had nothing to do with God.

The unexpected entry of Mother Percival made her feel hot and foolish. She clumsily tried to hide her Francis Thompson under the sheet, but it was too late. Mother Percival directed an unusually charitable smile at Nanda, but her eyes were on the book.

"Well, and how's Nanda?" she inquired affably. "Much better, by the look of her. Such red cheeks for an invalid."

"Oh, I'm nearly well," said Nanda feebly.

"Well enough to read, I see," smiled Mother Percival, seating herself by the bed. "A story-book, is it?"

"No, Mother," admitted Nanda. "It's just some poetry."

"Just some poetry, is it? I didn't know you had such a devotion to English literature. Perhaps you're learning something by heart to surprise me when you come back to class?"

She reached out a lean, capable hand for the book.

There was a silence while she opened it and scanned a few lines. Nanda felt the blood beating in her ears.

"Francis Thompson? That's not one of your school books, is it? I didn't know there was a copy in the infirmary."

"It's my own. Léonie gave it me for my First Communion," Nanda said boldly.

"I see. Francis Thompson was a great Catholic poet, but he did not write for little girls of eleven. How much of this do you imagine you understand?"

"Quite a lot," said Nanda recklessly.

"That's very interesting. Let me see." She glanced at the page. "Now what, for instance, does 'cymar' mean? Or 'effluence'? Or 'vertiginous'? Or 'panoply'?"

"I don't know," Nanda admitted sullenly.

"I thought as much. Did you ever hear about the little pig that died of trying to grunt like a grown-up pig when it could really only say 'wee-wee'?"

Mother Percival shut the book and laughed wholesomely.

"Now, you see, my dear child, that you're being just a little bit silly, aren't you? Some day you'll see the very wonderful religious meaning that's hidden in all this. But not yet. Francis Thompson was a mystic and no one expects little girls to understand the secrets of the saints. Not that Francis Thompson was a saint. He was not always a Catholic, you know, and there is often something a little morbid, a little hysterical in his work. But some of his poems are very simple and beautiful. I was going to let the Fifth Form learn *To a Snowdrop* for the Christmas wishing. But I think it would be better for you to let older people judge what is best for your little understanding."

"Please let me keep the book, Mother," she begged.

Mother Percival smiled again and turned over some pages.

"Well, perhaps there's no harm in keeping a book you so obviously don't understand. I suppose you want the others to think what a clever little person this Nanda Grey is?"

Suddenly her eye was arrested by a verse. Over her shoulder in a poem she had never looked at before, Nanda read:

> "I shall never feel a girl's soft arms
> Without horror of the skin."

But she read no more. Mother Percival hastily shut the book. The geniality had gone out of her face.

"This book goes straight to your trunk, Nanda," she said in her coldest voice. "There are things in it which are not fit for any decent person to read. If I had my way it should be burnt."

Nanda was trembling with indignation, but before she had time to speak, Mother Regan burst open the door.

"I'll have to move you back to your dormitory, child," she said. "I must have a good-sized room at once. Theresa Leighton is very ill indeed."

Meditation III. Dangers of the World.

Worldly pleasures, business, etc., tend to interfere with spiritual life. Things, not in themselves harmful may be harmful to soul. A saint said it was dangerous to walk through a beautiful wood. Tendency to regard things for their own sakes, rather than as manifestations of Creator's power, wisdom, etc. Sermons in stones. Dangers of nature-worship. Look for God in everything. Modern Pantheism. Believing everything to be God. Idea that it is better to go for country walk than attend mass. Dangerous nonsense and loose thinking. Devil responsible for part of creation after fall. Thistles, weeds, etc. Trying to upset God's scheme. Nature only beneficial to man before fall; now enemy. Even beauty often poisoned. Choose friends for solid piety, not for superficial good looks or accomplishments. Give up a friendship if it tends to hinder you in the practice of your religion. God hates exclusive personal loves. Mother love the highest of earthly loves, because essentially unselfish. Danger of idle conversation and frivolous reading. Never read books criticising Church. Priests must read them in order to refute them. Bad books do untold harm. Writer responsible for evil his books do; he shares in every sin occasioned by it. Cannot go to heaven until book has ceased to harm. Writer of bad book appeared in flames to saint. Tormented until last copy was destroyed. Oscar Wilde must now be suffering for untold evil done by his works. Books on the index. Kingsley, Macaulay, Huxley, etc. Abominable works exposed in Mayfair drawing-rooms. Zola, Anatole France, etc. Scientific works unsuitable for women. Puff up their vanity with ideas they only half understand. If science conflicts with religion, science must, by definition, be wrong. Garden of Eden a myth, perhaps; but true in essentials. Order of creation in Bible ratified even by modern scientists. Wrong to imagine Catholics not good scientists. Pasteur, Wassermann, etc. Jesuit astronomers. Read a spiritual book for every novel.

—from *Frost in May*

Miep Gies

(b. 1909)

In her memoir Anne Frank Remembered *Miep Gies recalls her role in hiding the Frank family in Amsterdam during the Nazi occupation and then, when they were discovered, in hiding the diaries of the younger daughter, Anne. Miep Gies put the bound notebooks and loose papers in an unlocked drawer of her desk and left them there untouched until the war was over. Otto Frank returned; his wife had died in Auschwitz. When news of the deaths of Anne and her sister Margot was received, Miep Gies gave Otto Frank the diaries. Eventually, at the urging of a fellow survivor, Otto Frank let a historian read them and they were published. All this time, Miep Gies had refused to read them, not wishing to "rekindle the terrible losses." She was doing other reading. She had originally been Catholic but had stopped attending church.*

. . . I never doubted the existence of God. That is, until the war. Then, by the time the war was finished, my sense of God had been poisoned and only an empty hole was left.

. . . I had a craving to read on the subject, and I began to read the Old Testament. Then I read the New Testament. Then, with deep interest, I read studies of many different religions: books on Judaism, books on Catholicism, Protestantism, anything I could lay my hands on.

I never spoke about my reading to anyone. I just read and read. Everything I read was rich and interesting, yet I was always hungry for more. The dark years had pulled down my inner supports, and I was looking for something to replace them.

Otto Frank, who was living with Miep Gies and her husband, continued to urge her to read the diaries. When the third Dutch

*printing was planned, Mr. Frank consented to the diary's translation
and publication in foreign countries.*

. . . Again and again, he'd say to me, "Miep, you must read
Anne's writing. Who would have imagined what went on in
her quick little mind?" Otto was never discouraged by my
continuing refusal. He would always wait awhile and then ask
me again.

Finally, I gave in to his insistence. I said, "All right, I will
read the diary, but only when I'm totally alone."

The next time I was totally alone on a warm day, I took the
second printing of the diary, went to my room, and shut the
door.

With awful fear in my heart, I opened the book and turned
to the first page.

And so I began to read.

I read the whole diary without stopping. From the first word,
I heard Anne's voice come back to speak to me from where she
had gone. I lost track of time. Anne's voice tumbled out of the
book, so full of life, moods, curiosity, feelings. She was no
longer gone and destroyed. She was alive again in my mind.

I read to the very end. I was surprised by how much had
happened in hiding that I'd known nothing about. Immediately, I was thankful that I hadn't read the diary after the
arrest, during the final nine months of the occupation, while
it had stayed in my desk drawer right beside me every day.
Had I read it, I would have had to burn the diary because it
would have been too dangerous for people about whom
Anne had written.

When I had read the last word, I didn't feel the pain I'd
anticipated. I was glad I'd read it at last. The emptiness in my
heart was eased. So much had been lost, but now Anne's voice
would never be lost. My young friend had left a remarkable
legacy to the world.

But always, every day of my life, I've wished that things had been different. That even had Anne's diary been lost to the world, Anne and the others might somehow have been saved.

Not a day goes by that I do not grieve for them.

—from *Anne Frank Remembered*

Jane Kenyon

(1948–1995)

Her early death robbed us of a poetic voice of particular beauty, wit, and—for all her familiarity with anxiety—peace. Jane Kenyon lived with her husband, Donald Hall, in New Hampshire and during her lifetime received many awards, among them a Guggenheim Fellowship.

Insomnia at the Solstice

The quicksilver song
of the wood thrush spills
downhill from ancient maples
at the end of the sun's single most
altruistic day. The woods grow dusky
while the bird's song brightens.

Reading to get sleepy . . . Rabbit
Angstrom knows himself so well,
why isn't he a better man?
I turn out the light, and rejoice
in the sound of high summer, and in air
on bare shoulders—*dolce, dolce*—
no blanket, or even a sheet.
A faint glow remains over the lake.

Now come wordless contemplations
on love and death, worry about
money, and the resolve to have the vet
clean the dog's teeth, though
he'll have to anaesthetize him.

An easy rain begins, drips off
the edge of the roof, onto the tin
watering can. A vast irritation rises. . . .
I turn and turn, try one pillow,
two, think of people who have no beds.

A car hisses by on wet macadam.
Then another. The room turns
gray by insensible degrees. The thrush
begins again its outpouring of silver
to rich and poor alike, to the just
and the unjust.

The dog's wet nose appears
on the pillow, pressing lightly,
decorously. He needs to go out.
All right cleverhead, let's declare
a new day.
                    Washing up, I say
to the face in the mirror,
"You're still here! How you bored me
all night, and now I'll have
to entertain you all day. . . ."

Bernard Malamud

(1914–1986)

Novelist and short story writer Bernard Malamud was particularly interested in the qualities of powerlessness, and often his characters are engaged in struggles to overcome their poverty, obscurity, and a lucklessness that makes them think God has forgotten them. In this story, reading gives a lover a weapon that works against the seemingly stronger pulls of duty and money.

The First Seven Years

Feld, the shoemaker, was annoyed that his helper, Sobel, was so insensitive to his reverie that he wouldn't for a minute cease his fanatic pounding at the other bench. He gave him a look, but Sobel's bald head was bent over the last as he worked, and he didn't notice. The shoemaker shrugged and continued to peer through the partly frosted window at the nearsighted haze of falling February snow. Neither the shifting white blur outside, nor the sudden deep remembrance of the snowy Polish village where he had wasted his youth, could turn his thoughts from Max the college boy (a constant visitor in the mind since early that morning when Feld saw him trudging through the snowdrifts on his way to school), whom he so much respected because of the sacrifices he had made throughout the years—in winter or direst heat—to further his education. An old wish returned to haunt the shoemaker: that he had had a son instead of a daughter, but this blew away in the snow, for Feld, if anything, was a practical man. Yet he could not help but contrast the diligence of the boy, who was a peddler's son, with Miriam's unconcern for an education. True, she was always with a book in her hand, yet when the opportunity arose for a college education, she had said no she would rather find a job.

He had begged her to go, pointing out how many fathers could not afford to send their children to college, but she said she wanted to be independent. As for education, what was it, she asked, but books, which Sobel, who diligently read the classics, would as usual advise her on. Her answer greatly grieved her father.

A figure emerged from the snow and the door opened. At the counter the man withdrew from a wet paper bag a pair of battered shoes for repair. Who he was the shoemaker for a moment had no idea, then his heart trembled as he realized, before he had thoroughly discerned the face, that Max himself was standing there, embarrassedly explaining what he wanted done to his old shoes. Though Feld listened eagerly, he couldn't hear a word, for the opportunity that had burst upon him was deafening,

He couldn't exactly recall when the thought had occurred to him, because it was clear he had more than once considered suggesting to the boy that he go out with Miriam. But he had not dared speak, for if Max said no, how would he face him again? Or suppose Miriam, who harped so often on independence, blew up in anger and shouted at him for his meddling? Still, the chance was too good to let by: all it meant was an introduction. They might long ago have become friends had they happened to meet somewhere, therefore was it not his duty—an obligation—to bring them together, nothing more, a harmless connivance to replace an accidental encounter in the subway, let's say, or a mutual friend's introduction in the street? Just let him once see and talk to her and he would for sure be interested. As for Miriam, what possible harm for a working girl in an office, who met only loudmouthed salesmen and illiterate shipping clerks, to make the acquaintance of a fine scholarly boy? Maybe he would awaken in her a desire to go to college; if not—the shoemaker's mind at last came to grips with the truth—let her marry an educated man and live a better life.

When Max finished describing what he wanted done to his shoes, Feld marked them, both with enormous holes in the soles which he pretended not to notice, with large white-chalk X's and the rubber heels, thinned to the nails, he marked with O's, though it troubled him he might have mixed up the letters. Max inquired the price, and the shoemaker cleared his throat and asked the boy, above Sobel's insistent hammering, would he please step through the side door there into the hall. Though surprised, Max did as the shoemaker requested, and Feld went in after him. For a minute they were both silent, because Sobel had stopped banging, and it seemed they understood neither was to say anything until the noise began again. When it did, loudly, the shoemaker quickly told Max why he had asked to talk to him.

"Ever since you went to high school," he said, in the dimly lit hallway, "I watched you in the morning go to the subway to school, and I said always to myself, this is a fine boy that he wants so much an education."

"Thanks," Max said, nervously alert. He was tall and grotesquely thin, with sharply cut features, particularly a beak-like nose. He was wearing a loose, long, slushy overcoat that hung down to his ankles, looking like a rug draped over his bony shoulders, and a soggy old brown hat, as battered as the shoes he had brought in.

"I am a businessman," the shoemaker abruptly said to conceal his embarrassment, "so I will explain you right away why I talk to you. I have a girl, my daughter Miriam—she is nineteen—a very nice girl and also so pretty that everybody looks on her when she passes by in the street. She is smart, always with a book, and I thought to myself that a boy like you, an educated boy—I thought maybe you will be interested sometime to meet a girl like this." He laughed a bit when he had finished and was tempted to say more but had the good sense not to.

Max stared down like a hawk. For an uncomfortable second he was silent, then he asked, "Did you say nineteen?"

"Yes."

"Would it be all right to inquire if you have a picture of her?"

"Just a minute." The shoemaker went into the store and hastily returned with a snapshot that Max held up to the light.

"She's all right," he said.

Feld waited.

"And is she sensible—not the flighty kind?"

"She is very sensible."

After another short pause, Max said it was okay with him if he met her.

"Here is my telephone," said the shoemaker, hurriedly handing him a slip of paper. "Call her up. She comes home from work six o'clock."

Max folded the paper and tucked it away into his worn leather wallet.

"About the shoes," he said. "How much did you say they will cost me?"

"Don't worry about the price."

"I just like to have an idea."

"A dollar—dollar fifty. A dollar fifty," the shoemaker said.

At once he felt bad, for he usually charged $2.25 for this kind of job. Either he should have asked the regular price or done the work for nothing.

Later, as he entered the store, he was startled by a violent clanging and looked up to see Sobel pounding upon the naked last. It broke, the iron striking the floor and jumping with a thump against the wall, but before the enraged shoemaker could cry out, the assistant had torn his hat and coat off the hook and rushed out into the snow.

So Feld, who had looked forward to anticipating how it would go with his daughter and Max, instead had a great worry on his mind. Without his temperamental helper he was a lost man, especially as it was years now since he had carried the store alone. The shoemaker had for an age suffered from a heart condition that threatened collapse if he dared exert himself. Five years ago, after an attack, it had appeared as though he would have either to sacrifice his business on the auction block and live on a pittance thereafter, or put himself at the mercy of some unscrupulous employee who would in the end probably ruin him. But just at the moment of his darkest despair, this Polish refugee, Sobel, had appeared one night out of the street and begged for work. He was a stocky man, poorly dressed, with a bald head that had once been blond, a severely plain face, and soft blue eyes prone to tears over the sad books he read, a young man but old—no one would have guessed thirty. Though he confessed he knew nothing of shoemaking, he said he was apt and would work for very little if Feld taught him the trade. Thinking that with, after all, a landsman, he would have less to fear than from a complete stranger, Feld took him on and within six weeks the refugee rebuilt as good a shoe as he, and not long thereafter expertly ran the business for the thoroughly relieved shoemaker.

Feld could trust him with anything and did, frequently going home after an hour or two at the store, leaving all the money in the till, knowing Sobel would guard every cent of it. The amazing thing was that he demanded so little. His wants were few; in money he wasn't interested—in nothing but books, it seemed—which he one by one lent to Miriam, together with his profuse, queer written comments, manufactured during his lonely rooming house evenings, thick pads of commentary which the shoemaker peered at and twitched his shoulders over as his daughter, from her fourteenth year, read page by sanctified page, as if the word of God were inscribed on them. To protect Sobel, Feld himself had to see that he received more than he asked for. Yet his conscience bothered him for not insisting that the assistant accept a better wage than he was getting, though Feld had honestly told him he could earn a handsome salary if he worked elsewhere, or maybe opened a place of his own. But the assistant answered, somewhat ungraciously, that he was not interested in going elsewhere, and though Feld frequently asked himself, What keeps him here? why does he stay? he finally answered it that the man, no doubt because of his terrible experiences as a refugee, was afraid of the world.

After the incident with the broken last, angered by Sobel's behavior, the shoemaker decided to let him stew for a week in the rooming house, although his own strength was taxed dangerously and the business suffered. However, after several sharp nagging warnings from both his wife and daughter, he went finally in search of Sobel, as he had once before, quite recently, when over some fancied slight—Feld had merely asked him not to give Miriam so many books to read because her eyes were strained and red—the assistant had left the place in a huff, an incident which, as usual, came to nothing, for he had returned after the shoemaker had talked to him, and taken his seat at the bench. But this time, after Feld had plodded through the snow to Sobel's house—he had thought of sending Miriam but the idea became repugnant to him—the burly landlady at the door informed him in a nasal voice that Sobel was not at home, and though Feld knew this was a nasty lie, for where had the refugee to go? still for some reason he was not completely sure of— it may have been the cold and his fatigue—he decided not to insist on seeing him. Instead he went home and hired a new helper.

Thus he settled the matter, though not entirely to his satisfaction, for he had much more to do than before, and so, for example, could no longer lie late in bed mornings because he had to get up to open the store for the new assistant, a speechless, dark man with an irritating rasp as he worked, whom he would not trust with the key as he had Sobel. Furthermore, this one, though able to do a fair repair job, knew nothing of grades of leather or prices, so Feld had to make his own purchases; and every night at closing time it was necessary to count the money in the till and lock up. However, he was not dissatisfied, for he lived much in his thoughts of Max and Miriam. The college boy had called her, and they had arranged a meeting for this coming Friday night. The shoemaker would personally have preferred Saturday, which he felt would make it a date of the first magnitude, but he learned Friday was Miriam's choice, so he said nothing. The day of the week did not matter. What mattered was the aftermath. Would they like each other and want to be friends? He sighed at all the time that would have to go by before he knew for sure. Often he was tempted to talk to Miriam about the boy, to ask whether she thought she would like his type—he had told her only that he considered Max a nice boy and had suggested he call her—but the one time he tried she snapped at him—justly—how should she know?

At last Friday came. Feld was not feeling particularly well so he stayed in bed, and Mrs. Feld thought it better to remain in the bedroom with him when Max called. Miriam received the boy, and her parents could hear their voices, his throaty one, as they talked. Just before leaving, Miriam brought Max to the bedroom door and he stood there a minute, a tall, slightly hunched figure wearing a thick, droopy suit, and apparently at ease as he greeted the shoemaker and his wife, which was surely a good sign. And Miriam, although she had worked all day, looked fresh and pretty. She was a large-framed girl with a well-shaped body, and she had a fine open face and soft hair. They made, Feld thought, a first-class couple.

Miriam returned after 11:30. Her mother was already asleep, but the shoemaker got out of bed and after locating his bathrobe went into the kitchen, where Miriam, to his surprise, sat at the table, reading.

"So where did you go?" Feld asked pleasantly.

"For a walk," she said, not looking up.

"I advised him," Feld said, clearing his throat, "he shouldn't spend so much money."

"I didn't care."

The shoemaker boiled up some water for tea and sat down at the table with a cupful and a thick slice of lemon.

"So how," he sighed after a sip, "did you enjoy?"

"It was all right."

He was silent. She must have sensed his disappointment, for she added, "You can't really tell much the first time."

"You will see him again?"

Turning a page, she said that Max had asked for another date.

"For when?"

"Saturday."

"So what did you say?"

"What did I say?" she asked, delaying for a moment—"I said yes."

Afterwards she inquired about Sobel, and Feld, without exactly knowing why, said the assistant had got another job. Miriam said nothing more and went on reading. The shoemaker's conscience did not trouble him; he was satisfied with the Saturday date.

During the week, by placing here and there a deft question, he managed to get from Miriam some information about Max. It surprised him to learn that the boy was not studying to be either a doctor or lawyer but was taking a business course leading to a degree in accountancy. Feld was a little disappointed because he thought of accountants as bookkeepers and would have preferred "a higher profession." However, it was not long before he had investigated the subject and discovered that Certified Public Accountants were highly respected people, so he was thoroughly content as Saturday approached. But because Saturday was a busy day, he was much in the store and therefore did not see Max when he came to call for Miriam. From his wife he learned there had been nothing especially revealing about their greeting. Max had rung the bell and Miriam had got her coat and left with him—nothing more. Feld did not probe, for his wife was not particularly observant. Instead, he waited up for Miriam with a newspaper on his lap, which he scarcely looked at so lost was he in thinking of the future. He awoke to find her in the room with him, tiredly removing her hat. Greeting her, he was suddenly inexplicably afraid to ask anything about the evening. But since she volunteered nothing he was at last forced to inquire how she had enjoyed herself. Miriam began something noncommittal, but apparently changed her mind, for she said after a minute, "I was bored."

When Feld had sufficiently recovered from his anguished disappointment to ask why, she answered without hesitation, "Because he's nothing more than a materialist."

"What means this word?"

"He has no soul. He's only interested in things."

He considered her statement for a long time, then asked, "Will you see him again?"

"He didn't ask."

"Suppose he will ask you?"

"I won't see him."

He did not argue; however, as the days went by he hoped increasingly she would change her mind. He wished the boy would telephone, because he was sure there was more to him than Miriam, with her inexperienced eye, could discern. But Max didn't call. As a matter of fact he took a different route to school, no longer passing the shoemaker's store, and Feld was deeply hurt.

Then, one afternoon Max came in and asked for his shoes. The shoemaker took them down from the shelf where he had placed them, apart from the other pairs. He had done the work himself and the soles and heels were well built and firm. The shoes had been highly polished and somehow looked better than new. Max's Adam's apple went up once when he saw them, and his eyes had little lights in them.

"How much?" he asked, without directly looking at the shoemaker, "Like I told you before," Feld answered sadly. "One dollar fifty cents."

Max handed him two crumpled bills and received in return a newly minted silver half dollar.

He left. Miriam had not been mentioned. That night the shoemaker discovered that his new assistant had been all the while stealing from him, and he suffered a heart attack.

Though the attack was very mild, he lay in bed for three weeks. Miriam spoke of going for Sobel, but sick as he was Feld rose in wrath against the idea. Yet in his heart he knew there was no other way, and the first weary day back in the shop thoroughly convinced him, so that night after supper he dragged himself to Sobel's rooming house.

He toiled up the stairs, though he knew it was bad for him, and at the top knocked at the door. Sobel opened it and the shoemaker entered. The room was a small, poor one, with a single window facing the street. It contained a narrow cot, a low table, and several stacks of books piled haphazardly around on the floor along the wall, which made him think how queer Sobel was, to be uneducated and read so much. He had once asked him, Sobel, why you read so much? and the assistant could not answer him. Did you ever study in a college someplace? he had asked, but Sobel shook his head. He read, he said, to know. But to know what, the shoemaker demanded, and to know, why? Sobel never explained, which proved he read so much because he was queer.

Feld sat down to recover his breath. The assistant was resting on his bed with his heavy back to the wall. His shirt and trousers were clean, and his stubby fingers, away from the shoemaker's bench, were strangely pallid. His face was thin and pale, as if he had been shut in this room since the day he had bolted from the store.

"So when you will come back to work?" Feld asked him.

To his surprise, Sobel burst out, "Never."

Jumping up, he strode over to the window that looked out upon the miserable street. "Why should I come back?" he cried.

"I will raise your wages."

"Who cares for your wages!"

The shoemaker, knowing he didn't care, was at a loss what else to say.

"What do you want from me, Sobel?"

"Nothing."

"I always treated you like you was my son."

Sobel vehemently denied it. "So why you look for strange boys in the street they should go out with Miriam? Why you don't think of me?"

The shoemaker's hands and feet turned freezing cold. His voice became so hoarse he couldn't speak. At last he cleared his throat and croaked, "So what has my daughter got to do with a shoemaker thirty-five years old who works for me?"

"Why do you think I worked so long for you?" Sobel cried out. "For the stingy wages I sacrificed five years of my life so you could have to eat and drink and where to sleep?"

"Then for what?" shouted the shoemaker.

"For Miriam," he blurted—"for her."

The shoemaker, after a time, managed to say, "I pay wages in cash, Sobel," and lapsed into silence. Though he was seething with excitement, his mind was coldly clear, and he had to admit to himself he had sensed all along that Sobel felt this way. He had never so much as thought it consciously, but he had felt it and was afraid.

"Miriam knows?" he muttered hoarsely.

"She knows."

"You told her?"

"No."

"Then how does she know?"

"How does she know?" Sobel said. "Because she knows. She knows who I am and what is in my heart."

Feld had a sudden insight. In some devious way, with his books and commentary, Sobel had given Miriam to understand that he loved her. The shoemaker felt a terrible anger at him for his deceit.

"Sobel, you are crazy," he said bitterly. "She will never marry a man so old and ugly like you."

Sobel turned black with rage. He cursed the shoemaker, but then, though he trembled to hold it in, his eyes filled with tears and he broke into deep sobs. With his back to Feld, he stood at the window, fists clenched, and his shoulders shook with his choked sobbing.

Watching him, the shoemaker's anger diminished. His teeth were on edge with pity for the man, and his eyes grew moist. How strange and sad that a refugee, a grown man, bald and old with his miseries, who had by the skin of his teeth escaped Hitler's incinerators, should fall in love, when he had got to America, with a girl less than half his age. Day after day, for five years he had sat at his bench, cutting and hammering away, waiting for the girl to become a woman, unable to ease his heart with speech, knowing no protest but desperation.

"Ugly I didn't mean," he said half aloud.

Then he realized that what he had called ugly was not Sobel but Miriam's life if she married him. He felt for his daughter a strange and gripping sorrow, as if she were already Sobel's bride, the wife, after all, of a shoemaker, and had in her life no more than her mother had had. And all his dreams for her—why he had slaved and destroyed his heart with anxiety and labor—all these dreams of a better life were dead.

The room was quiet. Sobel was standing by the window reading, and it was curious that when he read he looked young.

"She is only nineteen," Feld said brokenly. "This is too young yet to get married. Don't ask her for two years more, till she is twenty-one, then you can talk to her."

Sobel didn't answer. Feld rose and left. He went slowly down the stairs but once outside, though it was an icy night and the crisp falling snow whitened the street, he walked with a stronger stride.

But the next morning, when the shoemaker arrived, heavy-hearted, to open the store, he saw he needn't have come, for his assistant was already seated at the last, pounding leather for his love.

—from *The Stories of Bernard Malamud*

James Joyce

(1882–1941)

A Portrait of the Artist as a Young Man *(1916) is James Joyce's autobiographical novel that presents Stephen Dedalus, a noteworthy forerunner of alienated teens in English and American literature.*

In this passage, Stephen Dedalus is at a school in Dublin. For his weekly essay Stephen writes about the Creator and the soul. Mr. Tate, the English master, declares that the essay has heresy in it. Stephen is mortified and the class is thrilled. Stephen submits and rephrases his essay; Mr. Tate is appeased, but the other boys want blood.

A few nights after this public chiding he was walking with a letter along the Drumcondra Road when he heard a voice cry:

———Halt!

He turned and saw three boys of his own class coming towards him in the dusk. It was Heron who had called out and, as he marched forward between his two attendants, he cleft the air before him with a thin cane, in time to their steps. Boland, his friend, marched beside him, a large grin on his face, while Nash came on a few steps behind, blowing from the pace and wagging his great red head.

As soon as the boys had turned into Clonliffe Road together they began to speak about books and writers, saying what books they were reading and how many books there were in their fathers' bookcases at home. Stephen listened to them in some wonderment for Boland was the dunce and Nash the idler of the class. In fact after some talk about their favourite writers Nash declared for Captain Marryat who, he said, was the greatest writer.

——Fudge! said Heron. Ask Dedalus. Who is the greatest writer, Dedalus?

Stephen noted the mockery in the question and said:

——Of prose do you mean?

——Yes.

——Newman, I think.

——Is it Cardinal Newman? asked Boland.

——Yes, answered Stephen.

The grin broadened on Nash's freckled face as he turned to Stephen and said:

——And do you like Cardinal Newman, Dedalus?

——O, many say that Newman has the best prose style, Heron said to the other two in explanation. Of course he's not a poet.

——And who is the best poet, Heron? asked Boland.

——Lord Tennyson, of course, answered Heron.

——O, yes, Lord Tennyson, said Nash. We have all his poetry at home in a book.

At this Stephen forgot the silent vows he had been making and burst out:

——Tennyson a poet! Why, he's only a rhymester!

——O, get out! said Heron. Everyone knows that Tennyson is the greatest poet.

——And who do you think is the greatest poet? asked Boland, nudging his neighbour.

——Byron, of course, answered Stephen.

Heron gave the lead and all three joined in a scornful laugh.

——What are you laughing at? asked Stephen.

——You, said Heron. Byron the greatest poet! He's only a poet for uneducated people.

——He must be a fine poet! said Boland.

——You may keep your mouth shut, said Stephen, turning on him boldly. All you know about poetry is what you wrote up on the slates in the yard and were going to be sent to the loft for.

Boland, in fact, was said to have written on the slates in the

yard a couplet about a classmate of his who often rode home
from the college on a pony:

> *As Tyson was riding into Jerusalem*
> *He fell and hurt his Alec Kafoozelum.*

This thrust put the two lieutenants to silence but Heron went
on:

——In any case Byron was a heretic and immoral too.

——I don't care what he was, cried Stephen hotly.

——You don't care whether he was a heretic or not? said
Nash.

——What do you know about it? shouted Stephen. You
never read a line of anything in your life except a trans or
Boland either.

——I know that Byron was a bad man, said Boland.

——Here, catch hold of this heretic, Heron called out.

In a moment Stephen was a prisoner.

——Tate made you buck up the other day, Heron went on,
about the heresy in your essay.

——I'll tell him tomorrow, said Boland.

——Will you? said Stephen. You'd be afraid to open your
lips.

——Afraid?

——Ay. Afraid of your life.

——Behave yourself! cried Heron, cutting at Stephen's legs
with his cane.

It was the signal for their onset. Nash pinioned his arms
behind while Boland seized a long cabbage stump which was
lying in the gutter. Struggling and kicking under the cuts of the
cane and the blows of the knotty stump Stephen was borne back
against a barbed wire fence.

——Admit that Byron was no good.

——No.

——Admit.

——No.

——Admit.

——No. No.

At last after a fury of plunges he wrenched himself free. His tormentors set off towards Jones's Road, laughing and jeering at him, while he, torn and flushed and panting, stumbled after them half blinded with tears, clenching his fists madly and sobbing.

While he was still repeating the *Confiteor* amid the indulgent laughter of his hearers and while the scenes of that malignant episode were still passing sharply and swiftly before his mind he wondered why he bore no malice now to those who had tormented him. He had not forgotten a whit of their cowardice and cruelty but the memory of it called forth no anger from him. All the descriptions of fierce love and hatred which he had met in books had seemed to him therefore unreal. Even that night as he stumbled homewards along Jones's Road he had felt that some power was divesting him of that suddenwoven anger as easily as a fruit is divested of its soft ripe peel.

—from *A Portrait of the Artist as a Young Man*

VI
The Privileged
Pleasure

We take the direction and title of our final section from Robert Alter:

Reading is a privileged pleasure because each of us enjoys it, quite complexly, in ways not replicable by anyone else. But there is enough structured common ground in the text itself so that we can talk to each other, even sometimes persuade each other, about what we read; and that many-voiced conversation, with which, thankfully, we shall never be done, is one of the most gratifying responses to literary creation, second only to reading itself.

Oliver Wendell Holmes, Jr.
(1841–1935)
Harold J. Laski
(1893–1950)

The correspondence between Supreme Court Justice Oliver Wendell Holmes and the English political scientist Harold J. Laski began in 1916 with a bread-and-butter letter from Laski, then a 23-year-old instructor at Harvard. Holmes, the pre-eminent American judge, was 75.

There is scarcely a letter in the 20-year correspondence in which Holmes and Laski do not have something to say about reading books or collecting books, and the letters provide a record of the range of each man's reading. The letters, which range widely over the law, politics, and current events are full of lightheartedness, humor, and deep affection.

Washington, D.C., December 22, 1922

My dear Laski: No news since my last recently sent—so my answer to yours of the 5th received yesterday P.M. will be short. I found that Douglas and Orage *Credit Power and Democracy* was short and I am through it without waiting for you. I didn't follow its reasoning clearly, but felt that I could see the outside limits of its use to me and so put it in the shelves. To free me from scruples, the same or the next evening your Mr. Martin (clever chap) turned up and gave me an account of an evening with the authors at the Webbs with Bertrand Russell *et al.*—and brought peace to my spirit. The next evening he dined with us and I enjoyed talking with him very much, though I am far from sharing all his views. All manner of details present themselves as soon as one has a little leisure down to the clearing out of corners and making more room in one's bookshelves. My! I feel so clean—the result is that the days go by with little reading done. I have just past [*sic*] the middle of the one volume *Golden Bough*—the pages pitilessly snug with compact print—the ideas—I dare say to a considerable extent originating with Frazer—but familiar—the illustrations for the practice of the Bugaboos—the Wee Wees—the Beshitkas and manifold other savages—making as my father used to quote the Scotsman for saying about the calf's (sheep's) head—fine confused eating—the whole rather a reinforcement than an illumination—and heartbreaking to one who wanted to get through it—even though content to read. I can't bring my conscience to skimming—I have to read every word, though probably with no better result than if I just took the tips of the asparagus. So I shall be lucky if I have finished the damn thing by the time we go back to Court. You meantime will have eviscerated 100 pamphlets, and skun six folios, and eaten X octavos, all *en route* for a *magnum opus*. Fired by that thought I resume Frazer. My love and Christmas wishes to you both. *Affectionately yours, O.W. Holmes*

I sent you a decision in my last. I enclose another according to your request *(Jackman* v. *Rosenbaum Co.*, 260 U.S. 30 (Oct. 23, 1922).)—one other rather interesting one I have no spare copy of. In this one I send I coined the formula "average reciprocity of advantage" which I think neatly expressed the rationale of certain cases—not of all as Brandeis did vainly talk in his dissent that I sent you before.

Devon Lodge, 12.XII.27

My dear Justice: I imagine that this letter ought to arrive about Xmas. You know how warm are our good wishes to you both.

I was relieved to hear that you had received signs of life from Wu. I enquired at the Foreign Office here about him and they have sent out an enquiry. Could you let me have his exact address? They say that with it they can obtain exact information adding that it will take some time.

I was amused by your futher account of Zane. It reminds me a good deal of a colleague of mine at McGill University who used to commence his courses on English Literature by explaining that attendance thereat did not constitute a personal introduction to him as a man of his birth and breeding could not possibly know students outside the lecture room. Only last night I was told of a young man who applied for the post of secretary to Curzon. The latter asked if he was married. "Yes" said the applicant. Curzon hoped his wife was a lady; if so when they were in want of an extra woman for dinner she might be put on the list of availables. The candidate thereupon abruptly explained that he was no longer a candidate. "Dear me," said Curzon, "do you think it fair to deprive your wife of the social opportunities she could have by dining with us?" Could the sublimity of insolence really go farther than that?

The days since I wrote last have been very full of that disease of committees which accumulate about the end of term. And students have poured in relentlessly—including an American who only wanted me to ask Lloyd-George for him who had bought peerages while he was in office; and a German who presented me with an article upon the social theories of Graham Wallas in which in twenty odd pages (odd in a double sense) he compared him to thirty-one different German sociologists. Nor must I omit the Chinese student who wanted us to let him to an LL.D. and on investigation turned out to be the son of one of the most eminent pirates now operating in Chinese waters. You must admit that an academic life offers the prospect of very varied experience.

The most pleasant person I have encountered at all intimately these last weeks is our new professor of economics, Allyn Young, who comes to us from Harvard. I don't know if you ever encountered him in his Washington days. I find him learned, simple, and well-balanced. He agrees with my main feelings about education, especially in the view that half the people now doing research, especially on the co-operative plan are quite unfit for it. His affection for Felix and F. J. Turner is of the right intensity; and he entirely dislikes the Harvard Business School. These are the beginnings of wisdom. I had him in to dinner the other night with Bonar the economist and it was a delight to hear a series of conflicts about purely scholarly matters *e.g.* where the physiocrats got their ideas of natural law from, what is the most unintelligible sentence in Hegel (a good subject for an anthology) and the real nature of Mrs. J. S. Mill. I also had an adorable lunch with Birrell who told me he had been reading the early Fathers of the Church and had been completely converted to Manichaeism by the official proofs of its heterodoxy. He said he had been going through his fee-book and found that after he took silk all his biggest fees came from cases he had lost. We discussed the present bench and he took the interesting view that, on an average, the political appointments were vastly inferior to the non-political. I told him of Felix's arguments about the value of a grasp of affairs through political experience in his book and Birrell denied this with vigour. He insisted that the lawyer appointed direct from politics always showed hostility to experiments in the direction which ran counter to his own political views—that the word "reasonable" was something he could not interpret "reasonably." Which as he confirmed my private prejudices, please me much. With great deference, I submit that you, Learned Hand, and Cardozo would not have been better judges by coming to the Bench from a political career; and it is surely significant that Bowen, Blackburn, and MacNaghten were all non-political while Jessel was a dead failure in the House of Commons.

In the way of reading there is, I fear, but little to record, for I cannot, I fear, hope to persuade you to follow my footsteps through the dreary track of Saint Augustine. More pleasant was a good detective story by one Crofts called *Inspector French and the Starvel Tragedy* and a charming fantasy by an American writer named Thornton Wilder called *The Bridge of San Luis Rey*. Otherwise I have not found time for experiment on any

scale and Augustine produced in me a sense of irritation. Theology certainly needs faith as a compensation for its incredible
prolixity and any bigger draught of it would make me a mili-
tant atheist anxious to do battle with the credulous.

I had an amusing book-adventure. I found a nice copy of a
16th-century Aristotle—the *Politics*—with a coat of arms on the
binding. I paid ten shillings for it and then went on to a shop
where the bookseller prayed me to re-sell it to him. I changed it
there for a nice Locke in four quarto volumes. When these
came home Alexander, the philosopher, was having tea here. I
opened the Locke and he immediately sighed with envy and
offered to exchange something for them. I acquiesced and am
now the possessor of John Adams's *Works* in ten volumes. Frida
[Frida Laski] is urgent that the process of exchange should stop
there lest I end up with the Law Reports and drive her to found
a new house.

I go North on Thursday for a week to give two lectures at
Manchester University. Then home for Xmas and then a few
days on the Continent before term begins. I think Antwerp, and
if the money holds out, on to Amsterdam.

Our warm love to you both.

Ever affectionately yours, H.J.L.

Laski, who is little remembered in this country, was a true wunder-
kind. *When he met Holmes he was struggling to support his wife
and child. During the four years he spent at Harvard, he impressed
his students and colleagues with his gift for teaching and writing, his
intellect, his memory, and his passion for justice and the law. He
returned to England and was given the London School of Economics Chair of Political Science when he was thirty-three. In 1929,
Laski organized and campaigned for the Labour Government.
Laski's amazing energy and the range of his intellectual interests
gave him more in common with Justice Holmes than the fifty years
difference in their ages suggests.*

Harold Laski kept Holmes amused with anecdotes about his ob-
servations and about things that drifted his way.

30:XI.30:
I also went with Frida to a dinner to meet Virginia Woolf,
the novelist. She tickled me greatly; it was like watching someone organising her immortality. Every phrase and gesture was
studied. Now and again, when she said something a little out of
the ordinary, she wrote it down herself in a notebook. . . .
Really it was as good as an opera to see her put up a lorgnette
and say in a coy whisper "You write?" "Yes." "Ah, I read so
little—the effort of creation exhausts me." I wonder if you ever
met her? She is L. Stephen's younger daughter by his second
marriage.

Holmes envied and admired Laski's ability to read fast, to gut a
book, and he commented on it often.

You mention so many books that even with your swift eye I
think you must skim, relying on intuition to stop at anything
important—as I should skim through a legal document without
understanding it, feeling sure that any material passage would
arrest me. (August 27, 1925)
Your reading drives me mad. For even if I had as much time
you would be through six volumes while I was laboriously nib-
bling on Volume I. (May 9, 1925)
I don't read a book in a flash of gun powder, like you.
(March 27, 1923)

—from *Holmes–Laski Letters*

One wonders how these extraordinary people, each at the top of his
profession, each overworked and weighted with responsibilities,

could find time to read for pleasure as much as they did, to write so many wonderful letters to each other, and, of course, to others.

Justice Holmes was 85 when he died, and the correspondence with Harry Laski had continued until the end of his life. In his last letter to Holmes (17.II.35) Laski says he is coming to the United States for a sight of the New Deal and "I have booked my passage on March 20th—so I shall be in Washington sometime in the first part of April." Sadly, he did not make it before Holmes died on March 6, 1935.

Emily Dickinson

(1830–1886)

Emily Dickinson lived in Amherst, Massachusetts, most of her life. In her later years she stayed either in her house or garden, secluded from all but the most intimate family and friends. She carried on intense literary correspondences.

Emerson's essays were a major influence on her work. Her poetry, written in secret, is filled with ecstasies, bold imagination, and strong feeling. Only six of her poems were printed during her lifetime. As she aged, Dickinson became reluctant to allow the public to read her work. Long after her death more than 1,500 poems were carefully documented and numbered chronologically. She had penciled some poems on the backs of envelopes and scraps of paper. Others were carefully reworked and copied. Some remained as fragments and hasty jottings. Many were found in letters—1464, included here, was in a thank you letter to T. W. Higginson (a popular literary critic who had advised her against publication) for the gift of his Short Studies of American Authors.

604

Unto my Books—so good to turn—
Far ends of tired Days—
It half endears the Abstinence—
And Pain—is missed—in Praise—

As Flavors—cheer Retarded Guests
With Banquettings to be—
So Spices—stimulate the time
Till my small Library—

It may be Wilderness—without—
Far feet of failing Men—

But Holiday—excludes the night—
And it is Bells—within—

I thank these Kinsmen of the Shelf—
Their Countenances Kid
Enamor—in Prospective—
And satisfy—obtained—

(1862)

1263

There is no Frigate like a Book
To take us Lands away
Nor any Coursers like a Page
Of prancing Poetry—
This Travel may the poorest take
Without offence of Toll—
How frugal is the Chariot
That bears the Human soul.

(About 1873)

1464

One thing of it we borrow
And promise to return—
The Booty and the Sorrow
It's Sweetness to have known—
One thing of it we covet—
The power to forget—
The Anguish of the Avarice
Defrays the Dross of it—

(1879)

1587

He ate and drank the previous Words—
His spirit grew robust—
He knew no more that he was poor,
Nor that his frame was Dust—

He danced along the dingy Days
And this Bequest of Wings
Was but a Book—What Liberty
A loosened spirit brings—

(About 1883)

—from *The Poems of Emily Dickinson*

Henry James
(1843–1916)

In a letter to his nephew, Edward Holton James, a
student at Harvard, James wrote: "Read—read—read
much. Read everything."

SELECTED LETTERS

Alan Cheuse

(b. 1940)

Novelist Alan Cheuse's deep voice is heard on National Public Radio's "All Things Considered," sharing his latest reading with millions of listeners.

On a cold, rainy Washington night this past December, this traveler drove over to the Congressional Office Building on Capitol Hill to attend the Christmas party of a local literacy council. A group of young professionals, many of them lawyers and college teachers, who serve as tutors for the District's largest adult literacy project—not an official part of either the D.C. or federal government but rather a nonprofit organization that belongs to a national umbrella group that fosters the teaching of reading to adults—served plates of roast turkey and baked ham and many side dishes to a couple of dozen adults and a few teenagers, almost all of them black, who all share the desire to learn how to read.

One of these late bloomers was a fifty-three-year-old truck driver from South Carolina named James. James picked up a newspaper only about a year and a half ago after a lifetime of work and raising a family. He had dropped out of school at the age of six to pick crops at nearby farms and never went back. Though unable to read a word, he'd performed such tasks as stevedore and foreman at a shipping company; for the last two decades he has been working as a teamster, in some instances hauling his load as far away as the Canadian border without knowing how to read the road signs.

When I expressed my astonishment at this feat, James laughed and said, "Hey, once you pass the driver's test, the rest ain't all that hard. It's usually just a matter of counting. Counting the stop signs, things like that. You recognize land-

marks in town or out on the road and you sort of steer by
them."

But after a lifetime of living in his own country as though
it were a foreign land where he didn't know the language,
James decided that since all his children had learned to read
and had gone on to good jobs, he could take the time out to
learn how to read himself. This he told me over a plate of
food, his right leg moving up and down, up and down, his
plate shaking on his lap.

"I wanted to learn to read a newspaper, see? I wanted to
read about life, not just live it. So I can just about do that
now. And now I want to read a whole book. I want to read
a story. A good story." The desire for a good story—that
had been on my own mind ever since I could remember.
And for the last three decades reading and writing had become a large portion of my daily life. I write, usually, into
the early afternoon, and the rest of the day, when I'm not
leading a workshop or at the gym or the supermarket or the
movies, I give over to reading. Read, read, read, a rage to
read. It's an appetite as great as that for sex and food and
even for the air we breathe. Death will be a great disappointment if no love or family or friends come with it, but I'd
even forego food in the next life (if there is one) if I could
go on reading the good new novels as they come out. In the
last ten years I've reviewed nearly five hundred books for
National Public Radio's evening news magazine "All Things
Considered" and, like most people who love narrative,
whether fiction or history or politics or science (though fiction is the best narrative of them all), I've read a lot more
than those I've reviewed during this past decade, rereading
books as I teach them to my writing students (because as I
explain to them, thinking that at the same time if I have to
explain it to them then perhaps they are already lost, good
writers are good readers and great writers are great readers),
rereading as I write essays and articles as well as reviews.

But a lifetime—yours, mine—with books has to begin

somewhere. And while talking with James over our plates of turkey at the literacy party, I kept on trying to recall exactly when it was I first learned how to read. James could pinpoint his own beginning with the printed word: on a certain night in June, in Washington, at a restaurant where he had first met his tutor. Before that time, the printed language was a mystery to him, a cipher used by the rest of the world to keep him constantly on his toes. On the job he devised elaborate formulas to keep up with his work. In the supermarket he often depended on the kindness of strangers to tell him where certain foods were located. And as he was talking about his pre-literate life as an adult, I got carried back to one of the few pre-literate scenes in my own memory.

Once upon a time a young boy—he must have been about three years old—crawled into bed with his mother and father. It was a Sunday morning, in spring, probably, because even though it was light outside the window, his father still lay in bed rather than having gone to work. While his mother created a space between them where the boy might burrow beneath the covers, his father reached over to the night table and picked up a rectangular object about six by nine inches—it had an orange and sepia cover, an abstract design that suggested not quite formed stars and crescents—that he said he had just found in his old trunk from a place he called *Roosh-a*. The boy loved the sound of the word and asked his father to say it again: *Roosh-a*. There was a smell to the object too, this thing made of paper and bound in stiff board, the odor of dust and oranges that had been lying long in the hot sun.

When his father opened the front of it, the boy noticed strange designs stretched out in rows. The only thing he recognized was a drawing, that of a golden roosterlike bird. *The tale of the golden cockerel*, his father announced as he fixed his eye on the page and began to speak in a strange and incomprehensible fashion, making a series of globlike and skidding sounds, with a lot of phushes and ticks and bubblelike slurs and pauses.

The boy was me, of course, and the man was my father reading to me in Russian, a language I've never learned, from a book of fairy tales that has long ago been lost in the flood of years that rushes through a family's life. And he of course is gone, too, and I'm old enough now to have a while ago put aside such fairy tales and think instead about what novels to give as gifts to my children for Christmas and other occasions. But I still recall the way my father opened to the first page of that now lost volume and began to make those sounds with his mouth and tongue, interpreting the odd designs in front of him as if it were the easiest thing in the world. It was from this day on that I decided, I believe—if "deciding" is what children at that age I was then ever do—that I would learn to read for myself.

I don't actually remember when I first mastered this basic intellectual aptitude. As Roger Shattuck has pointed out in a recent essay, few of us do. "Most minds," he says, "bury those early faltering steps under recollections of later rewards—the fairy tales or comic books on which we perfected our new skill."

I don't recall seeing my parents read much at all. I do have the faint recollection of watching my father sit in a small alcove of a second-floor apartment on lower State Street in Perth Amboy, New Jersey, tapping on the keys of a small black typewriter, trying to write stories in English in the manner of the Russian satirists Ilf and Petrov. But I never saw him read anything other than the newspaper or a beat-up old copy of Richard Halliburton's *The Nine Wonders of the World*, the texture of whose cover and quality of photographs—waterfalls, drawings of statues—I recall rather than any text. My mother might have read the front page of the newspaper. I never saw her hold any book in her hand.

But I grew up reading, reading like a bandit. And no fairy tales for me. I went straight to comic books, *Archie*

Comics at first, and then the superheros, *Superman* and *Batman*, *Plastic Man*, *Wonder Woman*, and then on to the horror
comics, *EC Stories*, and *The Heap*, building a collection that
rivaled just about any in the neighborhood. Of a Saturday
you could see us comic fans, pushing baby carriages left over
from our younger siblings' infancies filled with our collections on our way to trade meets at someone's house. After a
while a quest for something more than *Archie*, etc. sent me
onward to better reading, which meant, of course, *Classics Illustrated*. The western world's greatest poems and stories
turned into comic books, from *The Iliad* and *The Odyssey* on
through the centuries all the way to Poe, that was my reading for years of early adolescence. . . .

Most of us find this period in which we encounter the
mental adventures of reading the most important part of our
maturation. Though to try and watch it happen is to see
nothing. Last spring, for example, I spent a few days behind
one-way glass observing an eighth-grade reading class at a
middle school in Huntsville, Texas. I'm not sure what I expected to find, but this is what I saw: several dozen kids
from around the ages eleven to thirteen seated at their desks
or sprawled on large cushions on the floor holding books
open in front of them. They moved their limbs and twitched
their eyes as they might have in sleep. Scarcely any of them
did more than change position on the cushions or cross or
extend their legs beneath their desks. Yet the internal processes in their minds, no more visible than coal changing under pressure into diamond, would change their lives. It will
help them discover the world in a way like no other, to learn
of history and philosophy and science and art, to acquire an
awareness of God and insects, of water and the nature of life
in a mining town in Belgium in 1900, to study Buddhism
and physics, or merely to keep boredom at arm's length on
an autumn evening in Great Falls, Montana; to become army
captains and sales managers and priests and cotton farmers,
and to ponder, in this case, Huntsville, Texas, and the rest of

the state, the country, the continent, the world, the solar system, galaxy, and cosmos.

However, you have only to observe a lower-level reading class in order to be reminded, if you need such an elemental tip, that this skill is not part of what we would call human nature. Kids study the shape of the letters and learn to sound each letter, groups of letters, then make words. We've sounded letters, vowels and consonants resounding and popping for our own kids. To watch a whole batch of them at once get this training is like witnessing the first hatch of tree frogs in a warm climate in early spring. The entire air fairly sings and squeaks with the wondering noise of it all. But despite the illusion of the naturalness of reading, an activity as everyday as breathing, this skill is, in the history of western culture, a relatively new invention. For the majority of humanity in Europe and the West verbal art was spoken or sung. And what we now call illiteracy was once the normal condition of culture in what we also name the Golden Age of Greece.

The thousand years or more prior to the sixth century B.C. in Athens was the time of the Homeric rhetors or rhapsodes, who chanted and sang the great poems of the culture to devoted audiences. It was only with the faltering of the Homeric tradition, when it seemed as though the transmission of the poems in memory from one generation to the next was in danger of dying out, that Pisistratus, the Greek tyrant, ordered that scribes record the performance of the two great epics, *The Iliad* and *The Odyssey*, on papyrus lest they be lost for all time.

Maybe that's when Paradise was truly lost, when it became necessary to read the great songs that had formerly been sung. Is it C. M. Ciorian who describes this transition as the culture's "fall into language"? Prior to this time no one read because there was no written language, but a hunger was present—present, it seems, from the beginnings of human culture—the hunger for story, for narrative, for the arrangement of incidents into action, even an action that might move the reader to feel pity and fear. This craving for order with emotional resonance was satisfied during the pre-classical period in the Mediterranean only by oral epic.

Drama arose during the fifth century B.C. and filled, among its other functions, the traditional need for a public gathering at which poetry was performed over an extended period of time. But by the first century A.D. poetry and drama were as often as not read on papyrus as performed. Prose narratives were composed as well, but these, like the *Satyricon*, seemed to take second place to the more engaging works of history in the mind of an audience looking, apparently, for a way both to restore a certain order to a life from which the formerly awesome power of the old gods had faded and for exciting and interesting stories that spoke to their own daily round.

Between the decline of Greece and Rome and the withering away of the Christendom that arose to take their place most westerners had to settle for one book, the Bible, with its multitudes of stories, as the storehouse of narrative. It wasn't really until the fourteenth century and the creation of *The Decamaron* that secular stories came to prominence as literary art—folk narratives were as plentiful as trees—in Europe. As every school kid used to know, the invention of movable type eventually made it possible for the wide dissemination of texts of all varieties, not just the Bible for which the printing press was first widely used. After Luther's revolt against Rome's authority as the prime interpreter of the Holy Book, literacy became a necessity in his part of Europe for the religious man, and soon evolved into a means of power among the rising merchant class, and reading became a sign that a person was wholly civilized.

With the breakup of oral culture and the rise of scriptural authority, reading became a prized activity, not just for the priesthood but for the elite of the continent's court and fief. The book became a metaphor for the world, and reading emerged as a method for interpreting God's creation. To be illiterate meant one stood several stages removed from a knowledge of sacred reality. The idea that one listened to the words of the epic poet and thus heard the language of the muses directly in one's ears became, in this thousand-year interregnum between the demise of oral poetry and the establishment of a secular reading culture, static and sterile when the priest, rather than the poet, served as conduit between holy work and worshipper. With the secularization of storytelling, from Boccaccio forward, the printed word became even further detached from its sacred origins in theodicic poetry, telling stories of the death of kings and then barons and then squires, so that by the time of Balzac, say, readers learned of the lives, loves, and sorrows of the denizens of a great secular city, which is to say, themselves.

As the story evolves—some might want to say descends—from scripture to secular tales of middle-class life, the relation of text to reader evolves as well. Christian theology demanded a singular oath from its worshippers, the acceptance of Christ on the part of the individual as his savior. Eighteen hundred years later the individual picks up a copy of *Tom Jones* and finds that the story illuminates part of his or her daily round, a far cry from any hint of salvation. In fact, quite the opposite, if you consider the distance between the hope of heaven and the worlds in contemporary fiction. To pass one's eyes across the lines of the Holy Writ was an act of prayer. What is it then to read modern fiction?

It may well be that putting together in our own minds a lifetime of novel reading is close to knowing what it must be like in the mind of God. From these simple stories, of a foolish hidalgo in search of a phantom lover, of the way the past rises up against the present in an English village called Middlemarch, of a Jewish advertising salesman wandering about Dublin looking for sympathy, of a Mississippi family plagued by alcoholism, madness, and imagined incest, of a woman named Maria who aimlessly drives the L.A. freeways, we make up a cosmos.

Think of reading then as an act of praise, of prayer, even,

in which individuals reassert their devotion to creation and to the immanent world in which we reside, a world in which every aspect of life, from old used tires piled high in a trash heap to the multiform patterns of snowflakes on a day in high winter, from the sickness of murder to the charity of parenthood, all make up part of a larger pattern. And when we read, we reenact that pattern, an activity that may be as close to serious prayer as most of us will get. Or want to. The organized modern religions hold no patent on expressing devotion to the universe. In fact, the pagan poets, the epic Homers of the oldest stories of the western Mediterranean, show a lot more imagination when it comes to creating great characters and overarching plots than the lyricists and lamenters of the Old and New Testaments. Some great poetry in the former, but nothing much in the latter unless you're spiritually bound to the text. Apply the test of narrative coherence and the pagan epics win hands down. And if the response of the reader, the immersion into a story that delights and instructs in the deepest fashion we know, is any test of the presence of godliness, there's no doubt in my mind which stories show the mark of real deity.

Franz Kafka
(1893–1924)

In a better state because I read Strindberg *(Separated)*. I don't read him to read him, but rather to lie on his breast. He holds me on his left arm like a child. I sit there like a man on a statue. Ten times I almost slip off, but at the eleventh attempt I sit there firmly, feel secure, and have a wide view. [May 4, 1915]

THE DIARIES OF FRANZ KAFKA, 1914–1923

Reading—reading is home itself, the place where we go when we wish to be with ourselves and our own minds and our own hearts. It is an act of the eye which, unlike the viewing of painting or film, has little to do with what the eye perceives before it. Theater and film are the imagination externalized, the created images of the mind or minds of other parties performed objectively before us. While viewing a dance or a play, our eye is captive. Narrative prose or poetry, like music, is a different, and I believe, higher form of representation. The words, like musical notation, are mere potential art, waiting to be performed by the reader on the interior stage of the imagination. And just as nothing could be more public than the performance of a play, nothing could be more private than reading a novel or story. Neurologically one can distinguish the act of reading from the perception of art in other forms, such as dance or drama, and one can see how is has a social reality distinct from the external performance, and perception, of ancient oral poetry, medieval drama, and all the other theatrical and visual art that has come after. Unlike oral poetry, which presumed the presence of a community ethos and the absence of what we would call individual ego, prose on the page demands individual participation and, ever since the advent of symbolism, individual interpretation. Everyone in the Homeric audience understood the explicit meaning of the poems—there was no *im*plicit meaning—and celebrated these values and beliefs by means of listening. Since the middle of the eighteenth century, readers have pondered the implicit values of a work within the confines of their own imaginations, and sometimes despaired of a world in which such solitariness is the norm and values are determined by the situation of the individual.

It's no wonder then that we all know so many people who never dare venture seriously into the world of reading. For most people a functioning imagination can be a treacherous and even frightening possession, generating such trivial but annoying conditions as hypochondria on the one hand and much more dangerous situations such as jealousy, paranoia, and megalomania on the other. In this regard, we read *Don Quixote*, the first modern novel, as a book about the dangers of taking books literally. Logos detached from its divine origins is a symbol awaiting interpretation by the god within us, which is to say, our imaginative powers. Woe to him—look at poor Quixote— who takes it at face value.

. . . Having grown up in the time of the Big Talk about the Death of the Novel and now finding myself on the verge of an epoch in which the Big Talk focuses on the Death of Literature and possibly even the Death of the Book itself, all the Jersey rises up in me and wants to spit on the Reeboks of whatever current theologian of culture makes this argument. And there's no help from the academy either. In exactly that quarter where you'd think you might find people professing their love of liter- ature and the importance, if not primacy, of the art of fiction and poetry, you meet instead theory-fraught ideologies, waving foreign paradigms about in place of scripture, telling us of every reason under the sun for spending time with a book except the necessary ones.

Virginia Woolf
(1882–1941)

Sometimes I think heaven must be one continuous unexhausted reading.

SELECTED LETTERS

To know another mind. To know another life. To feel oneself in the heart of another age, in the heart of another human being. To live out the entire trajectory of a human motivation and understand its fullness in time. To move out of ourselves, lifted into another scene, another action, another destiny, so that we might gain a better sense of our own. To warm our spirits by the heat of a fine story, to help us keep the vision (even if illusion) of order in a world constantly on the verge of chaos. Bored theoreticians, losing hold of their own humanity, turn away from these blessings that the novel offers in order to further their own pallid fantasies of the modern spirit. And by shirking their responsibility towards the very humanist tradition that spawned them, they show their contempt not only for their own best (now sadly blighted) tendencies as readers but also for the new generations of potential readers to come who even now in the elementary schools of urban America are doing their best to prepare themselves—sounding their vowels, making out their letters, clumping them together into stumbling words on the page—to partake of the riches of our culture from Homer to Virginia Woolf to John Edgar Wideman. And for the potential new readers among our immigrant populations. And for the newly educated adults, born here but not born free enough to learn to read as children, new readers such as James the truck driver, my companion at the literacy council Christmas supper.

"TV gets to you after a while," James said to me as we were finishing up our turkey. "And let me tell you, life is tough enough without finding out a way to see it a little better. I learned the hard way, by not learning until now. My Mama told us good stories when we were children, but she couldn't write them down. I'm missing a good story like in the old days. So when I get good enough with my reading, that's what I'm going to do."

"Write them down?" I said.

James laughed and chewed a bite of food.

"I don't know if I'd ever get that good. But I could like to read one."

"Talking here with you," I told him, "made me remember the first time I ever heard a story, the first time I ever thought about learning how to read."

"Tell me the story," he said.

I explained that I couldn't because it had been in Russian and all these years I had never found the English version of that tale.

"Well, that's a story by itself," he said. "Remembering it, trying to find it, not finding it. Write that one down. And maybe sometime when I get good enough I'll see it on a page."

So this is what I've done.

—from "Writing It Down for James: Some Thoughts on Reading Towards the Millennium"

Mary McGinnis

(b. 1946)

*Poet Mary McGinnis lives in Santa Fe, New Mexico, where she is a
counselor for people with disabilities.*

READING BRAILLE

It wasn't my stomach that liked to read, but those socially
    acceptable parts:
the orderly hands, the thin shapely wrists, the neck with its pocke
    of deceit,
the mouth with its tiny partitions, the eyes with their flower cente
it wasn't the nose, it wasn't the legs in their sheaths of skin,

the ankle bones that protruded—it was the head,
the brain with its secret lobes,
the spine with its little curvatures,
all of these parts read and read when I was a child,
their parts with their clear black and white English names, not

*la cabeza, o los manos o los ojos,
o la cara o las piedras o la primavera blanca;*
not the knee but the fingertips, not the thigh but the petite ear;
all of me sank into my lap where the book was;
they talked about the ambulance coming, about my great aunts
    who were sick,
my mother talked on the phone about what the hairdresser said
    about sex,
my father answered my mother in mumbled syllables over the
    blare of the television
and I sat very still on the couch so they wouldn't notice
that I hadn't gone to bed.

I read and dreamed of wild, dark places near the water,
pearl divers who dove for pearls and had seaweed on their arms;
I was not at home in my body then,
and I read until my fingers were raw, and there were
words racing through my head and I didn't have to talk
or ask too many questions.
I loved the quiet in the house when my parents were sleeping—
when I was alone with my hands.

—from *The Disability Rag*

John Keats

(1795–1821)

Keats wrote this sonnet in 1815 after a night spent reading the translation of Homer by George Chapman (1559?–1635), and it was published the next year when he was twenty-one. Note that the young Keats wrote Cortez *instead of* Balboa.

On First Looking into Chapman's Homer

Much have I travelled in the realms of gold,
    And many goodly states and kingdoms seen;
    Round many western islands have I been
Which bards in fealty to Apollo hold.
Oft of one wide expanse had I been told,
    That deep-browed Homer ruled as his demesne:
    Yet did I never breathe its pure serene
Till I heard Chapman speak out loud and bold:
Then felt I like some watcher of the skies
    When a new planet swims into his ken;
Or like a stout Cortez when with eagle eyes
    He stared at the Pacific—and all his men
Look'd at each other with a wild surmise—
    Silent, upon a peak in Darien.

—from *The Home Book of Verse*

Sylvia Townsend Warner

(1893–1978)

*When she heard she was to become a fellow of the Royal Society of
Literature, Warner said ". . . it is the first public acknowledge-
ment I have received since I was expelled from my kindergarten for
being a disruptive influence."*

*Sylvia Townsend Warner was born in 1893, the daughter of a
master at Harrow House. Her mother taught her to read at home
and she had the run of her father's library.*

*After World War I, she went to live in London where she was
drawn to musicology and poetry. During her lifetime, she wrote
seven novels, volumes of poetry and short fiction, and a biography of
T. H. White.*

William Maxwell, her editor at The New Yorker, *who collected
Warner's letters in 1982, tells us in the Introduction that Sylvia
Townsend Warner was reading* Vanity Fair *when she died:
". . . she found and read half-way through* Vanity Fair *before she
was ten. Also Mackay's* Popular Delusions. *And she remembered
sitting on the stairs repeating the spells for raising the devil, from the
chapter on witchcraft, to her black cat and 'feeling a black hope that
they would work.' "*

Rainer Maria Rilke

(1875–1902)

Rilke's portrait of the reader as he exists in two worlds at once is part of Das Buch der Bilder *(The Book of Images, 1902). The poem was translated especially for* Bookworms *by Markus Frank and John Zuern.*

The Reader

I have read for a long while. Since this afternoon,
rustling with rain, lay on the windows.
I no longer heard the wind outside:
my book was hard.
I looked into its leaves as into faces
that grow somber with thought,
and, all around my reading, time piled up.
Suddenly the pages shine with light
and instead of the anxious entanglements of words
evening, evening . . . is written all over them.
Even now, I do not look outside, and yet the long lines
snap, and the words roll
from their threads, wherever they wish to go. . . .
Then I know: above the overgrown,
glistening gardens the skies are wide;
the sun has had to come out one last time.
And now the summer night is falling, as far as one can see:
what was scattered gathers in sparse groups,
people walk long paths, somber,
and far and wide, oddly, as if it might mean more,
one hears the few things that still are going on.

And now when I lift my eyes from the book,
nothing will be disturbing, and everything grand.
There outside is what I, here inside, am living,
and here and there it all is without bounds;
only that I weave myself into it even more
when my gaze aligns itself with things,
and with the solemn simplicity of mass—
then the earth grows out beyond itself.
It seems to comprehend the whole night sky:
the first star is like the final house.

—from *The Book of Images*

Wallace Stevens

(1879–1955)

In 1904, when Wallace Steves was courting his future wife, he wrote to her: "Are you really fond of books—paper valleys and far countries, paper gardens, paper men and paper women? They are all I have, except you; and I live with them constantly."

Like other American writers such as Louis Auchincloss and William Carlos Williams, Wallace Stevens worked outside the literary world his whole life. A lawyer, he became an insurance company executive and remained with the same company until he retired. He won the Bollingen Prize in Poetry in 1949, and in 1950 he received a National Book Award for Poetry. "The Reader" *(1936) is Stevens' reading, not a translation, of Rilke's poem.*

The Reader

All night I sat reading a book,
Sat reading as if in a book
Of sombre pages.

It was autumn and falling stars
Covered the shrivelled forms
Crouched in the moonlight.

No lamp was burning as I read,
A voice was mumbling, "Everything
Falls back to coldness.

Even the musky muscadines,
The melons, the vermilion pears
Of the leafless garden."

The sombre pages bore no print
Except the trace of burning stars
In the frosty heaven.
—from *Ideas of Order*

Rex Stout
(1886–1975)

Archie Goodwin to Nero Wolfe: "Go to hell. I'm reading."

FER-DE-LANCE

Isabel Fonseca

(date unknown)

Fonseca's research for her account of Gypsy life in eastern Europe
included living with the Dukas, a Roma family in Albania. She was
not permitted to make herself useful by helping with the housework,
and was cut off from a customary occupation of reading. Even
literate Gypsies, themselves a minority, were not readers.

. . . and so, while the women worked, I sat, and I watched,
and sketched, and wrote in my notebook. Reading was out of
the question. Reading plain worried the Dukas. *So keres? —*
What are you doing?—was the usual puzzled response to an
upheld book. But as often I would be asked: *Chindilan? —*Are
you fed up, weary?—as if any quiet, or stillness, was a sign of
infirmity or depression.

—from *Bury Me Standing*

Emily Post

(1873–1960)

In her advice on the requirements of a properly equipped guest room, Mrs. Post does not forget the reader. We can only assume that 40 watts was the best to be had in 1934.

There must of course be a night light at the head of the bed. Not just a decorative glow-worm effect, but a 40 Watt light with an adjustable shade that is really good to lie in bed and read by. And always there should be books—chosen more to divert than to strain the reader's attention. The sort of selection appropriate for a guest room might best comprise two or three books of the moment, a light novel, or a mystery novel, a book of essays, or poetry, another of short stories, and a few of the best magazines. Better yet, books ought to be chosen particularly, for even though one may not guess accurately the tastes of another, one can at least guess whether the visitor is likely to prefer transcendental philosophy or detective stories, and provide accordingly.

—from *Etiquette*

E. M. Forster
(1879–1970)

1932: *I have to read* a book at a certain rate and cannot look backwards or on. One of the pages turns out to be gold. I come to it with surprise, joy and terror, and know it must be turned over like the others. How lovely if the next page could be The End.

THE COMMONPLACE BOOK

WORKS CONSULTED

For the reader who wishes to pursue the selections included in this book, we offer a brief bibliography. The list is neither inclusive nor systematic; it is meant to be a sampler of writing that has contributed to *Bookworms*.

Adler, Mortimer. *How to Read a Book.* New York: Simon, 1940.

Alpers, Antony. *Katherine Mansfield: A Biography.* London: Jonathan Cape, 1954.

Alter, Robert. *The Pleasures of Reading in an Ideological Age.* New York: Simon, 1989.

Auden, W.H. *The Dyer's Hand and other essays.* New York: Random, 1948.

Austen, Jane. *The Complete Novels of Jane Austen.* New York: Random, 1931.

Bennett, Alan. "The Treachery of Books." *Writing Home.* London: Faber, 1994.

Bennett, Arnold. *Literary Taste and How to Form It.* London: Hodder, 1909.

Berman, Paul. "Dos Misérables: After Quasimodo and Gutenberg, it's Microsoft Bob." *The New Yorker.* 01 Apr. 1995, 8–9.

Birkerts, Sven. "Fiction in a Media Age." *American Energies.* New York: Morrow, 1992.

———. "Paging the Self: Privacies of Reading." *The Gutenberg Elegies: The Fate of Reading in an Electronic Age.* Boston: Faber, 1994.

Bloom, Harold. *The Western Canon.* New York: Harcourt, 1994.

Boorstin, Daniel. "A Nation of Readers." Library of Congress. DC. 21 Apr. 1982.

Borland, Hal. *High, Wide and Lonesome.* Philadelphia: Lippincott, 1959.

Brodkey, Linda. "Writing on the Bias." *College English.* 56.5 (1994): 527–547.

Cambor, Kathleen. "Taped Books: The Reader Listens." n.p. n.p. 1996.

Cheuse, Alan. "Writing it Down for James: Some Thoughts on Reading Towards the Millennium." *The Antioch Review.* Summer 1993: 487–502.

Ciresi, Rita. "Paradise Below the Stairs." *Italiana Americana.* 12.1 (1993) 17–22.

Coleridge, Samuel Taylor. *The Collected Works of Samuel Taylor Coleridge: Lectures 1808–1819 On Literature.* Vol. I. ed. R. A. Foakes. Princeton: Princeton UP, 1987.

Delacroix, Eugène. *The Journal of Eugène Delacroix.* 1893. Trans. Walter Pach. New York: Grove Press, 1961.

Denby, David. "Queen Lear." *The New Yorker.* 03 Oct. 1994: 88–96.

Dickinson, Emily. *The Poems of Emily Dickinson.* Ed. Thomas H. Johnson. Cambridge: Belknap-Harvard UP, 1955.

Douglass, Frederick. *My Bondage and My Freedom.* New York and Auburn, 1855.

Emerson, Ralph Waldo. *The Early Lectures of Ralph Waldo Emerson,* Eds. Robert E. Spillar and Wallace E. Williams. Vol. 3. Cambridge: Harvard UP, 1972.

———. *The Journals and Miscellaneous Notebooks of Ralph Waldo Emerson.* Eds. William H. Gilman and Alfred R. Ferguson. Vol. 3. Cambridge: Harvard UP, 1963.

Epstein, Joseph. "Waiter, There's a Paragraph in My Soup!" *The American Scholar.* Summer 1989. 327–336.

Fitz, Earl. E. *Clarice Lispector,* Boston: Twayne, 1985.

Flaubert, Gustave. *Madame Bovary.* 1857. New York: Book League, 1941.

Fonseca, Isabel. *Bury Me Standing: The Gypsies and Their Journey.* New York: Knopf, 1995.

Franzen, Jonathan. "The Reader in Exile: The Writen Word Versus the Digital Revolution." *New Yorker.* 06 Mar. 1995. 119–124.

Freed, Lynn. "A Child's Reading in South Africa." *Washington Post Book World.* 10 December *1995.*

Forster, E. M. *The Commonplace Book.* Ed. Philip Gardner. Stanford: Stanford UP, 1985.

Fowler, Don. "Beyond the Book" *Times Literary Supplement.* 10 May 1996: 11.

Furman, Laura. "Mrs. Darling's Kiss." n.p. n.p. 1996.

Gies, Miep with Alison Leslie Gold. *Anne Frank Remembered.* New York: Simon, 1987.

Gill, Eric. *Autobiography.* New York: Devin-Adair, 1941.

———. *The Engravings.* Ed. Christopher Skelton. Boston: Godine, 1990.

Greene, Jonathan. "The Ideal Reader." *Idylls,*. Rocky Mount: North Carolina Wesleyan College Press, 1990.

Gregorian, Vartan. "A Place Elsewhere: Reading in the Age of the Computer." AAAS Stated Meeting. NYU. New York. 03 Apr. 1995.

Hadas, Rachel. "The Cradle and the Bookcase." *Living in Time*. New
Brunswick: Rutgers, 1990.

Hamilton, Ian, "An Oxford Union" *The New Yorker*. 19 February 1996:
74.

Hoffman, Eva. *Lost in Translation: A Life in a New Language*. New York:
Dutton, 1989.

Hoggart, Richard. *The Uses of Literacy*. Boston: Beacon, 1961.

Holmes, Oliver Wendell, Jr. and Harold J. Laski. *Holmes-Laski Letters
1916–1935*. Ed. Mark DeWolfe Howe. Cambridge: Harvard UP, 1953.

Holroyd, Michael "Diary." *London Review of Books*. 07 March 1996: 24.

Hurston, Zora Neale. *Dust Tracks on the Road: An Autobiography*. Urbana:
U Ill. P, 1984.

———. *I Love Myself When I Am Laughing—And Then Again When I Am
Looking Mean and Impressive*. Ed. Alice Walker. Old Westbury: Feminist Press, 1979.

James, Henry. *Selected Letters*. Ed. Leon Edel. Cambridge: Belknap-Harvard UP, 1974.

Jensen, Laura. "Destinations." *Shelter*. Port Townsend, WA.: Dragon
Gate, Inc., 1985.

John, Richard R. "Remembering McLuhan." *Reviews in American History*. 18.3 (1990): 419–424.

Joyce, James. *A Portrait of the Artist as a Young Man*. 1916. New York:
Viking, 1964.

Kafka, Franz. *The Diaries of Franz Kafka, 1910–1913 and 1914–1923*.
Trans. Joseph Kresh. Ed. Max Brod. 2 vols. New York: Schocken,
1948.

Katz, Jon. "Return of the Luddites." *Wired*. 06 Mar., 1995.

Keats, John. "On First Looking Into Chapman's Homer." 1817. *The
Home Book of Verse*. Ed. Burton Egbert Stevenson. 9th ed. New York:
Holt, 1953.

Kelly, Kevin. "Interview with the Luddite." *Wired*. 03 Mar. 1995.

Kenyon, Jane. "Insomnia at the Solstice." *Constance*. St. Paul: Graywolf,
1993.

Lamb, Charles. "Detached Thoughts on Books and Reading." *The Last
Essays of Elia*. 1823. New York: Random, 1935.

Lamott, Anne. *Bird by Bird: Some Instructions on Writing and Life.* New York: Pantheon, 1994.

Langer, Jiri. *Nine Gates to the Chassidic Mysteries*, 1937. Cambridge: James Clarke & Co., 1961.

Lewin, Tamar. "Hooked on Boy Books." *New York Times Magazine.* 23 July, 1995: 12.

LeGuin, Ursula K. "Texts." *American Short Fiction.* 1.1 (1991): 91–94.

Leonhardt, Mary. *Parents Who Love Reading, Kids Who Don't: How It Happens and What You Can Do About It.* New York: Crown, 1993.

Leopardi, Giacomo. "Pensieri XX." *Essays, Dialogues and Thoughts.* Trans. James Thomson. Ed. Bertram Dobell. London: Routledge, 1905.

Lively, Penelope. *Oleander, Jacaranda. A Childhood Perceived.* New York: Harper, 1994.

Lispector, Clarice. "The First Book of Each of My Lives" *Discovering the World.* Trans. Giovanni Pontiero. Manchester: Carcanet, 1992. 598–599.

———. "Torture and Glory." *Discovering the World.* Trans. Giovanni Pontiero. Manchester: Carcanet, 1992.

Mansfield, Katherine. *Journal.* Ed. John Middleton Murry. New York: Knopf, 1946.

———. *The Scrapbook of Katherine Mansfield,* Ed. John Middleton Murry. London: Constable, 1939.

———. *The Letters of Katherine Mansfield,* Ed. John Middleton Murry. London: Constable, 1928.

———. *The Letters and Journals of Katherine Mansfield*, Ed. C.K. Stead. London: Allen Lane, 1977.

McCarey, John. *The Intellectuals and the Masses: Pride and Prejudice Among the Literary Intelligentsia, 1880–1939.* New York: St. Martin's, 1992.

McGinnis, Mary. "Reading Braille." *The Disability Rag.* July–Aug. 1993: 100.

Meyers, Jeffrey. *Katherine Mansfield: A Biography*, London: Hamish Hamilton, 1978.

Moore, Leslie. *Katherine Mansfield: The Memories of LM,* London: Michael Joseph, 1971.

O'Keeffe, Phil. *Down Cobbled Streets: A Liberties Childhood.* Dingle, Ire.: Brandon. 1995.

Origo, Iris. *Leopardi: A Biography.* London: Oxford University Press, 1935.

Pastan, Linda. "McGuffey's First Eclectic Reader." *PM/AM: New and Selected Poems.* New York: Norton, 1983.

Powell, Anthony. *Books Do Furnish A Room.* Boston: Little, Brown, 1971.

Pritchett, V.S. *A Cab at the Door*. London: Chatto & Windus, 1970.

Richardson, Robert D. Jr. *The Mind on Fire: A Biography of Ralph Waldo Emerson*. Berkeley: U of Cal. P, 1995.

Rilke, Rainer Maria. *"Der Lesende"* (The Reader). *Das Buch der Bilder* (The Book of Images). 1902. Trans. Markus Frank and John Zuern, n.p. n.p. 1996.

Rodriguez, Richard. "The Achievement of Desire." *Hunger of Memory*. Boston: Godine, 1981.

Rose, Mike. "Reclaiming the Classroom." *Lives on the Boundary*. New York: Free Press, 1989.

Sale, Kirkpatrick. *Rebels Against the Future: The Luddites and Their War on the Industrial Revoltuion*. Reading, MA: Addison, 1996.

Sayers, Dorothy L. *Gaudy Night*. New York: Harper, 1936.

Silko, Leslie Marmon. "Books: Notes on Mixtec and Maya Screenfolds, Picture Books of Pre-Conquest Mexico." *Yellow Woman and a Beauty of the Spirit, Essays of Native American Life Today*. New York: Simon, 1996.

Silver, Brenda. *Virginia Woolf's Reading Notebooks*. Princeton: Princeton UP. 1983.

Standard, Elinore. "My Reading Life." n.p. n.p. 1996.

Stevens, Wallace. *The Collected Poems of Wallace Stevens*. New York: Knopf, 1954.

———. "The Reader." *Ideas of Order,* New York: Knopf, 1936.

———. *Letters of Wallace Stevens*. Ed. Holly Stevens. New York: Knopf, 1966.

Stout, Rex. *Fer-de-Lance*. 1934. New York: Pyramid, 1962.

Trollope, Anthony. *Autobiography*. 1883. New York: Oxford, 1950.

Tuohy, Frank. *Yeats,* New York: Macmillan, 1976.

Turk, Rob. Letter. *Austin Chronicle* 14, 23 (10 Feb. 1995): 2, 4.

Welty, Eudora. *One Writer's Beginnings*. New York: Warner, and Cambridge: Harvard UP, 1983.

White, Antonia. *Frost in May*. 1933. New York: Dial, 1982.

Wolff, Tobias. *This Boy's Life: A Memoir*. New York: Atlantic, 1989.

Woodbury, Charles J. *Talks with Emerson*. 1890. New York: Horizon, 1971.

Wright, Richard. *Black Boy: A Record of Childhood and Youth*. New York: Harper, 1945.